Seoul

World Cities Series

Edited by
Professor R. J. Johnston and Professor P. Knox

Published titles in the series:

Forthcoming titles in the series:

Other titles are in preparation

Seoul

The Making of a Metropolis

Joochul Kim

Arizona State University, USA

and

Sang-Chuel Choe

Seoul National University, Korea

JOHN WILEY & SONS

Chichester • New York • Weinheim • Brisbane • Singapore • Toronto

Published in 1997 by John Wiley & Sons Ltd,
Baffins Lane, Chichester,
West Sussex PO19 1UD, England

National   01243 779777
International (+44) 1243 779777
e-mail (for orders and customer service enquiries):
cs-books@wiley.co.uk.
Visit our Home Page on http://www.wiley.co.uk
or http://www.wiley.com

Other Wiley Editorial Offices

John Wiley & Sons, Inc., 605 Third Avenue,
New York, NY 10158-0012, USA

VCH Verlagsgesellschaft mbH, Pappelallee 3,
D-69469 Weinheim, Germany

Jacaranda Wiley Ltd, 33 Park Road, Milton,
Queensland 4064, Australia

John Wiley & Sons (Asia) Pte Ltd, 2 Clementi Loop #02-01,
Jin Xing Distripark, Singapore 129809

John Wiley & Sons (Canada) Ltd, 22 Worcester Road,
Rexdale, Ontario M9W 1L1, Canada

Library of Congress Cataloging-in-Publication Data

A catalogue record for this book is available from the Library of Congress

British Library Cataloguing in Publication Data

A catalogue record for this book is available from the British Library

ISBN 0-471-94936-1

Typeset in 10/12pt Palatino from author's disks by Mayhew Typesetting, Rhayader, Powys
Printed and bound in Great Britain by Biddles Ltd, Guildford and King's Lynn

This book is printed on acid-free paper responsibly manufactured from sustainable forestation, for which at least two trees are planted for each one used for paper production.

Contents

To our friends, family and Tampico
who have endured this arduous task with us

List of figures

List of tables

Preface

When we first began the task of writing this book, our interests and expectations were somewhat different. For Professor Choe, a senior scholar who wrote frequently about Seoul, it was his moment of reflection and appreciation. During the 1960s when Seoul showed the first sign of tremendous growth, Professor Choe was a city official working on a general plan of the City of Seoul. As an insider, he participated actively in the process of change and was instrumental in many cases in shaping and guiding the development and growth of the capital city. After he was appointed as an urban scholar at Seoul National University, he became a willing critic who stated his positions not merely for the sake of arguing but for problematic engagement in the planning process. By writing this book, he has been able to consolidate his integral involvement with Seoul's change and growth.

For Professor Kim, writing this book was like coming home; a journey into learning and understanding more about the city in which he grew up and was somewhat familiar with. Having left Korea in 1969, his experience of the city was clearly limited and, in fact, his comprehensive knowledge of the city from when he was a young man did not extend beyond familiarity with his surroundings of that particular time period. Only after he was able to make frequent visits to Seoul, beginning in 1984, did he realize the fast pace of change and growth that had taken place. He developed an urge to document the process of change and what impacts it was making on residents in Seoul. During a one-year sojourn as a Fulbright scholar to Korea between 1986 and 1987, he was able to conduct research into the areas of urban renewal and urban redevelopment, and actively immersed himself into various aspects of the issues and urgent problems facing the city. Thus, with the completion of this book, he feels that he has just begun another stimulating journey into finding new meaning for a modern metropolis, a city in transition.

When we began this exciting project, our main purpose was not only to provide pertinent data concerning the growth of Seoul but to tell a story: how Seoul became a giant international city with the current flavour. To some urban scholars and visitors alike, Seoul is a city with strong vitality and excitement. The capital city holds old charms, attractive physical surroundings and widely available international culture. To others, Seoul has lost its soul. Overcrowding, pollution, traffic congestion and other urban ills have become too serious to provide the quality of urban life that they have aspired to. We hope that our stories will help them understand the issues facing the capital city as well as make their assessment about the current and future condition of Seoul easier.

We start our story by describing the initial beginning of Seoul over 600 years ago. It was a small village, but nevertheless an important place for Yi dynasty. However unpleasant, the colonial experience during the Japanese domination is also discussed. In Chapter 1, we conclude with theoretical discussions about the formation of the city. Then, both economic and population growth of the city are extensively analysed in Chapter 2. We also explain the main reasons for the emergence of the Seoul Metropolitan Region and its economic and regional dominance in present-day Korea. In Chapter 3, historical patterns of land use and their associated transportation networks and problems are discussed. Based on some actual case studies, an equity issue facing urban housing and redevelopment problems is carefully debated, while various recommendations are presented to deal more effectively with some of the critical issues (Chapter 4).

In Chapter 5, we provide historical perspectives on how the process of city planning has affected the growth of Seoul. The relationship between the central government and the city government during the planning process is shown, while at the same time the mechanisms of municipal finance are described. Korea is currently undergoing fundamental changes with respect to local government autonomy; local governments are breaking away from their historically centralized government control. What impact this new trend will have on the general affairs of Seoul's municipal government is also included in Chapter 5. How does the city physically look now? Are there any unique design characteristics illuminating 600 years of urban formation? Is there a clash between western influences and traditional Korean culture in terms of developing livable urban space? These questions coupled with some constructive suggestions are presented in Chapter 6. Chapter 7 details some difficult challenges facing the capital city, recognizing that any solutions may require diligent efforts from both politicians and citizens alike.

We wish that our efforts have resulted in a book that is both informative and enjoyable to read. To academic scholars and interested students in Korean affairs, we are hopeful that this book contains enough data and materials for critical analysis of issues facing Seoul and Korea. On the other hand, we also hope that this book will be intriguing enough to capture attention from prospective future visitors to Seoul and Korea so that they will be better informed once they find themselves in an unfamiliar territory in the Far East.

Joochul Kim in the desert
Tempe, Arizona, USA
Sang-Chuel Choe at Kwanak San
Seoul, Korea
December 10, 1996

Acknowledgments

During the six years taken to complete this book, we often felt that we were climbing a mountain. When faced with going downhill, we thought things were moving along smoothly. Other times going uphill, we became out of breath thinking that we would never recover to see the familiar path downhill. When discouraged, many individuals and institutions encouraged us to move on. We are grateful to our friends and colleagues who motivated us to see the end of this task.

For Professor Choe, it has been a lasting passion to write a book on Seoul after his encounter with the City Hall in the mid-1960s. Since then many colleagues and city officials have provided constant sources of encouragement to complete this book. Professor Choe also wishes to extend his warmth thanks to his graduate students and colleagues at the university.

Both Seoul National University and Arizona State University have provided institutional support during the years of writing this book. Professor Kim would like to express his sincere gratitude to all his friends in the Office of the President at ASU for providing him with a human touch and a caring environment when needed. His students and colleagues often provided critical comments when needed. The City of Phoenix, particularly the Aviation Department, provided great institutional support while he was assigned there to work in the Office of the City Manager.

Gigi Chan was instrumental in reading over our first draft of all the chapters. It was delightful to receive her insightful comments, humour and editorial guidance. Professor Manuel Castells suggested to me the concept of floating urbanscape in Seoul. Professors Chunghee Moon, Sooyong Park Jeongsoo Kim, Sungkyu Ha and Sangjoon Kwon made frequent comments and suggestions. Dongho Han guided us through the city streets when we need to reassure our ideas. Our colleagues at Korea Research Institute for Human Settlements often provided the necessary materials for analysis. Dr Woobae Lee has had a long standing involvement in this project.

When Professor Kim needed a few months to concentrate on this project, Seoul Development Institute (SDI) provided him with a home so that he could dwell on data collection and writing. At SDI, many individuals were instrumental in making this task more enjoyable. Director Dr Saewook Chung provided us with support staff. Sang-dae Lee and Young-sun Choe were excellent in preparing the figures and maps. Kwang-joo Park was a central figure at SDI, putting missing pieces together for our project. With his relentless visits to local and national offices to obtain necessary pictures for the book, we are certain that Chapter 6 is better presented. Young-eun Lee was instrumental in preparing all tables and figures on the computer. When a bug was found in the computer program, she was persistent in correcting it rather than being discouraged by endless hours of labour. Her wit and enthusiasm made our project more enjoyable.

We would like to express our sincere appreciation for the following institutions for allowing us to use pictures and figures in the book: Seoul Metropolitan Government, Seoul Development Institute, Office of Culture Properties, Ministry of Culture and Sports and Bank of Korea. Mr Jongil Kim of the Public Relations and Planning Division in Seoul Metropolitan Government was an essential figure in guiding us with most of the pictures used in the book.

Editorial and production staff at John Wiley & Sons were simply exceptional in providing the necessary support for us. Over the years, Tiffany Robinson, Katrinia Sinclair and Louise Portsmouth were instrumental in keeping the communication channel open. They kept us informed of the things we needed to do. Anne Horscroft did an excellent job of editing the book. Her professional skills and inquiries were greatly appreciated. Isabelle Strafford and Claire Walker, with their highly competent professionalism kept our production schedule on-time. Last, but not least, we want to express our warm thanks to Paul Knox and R.J. Johnston, co-editors of the series, and Iain Stevenson, Publisher. They never gave up on us, when we met with the uphill struggle. Their constant support and encouragement made the task much easier for us.

1

Seoul: an emerging international city

Historical process of growth

The recent economic success of Korea has taken the world-wide community by storm.[1] Korean-made automobiles such as Hyundai Excels and Daewoo Lemans are driven in many parts of the world, while a variety of electronic goods such as VCRs, camcorders, and televisions are produced by such Korean conglomerates (*Jaebols*) as Daewoo, Goldstar and Samsung. Other consumer products have also become familiar household items to many consumers outside Korea. Naisbitt, a leading futurologist, states that countries such as Korea now challenge the USA and Japan with an increasing variety of export goods, and further observes that newly industrializing countries (NICs) such as Korea, Taiwan, Hong Kong, and Singapore have revolutionized the theory of economic development by skipping over much of the industrialization phases and plunging directly into the information and service based economy (Bello and Rosenfeld, 1990).

As recently as a few years ago, images of Korea as a country in conflict persisted: war-torn, plagued with severe poverty, repressed by a

---

[1] Historically Korea was one country. After Korea was liberated from a long period of Japanese domination (1909–1945) in 1945, Korea was divided into two: the Soviet-influenced North Korea (Democratic People's Republic of Korea) and the American-influenced South Korea (Republic of Korea). Between 1950 and 1953, the Korean peninsula was devastated by the most painful civil war in her modern history. Although Korea is still divided, and remains the only divided country in the world, the Korea we refer to in this book denotes South Korea.

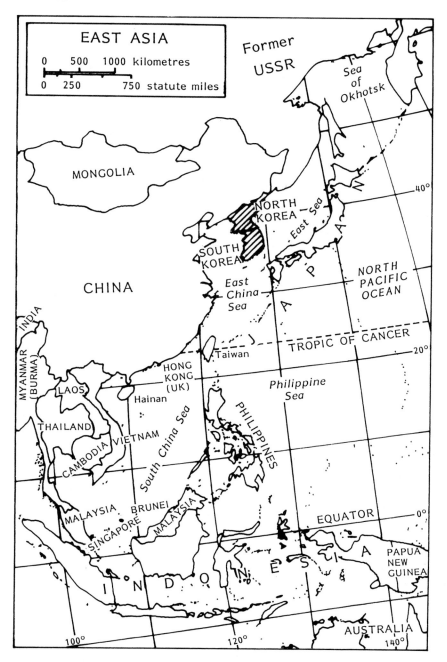

Figure 1.1 Korea in the Far East. Reproduced from Macdonald (1990) *The Koreans* by permission of Westview Press

dictatorial government, and rocked by daily student demonstrations on the street. These images have now been replaced, however. Many now see Korea as a country with a rapidly growing economy, an emerging economic and political power in the Far East. Another indicator of Korea's strong economic status was its delivery of economic aid packages in 1991 to the now dismantled Soviet Union. The successful completion of the 1988 Summer Olympics also bolstered Korea as an important member of the international community. From the early 1980s, government officials prepared for both the 1986 Asian Games and the 1988 Summer Olympics by modernizing and beautifying the City of Seoul. Before the impressively staged showcase of the 1988 Summer Olympics, however, very few people, particularly in the Western world, knew anything about Seoul and its rich history.

Today, Seoul is a fast-paced, large metropolitan city with a population of more than 11 million people. Most of the growth has occurred during the last 30 years, spurred by the intense flow of migration from rural to urban centers, particularly to Seoul; during the 1960s and 1970s, about 300 000 people migrated annually into Seoul (City of Seoul, 1992). The concentration of political and economic power in Seoul has also contributed to this unmatched growth in her history. Unless drastic government-induced measures curtailing this constant influx of people to Seoul are introduced, it is expected that Seoul will continue to grow to a point where the quality of life seriously deteriorates: Seoul already experiences and severely suffers from many negative aspects of urban sprawl such as air pollution, environmental degradation, overcrowding, traffic jams, housing shortages, and crime (see Figure 1.3 for a brief illustration of physical expansion since 1920).

If we look at the Seoul Metropolitan Region (SMR), which includes the surrounding satellite towns and cities, the total population of the SMR is rapidly approaching 20 million, representing more than 46% of Korea's total population (City of Seoul, 1993). This burgeoning growth of Seoul and the SMR in both population and physical size (Figures 1.3 and 1.4) is impressive. In 1960, the total populations of Seoul and the SMR were, respectively, about three and 5.5 million. The SMR was placed about sixteenth among the most populous regions in the world. By 1980, the SMR ranked fourth with 13.3 million people, behind Mexico City. It is also estimated that by the year 2000, the SMR will rank third in total population, preceded only by Mexico City in Mexico and São Paulo in Brazil, as indicated in Table 1.1.

Throughout the history of modern Korea, Seoul has been the most dominant city. Traditionally, most economic and political bases have located in Seoul and, because the national government has engineered and guided the city's development so actively, it was very closely tied to

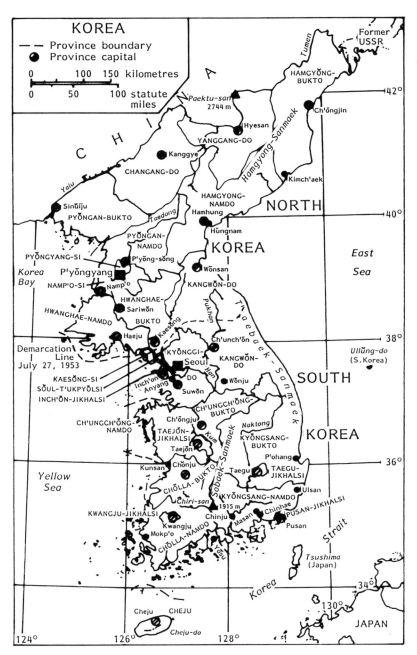

Figure 1.2 Map of Korea. Reproduced Macdonald from (1990) *The Koreans* by permission of Westview Press

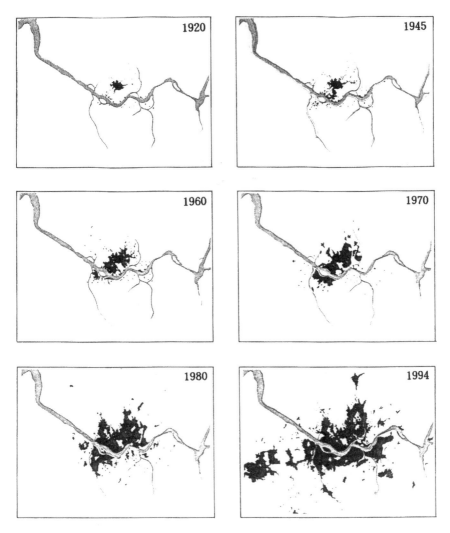

Figure 1.3 Physical growth of Seoul. *Source:* Seoul Metropolis (1962a, 1962b, 1977, 1990a)

the nation's economic development. Therefore, much of the growth and development of Seoul has occurred since the mid-1970s when Korea's economy, heavily dependent on export-oriented manufacturing indus-tries, showed remarkable growth.

Many international firms now maintain their branch operations in Seoul. Following trade missions from China and some Eastern European countries in the late 1980s, once considered communist enemies and

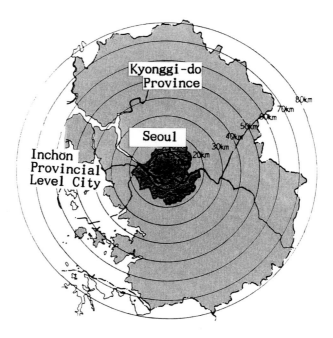

Figure 1.4 Spatial boundaries of Seoul and the Seoul Metropolitan Region. *Source:* Seoul Metropolis (1991)

Table 1.1 Growth of metropolitan cities by rank. Population (in millions) given in parentheses

1960	1980	2000
1 New York (14.2)	1 Osaka, Kobe (17.7)	1 Mexico City (25.8)
2 London (10.7)	2 New York (15.6)	2 São Paulo (24.0)
3 Shanghai (10.7)	3 Mexico City (14.5)	3 **Seoul (21.7)**
4 Tokyo (10.7)	4 **Seoul (13.3)**	4 Osaka, Kobe (20.0)
5 Rheinrhuru (Africa) (8.7)	5 São Paulo (12.8)	5 Calcutta (16.5)
6 Beijing (7.3)	6 Shanghai (11.8)	6 Bombay (16.0)
7 Paris (7.2)	7 London (10.3)	7 New York (15.8)
8 Buenos Aires (6.9)	8 Buenos Aires (10.1)	8 Tehran (13.6)
9 Los Angeles (6.6)	9 Calcutta (9.5)	9 Shanghai (13.3)
10 Moscow (6.3)	10 Los Angeles (9.5)	10 Rio de Janeiro (13.3)
11 Chicago (6.0)		
12 Tianjin (6.0)		
13 Osaka, Kobe (5.7)		
14 Calcutta (5.6)		
15 Mexico City (5.2)		
16 **Seoul (5.2)**		

barred from entering Korea, Russia, China and most former Eastern European countries now have normal diplomatic relationships with Korea and have continued an increasing interest in exploring future economic ventures. International arts and culture are routinely displayed in Seoul and have solidly established Seoul as an international city. In 1994, Seoul celebrated 600 years as the capital city in Korea.

Growth during the Yi Dynasty, 1394–1909

Although Korea's long history dates back well over 5000 years, the emergence of the Yi Dynasty (Chosun Dynasty) in 1394 gave birth to the historical beginning of Seoul as the capital city. Until then, Seoul was recognized as a major provincial city from time to time, due largely to its strategic location, particularly during the unified Shilla and Koryo Kingdoms (668–1392 AD).[1] During the Yi Dynasty, however, Seoul, known then as Hanyang, was a walled-in city (castled city), a main characteristic of the traditional cities for most of Korea's dynasties (Seoul Metropolis, 1977).

The site for Seoul as the capital city was deliberately scrutinized from the beginning, however. The capital city, which was supposed to be superior to as well as different from other conventional cities, was developed based on the concept of geomancy (the Fengshui Principles) along with the ancient Chinese spatial concept that was used for the layout of the city of Changan (now Xian) during the Tang Dynasty in China. The basic concept of geomancy emphasizes the harmonious use of all local currents of the cosmic breath. It is widely interpreted to mean that the site of a capital city has to be bound on the north by elegant mountain ranges and encompassed on the south by an ever-flowing river (Seoul Metropolis, 1977; Sohn, 1987). Indeed, Seoul is surrounded by various mountain ranges and the Han River flows into the western sea. Figure 1.5 illustrates how well Seoul was suited to be the capital city based on these ancient spatial principles.

The total population of Seoul fluctuated between 100 000 and 120 000, and Seoul remained a pastoral mandarin city for almost 500 years. The physical size of Seoul did not show any sign of measurable growth, staying at approximately 16.5 km². Subsequently, the population density was maintained between 60 and 120 people per hectare during this period (Seoul Metropolis, 1977; Sohn, 1987). Deeply rooted in the tradition of

---

[1] Before Shilla Kingdom unified Korea, the country was divided into three Kingdoms: Koguryo in the north, Shilla in the southeast and Paekche in the southwestern part of the country. The three Kingdom period lasted from 57 BC to 668 AD, and Seoul was often mentioned as an important place in the ancient records during this particular period.

Figure 1.5 Ancient layout of Seoul based on the Fengshui principles

Confucianism and an agrarian economic system, coupled with very limited contact with the outside world, particularly Western influences, most residents in Seoul were not predisposed to commercialism, industrial development, or citizen input into local government affairs. This situation was particularly acute, as most government activities were heavily centralized and the ideal of democratic rule was a completely foreign concept to Korea.

Most rulers in the later period of the Yi Dynasty adhered to a closed-door policy that prohibited people from making any contact with foreign nationals; Korea was known as the "Hermit Kingdom" during this period. The opening of its doors to the modern world occurred in 1876 with the signing of the Kanghwa Treaty with Japan. Some scholars believe that this treaty marked the significant beginning of Korea's entrance into the new international economic and political system (Lim, 1985).

Growth during the colonial period, 1909–1945

In 1909, a tragic event in Korea's modern history occurred – the beginning of 36 long, brutal years of Japanese colonial rule. The Japanese colonial government changed the name of the capital from Hanyang to Kyongsong and immediately began the process of dismantling its walled-in city (castled city) character, a symbol of the nation traditionally made by the royal palace.

Under Japanese domination, capitalist economic patterns of industrialization and trade, along with a modern bureaucratic system of government, were introduced to Korea. As Seoul underwent the initial stages of an early urbanization process, the total population of Seoul continued to grow, but was eventually limited to about one million (Macdonald, 1990). Clearly, the gradual expansion of commerce in Seoul, coupled with worsening living conditions for a large proportion of the rural villages, was a major factor contributing to a substantial growth in the total population. In an attempt to accommodate the steady increase in Japanese residents and military personnel, a significant section of the city, mainly its central city core, had to be designated as special residential quarters.

The introduction of streetcars and trains quickly supported the expansion of urban structure. A Japanese shrine was built on top of Mount Namsan, and a building for the newly instituted colonial government office was constructed in front of the Kyongbok Palace that had been a royal residence during the Yi Dynasty. Various other modern urban structures were juxtaposed on the existing traditional cityscape, but many of the buildings were primarily designed to smear national pride and identity for Koreans. The physical size of the city also expanded to about 134 km^2 by 1936, almost ten times bigger than the original size of Seoul (City of Seoul, 1961–1994).

The economic growth and structural changes during the colonial period were indeed substantial, and Seoul became a dominant center for business, financial, and administrative activities. However, they were mostly designed to meet the needs of the Japanese, consequently contributing very little to the needs of Koreans (Kim and Roemer, 1981). It must be mentioned, however, that the modern treatment facility for drinking water was constructed during the early years of the colonial period and contributed significantly to the reduction of mortality from a cholera epidemic in Korea.

Growth during the early modernization period, 1945–1970

After 36 years of oppressive Japanese rule, Korea was liberated in 1945 by Japan's surrender in the Second World War. In 1949, the government renamed the capital from Kyongsong to Seoul.

Immediately following the end of Japanese colonial rule was the most turbulent and chaotic five-year period in the history of Korea. The forced partition of the Korean peninsula by outside forces (America and then the former Soviet Union) along political ideologies left the country unstable and increased political bickering and confrontation by both sides to an immensely dangerous level. During this difficult period, Seoul was immediately inundated by a high volume of in-migration from rural areas and from expatriates returning to the capital city, mainly from Manchuria, Japan, and other parts of China. By 1949, the total population of Seoul exceeded 1.6 million and the physical size grew to 268.4 km^2, doubling the existing city size (City of Seoul, 1961–1994). Makeshift dwellings and squatter settlements began appearing in many parts of the city.

At that time Seoul, which inherited much of the Japanese colonial culture and bureaucracy, had seven districts (wards) and was served by a very small central city government structure of seven bureaus and 34 divisions. Today, Seoul, with more than 11 million people, has grown into a metropolitan city with 25 districts. The city government structure has also grown into a giant bureaucracy with one main office, two coordinating offices, 13 bureaus, five headquarters, one board, 71 divisions, and 69 field offices (Seoul Development Institute, 1994).

Between 1950 and 1953, Korea was engaged in the most tragic civil war in her history. Seoul was devastated during the war, approximately 47% of her standing buildings were destroyed, and at one point the operation of the capital city had to be temporarily moved to Pusan, a southeastern port city. After an armistice agreement in July 1953, Seoul again functioned as the capital city and a tremendous population surge ensued. After the war, a stream of people from all parts of the country, particularly from rural areas and small cities, came to Seoul for better employment opportunities and an improved quality of life.

As Korea was still in the process of rebuilding both from the war and Japanese colonialism, Seoul had very limited financial resources and could not accommodate this suddenly burgeoning population growth with well-prepared development plans. Much of its physical infra-structure was in dire need of repair, the provision of housing and public services lagged well behind population growth, and its city government lacked a well-prepared plan even for the immediate future. Many city development plans, such as the clearing of most squatter settlements, were carried out in an abrupt, bulldozing manner.

A turning point in the direction of national economic development policies came in the 1960s. After the military coup of 1961, the national government launched a new industrial policy, emphasizing the development of heavy and other manufacturing based industries. The national agenda indeed shifted from a widely practised agrarian economy to export-oriented industries. Urban centers attracted newly emerging manufacturing factories and consequently accelerated rural to urban migration during this particular period. The total population in Seoul increased substantially to almost five million and the physical size of the city expanded to 613 km^2 by 1969 (City of Seoul, 1961–1994). Most growth in Seoul during the 1950s and 1960s, however, was limited to areas north of the Han River (see Figure 1.3). Not only was the Han River considered as an important natural asset, but it was seen as a physical barrier to the future development of Seoul. As more and more people began settling in Seoul, urban sprawl accompanied by undesirable land speculation began to spread throughout the city.

Growth during the rapid modernization period, 1970 to present

By the year 1970, the rate of national urbanization surpassed 50%, and the total population for Seoul reached more than 5.5 million. In fact, the annual population increase for Seoul averaged about 300 000 people during the 1970s (City of Seoul, 1984). To prevent explosive population growth in Seoul, a variety of national policies that emphasized the decentralization of the population and government functions in the capital city were initiated in the 1970s. The sheer existence of Seoul and its magnetic pull-factor proved to be simply too strong for many of the policies to be effective, however.

In 1971, city officials, in a deliberate attempt to restrict, yet accommodate, the influx of newcomers, decided to adopt a greenbelt policy in and around the city limit. Encircled by the greenbelt area, the physical expansion of Seoul had to find its own way. Development, south of the Han River, then mostly undeveloped farmland and open space, was thus initiated. For most of the 1970s and 1980s, a series of new urban developments following Western style grid-street patterns was implemented in the area south of the Han River. During this period, large-scale, monotonous apartment buildings emerged as a prevailing development norm and became the predominant cityscape in Seoul. Unlike the many single-story residential homes reflecting traditional Korean architecture north of the Han River, most of the housing and commercial development south of the Han River exemplified Western-style, at times post-modern architecture. Typifying this architecture were the large high-rise apartment complexes that tended to ignore a sensible and acceptable human scale.

During the 1980s, Seoul prepared for the 1988 Summer Olympics. Urban redevelopment projects, along with the expansion of the existing public infrastructure, received higher priority. The face-lifting of Seoul was further advanced by the development of several new towns, urban renewal projects surrounding the Olympic Stadium, expressway construction along the Han River, and the opening of subway lines. Seoul's total population exceeded more than 11 million and urban sprawl approached uncontrollable dimensions, reaching beyond the designated greenbelt areas and new satellite cities which sprung up around the outer boundaries of the city (City of Seoul, 1992).

At present, the size of Seoul is enormous; its physical size is about 605.4 km² with 25 districts (wards) and 50 000 city employees. There are five lines of underground subways for commuters that serve most areas of the city, with two additional lines currently under construction. With over 11 million people, about 16 000 people per square kilometer, Seoul is one of the most densely populated cities in the world. About 2711 people move daily to Seoul, while 2231 leave (Macdonald, 1990; Seoul Development Institute, 1994). Following the nation's recent economic success, more people are participating in the new trend of owning a private automobile; every day, more than two million automobiles clog up already overcrowded city streets. The price of real estate has been escalating in recent years and Seoul is rapidly becoming like Tokyo, Japan where the price of real estate is nearly prohibitive to most residents. Residential segregation is a common phenomenon and the gap between "haves" and "have-nots" appears to be substantially widening.

Seoul is also heavily populated by those who do not have historical roots; more than 80% of the city residents settled here only during the last 30-year period. Moreover, this giant capital city shows all the symptoms of urban ills; overcrowding, traffic jams, air pollution, urban decay, and environmental degradation. Yet, for the foreseeable future, Seoul remains the most dominant and important city in Korea.

The formation of cities

We have briefly discussed the historical development of Seoul. There are many theories that have attempted to describe the formation of cities, but there is very little consensus among these theories in explaining how most cities have become what they are now. Traditional theories summarized in both Ward (1990) and Smith (1979) have shown that the changes and formation of a city can generally be seen as certain products stemming from unplanned, symbiotic ties evolved within the city as well as from particular spatial relations with the qualities of the city. Historically, cities with such natural assets as rivers, oceans, or canals have developed into dominant cities. These theories do not, however, relate a city's evolution to the outcome of the operation of the wider influences of national and international development (Smith, 1979; Ward, 1990).

Additionally, there has not been a unified explanation as to whether the process of urban growth for cities in today's developing world is similar to or essentially different from the experiences of the cities in Europe and the USA during the 19th and 20th centuries (Dogan and Kasarda, 1988). Castells (1983) has argued that cities are living systems and their forms and functions are produced and managed by the interaction between space and society; urban structures are, therefore, the expression of some institutionalized domination. The new international and interregional spatial divisions of labor, the growing importance of collective consumption through urban services and the intervention of the state have become even more important factors in understanding the formation of a city, particularly in the developing nations (Castells, 1977; 1983).

An important aspect of collective consumption (i.e. goods and services directly or indirectly provided by the state) in the formation of a city is illuminated by Castells et al. (1990) based on successful examples of public housing projects in Hong Kong and Singapore. Their work has also shown that a lack of state intervention in collective consumption in a given society could produce a higher level of conflict, thereby creating many forms of urban protest movement, and that only through an innovative method of meeting such demands from citizens could cities develop into a meaningful urban form. The process of state-led economic development that can be seen as a new condition of the world economy could therefore create an environment that includes the essential values of human capital formation and social integration (Castells et al., 1990). The formation of a city is, hence, determined by the interplay of economic growth, political power and cultural values, coupled with historical variations within the particular system (Castells, 1983; Castells et al., 1990). Though recognizing the importance of analytical and conceptual tools developed by Castells, Saunders (1983) argues that the concept of collective consumption should be understood within the framework of existing systems of the individualistic mode of consumption and of strong private sectors for many areas of the collective consumption; housing, in particular.

Based on the concept of time and space, Hall (1984) has emphasized that we should look sequentially at urban population growth. He has introduced a five-stage model of urban population evolution. With very limited economic and natural resources, a primary city is seen as the major source of the nation's economic and industrial activities, thereby forcing a large volume of rural to urban migration. A primary city receives an uneven share of the nation's population growth. Most cities in the developing world have experienced or are still in the process of completing this first stage of growth. With the moderate development of transportation systems, a spread of industrialization is possible throughout different regions of the nation, and population movement, still involving rural migrants, is now responsible for developing secondary cities. During this second stage, the primary city still dominates the nation's economic and industrial scene and its population continues to grow. Over time, the primary city becomes too densely populated and the surrounding towns and cities begin to receive spillover population. In the third stage, the primary city, particularly in the core areas, starts losing some population, and the surrounding towns and cities (peripheral areas) begin to exhibit a faster rate of population growth than the primary city. The fourth stage can be explained by a further loss of population from the primary city, whereas the secondary cities begin to receive more migrants, along with industries, and emerge as important economic centers. In the mean time, the population from the primary core areas continues to move to the peripheral areas. In the final stage, the decline of the primary city both in population and in significance accelerates, whereas secondary cities and non-metropolitan areas continue to grow. Although the peripheral areas suffer a little population loss, it symbolizes the end of the urban life cycle (Hall, 1984; Dogan and Kasarda, 1988).

Hall (1984) suggests that most of the cities in the current developing world fall under stages one and two, whereas some of the NICs such as Brazil, Mexico, and Korea, including many southern and Eastern European cities, are in stages two and three. Other European countries can be classified as stages four or five, whereas the USA and the UK are clearly in stage five (Hall, 1984). This model is similar to an earlier ecological theory that described a particular pattern of spatial dispersion by various income groups. This theory was originally developed by human ecologists such as Park et al. (1925), who state that cities are the outward manifestation of processes of spatial competition and adaptation by social groups which correspond to the ecological struggle for environmental adaptation found in nature (Cooke, 1983). Similar land use development patterns tend to create "zones of deterioration" or "concentric rings" on moving away from the central business districts. The central business districts are surrounded by a series of zones, depicting an increase in socio-economic status as the distance of each zone from the central business district increases. Although this theory describes a certain homogeneous land use segregation pattern, it does not explain the social determinants of such a ring pattern of growth (Tabb and Sawers, 1978).

Some additional theories that have relied on spatial determinism and consumer choice have stated that urbanization is a finite process, a cycle through which nations go in their transition from agrarian to industrial society. Along the way, cities with a more intensified division of labor and increased productivity become continuously larger, more complicated, and more interdependent (Blumenfeld, 1967; Davis, 1965). Raban (1974), whose work was based on London and was summarized in Harvey (1990), goes further by stating that cities show a widespread individualism and the marks of social distinction are broadly conferred by possessions and appearances. The cities are like a theatre, a series of stages where individuals could work their own distinctive magic, while performing a multiplicity of roles.

Others have argued that the development of spatial forms is conditioned by particular stages of capital accumulation, especially in the advanced capitalist countries (Gordon, 1978; Harvey, 1973; 1985). Gordon (1978), in particular, has described the urban development process by three main stages of capital accumulation – commercial accumulation, industrial accumulation, and corporate accumulation – and argues that the process of capital accumulation is the most important factor for structuring the growth of cities. Based on some historical evidence of cities in the USA, Gordon (1978) has shown that under commercial accumulation during the period 1800–1850, merchant capitalists sought to increase their capital through the exchange of commodities in the market place. Cities retained their heterogeneity and new immigrant groups were rapidly assimilated into the flowing central city life. The stage of commercial accumulation tended to generate uneven development among buyers and sellers and, consequently, stimulated popular demands for more economic and political equality.

Between 1850 and 1900, the stage of industrial accumulation became a dominant force as capitalists increasingly turned towards making profits through industrial production itself. Cities became the central locus for factory production, provided easy access to markets, and facilitated the scale of production necessary to support homogenized labor processes. As more huge factories were concentrated in downtown factory industrial districts, the central city was increasingly occupied by dependent wage-earners instead of independent property owners, thereby creating a separation between job and residential location. Unlike cities under commercial accumulation, cities no longer maintained residential heterogeneity and created a sharp residential segregation by economic class. A stage of corporate accumulation actually began during the turn of the century, between 1898 and 1920; corporate skyscrapers became a dominant cityscape in downtown areas and many factories left the central city. With the decentralization of manufacturing, many corporations were large enough to separate administrative functions from the production process and began controlling their labor forces in newly established suburban communities. Many new cities during the stage of corporate accumulation could be constructed from scratch to fit the needs of a new period of accumulation process. Manufacturing activities were scattered throughout the city plane; no dominant business centers anywhere, only diffuse economic activities everywhere (Gordon, 1978).

The development process of Seoul could probably be explained by some aspects of, or a combination of, these theories. Although a close interrelationship between the state and international capitalism in recent years has become a dominant force in creating the modern urban structure for Seoul, we must accept that the role of the state that was largely based on persuasion, coercion, and mediation was truly instrumental in shaping most of what Seoul is currently. With the sweeping, often brutal, intervention of the state for most urban redevelopment projects, local authorities were able to control the process of urban development and suppress any slight sign of urban politics of any kind of grassroots movement. In many areas of Seoul, major industrial giants such as Hyundai, Daewoo, Goldstar, and Samsung have competed to create their own physical identities by developing their headquarters through urban redevelopment projects. The ensuing result is a disjointed cityscape with individual corporate headquarters seeming to float in various districts of the city. In the following chapter we describe both the population and economic growth of Seoul and the SMR.

2

Population and economic growth in Seoul and Seoul Metropolitan Region

Like many other highly populated Asian cities, a seemingly endless flow of people waves with a great intensity through the physical plane of Seoul. Often, particularly during the morning and evening rush hours, huge throngs of people participate in the daily war of commuting. There appears to be no specific direction, much like the movement of amoebas, as to where all these people are coming from and going, but the existence of the city seems to be punctuated by a chaotic, yet routine, movement of people. By the late evening, however, the entire city again becomes a quiet, serene place, as if the great volume of people can only be discerned by an ever-increasing physical presence of high-rise apartments and tall, modern commercial skyscrapers.

As the capital of Korea, Seoul has always been an important city, but its impressive growth did not take place until the mid-1960s. Until then Seoul was essentially a small city with a heavy concentration of mercantile activities covering a very limited physical area. What then contributed to the rapid growth of Seoul, and which underlying factors were so important to the birth of both present Seoul and the Seoul Metropolitan Region (SMR)? In this chapter we will attempt to answer some of these intriguing questions by examining various contributing factors.

Population growth factors

There are many factors that have contributed to the growth of some great cities: the natural environment, natural population growth, inter-regional migration, economic opportunities, family ties, cultural activities, political institutions, and others. It appears that a boom and bust cycle of a certain historical period is also responsible for growth, as many cities have emerged with their own distinctive characteristics and identities throughout their historical growth process. There have always been push and pull factors in regional migration, mainly from rural to urban areas, with both the origin and destination exhibiting different strengths of economic, social, and political conditions.

Over the entire growth cycle of the city, Seoul has experienced a number of different growth factors. Chief among these is the social factor, which is largely explained by human migration. When a city experiences a high rate of urbanization, a natural growth factor that is the difference between the total number of births and deaths may not significantly contribute to the total growth.

Figure 2.1 clearly illustrates that since 1975 the total population growth for Seoul can be largely attributed to this social factor. Although not shown in the figure, it was particularly noted that between 1960 and 1975, most of the increase in population was caused by the social factor, the major reason for explosive growth. At one point, for example, the social factor was responsible for almost 90% of the total growth (Seoul Metropolis, 1977). During the early 1980s, however, the natural rate of growth outweighed the social factor until the rate of growth was again significantly reversed in 1988. Given the fact that birth control measures in Korea have been successful since the early 1960s, and that the natural growth rate has remained almost constant over the years, this might be an indication that the current population in Seoul has become a large enough pool of resources for natural growth. Even with a slow down in the population movement between the regions, particularly from rural areas, the rate of natural growth with this large pool of the present population may continue to be a significant factor for some time to come.

Growth during different historical periods

After Seoul was created as the capital city of the Yi Dynasty in 1394, the total population of the city fluctuated between 100 000 and 200 000 throughout most of the Yi Dynasty. In fact, until the early 1900s, the total population was about one million and was limited to this small

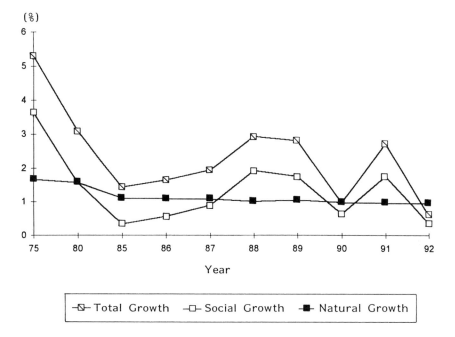

(%)

Figure 2.1 Growth factors in Seoul since 1975

size during most of the Japanese colonial period. As discussed in the previous chapter, the growth of Seoul can be distinguished by some clearly defined historical periods. Until the late 19th century, most cities, including Seoul, under the Yi Dynasty were small in size and evenly developed throughout the country, primarily according to their import-ance in political, administrative, and military functions. As the country was heavily dominated by an agrarian economic system, it was believed that an orderly distribution of small and medium-sized cities could contribute to the stability of the Kingdom. As the capital of the King-dom, Seoul always retained a special meaning for most people, as all important administrative, military, and educational decisions were made and carried out there.

To a large number of the country's residents, Seoul was the most admired and celebrated city to visit or reside in. After all, the palace was in the heart of the city, and as the country was under a heavily central-ized government system, most important political decisions affecting all aspects of their daily lives were decided in the palace. For example, in an attempt to find and cultivate hidden talents in the country, an annual civil service examination took place in the palace during most of the Yi Dynasty. This civil service examination, known as the *Kwageo* was the most prestigious and important event for young people who were aspiring to become civil servants and serve the Kingdom. Under the tradition of Confucianism, the country and her bureaucratic system rewarded bright young minds with higher levels of education. Crowds of young men came to Seoul and spent many years preparing for the examination at local room and board facilities. Those who were successful in passing the exam were usually rewarded by allowing their immediate families to relocate to Seoul.

Under the same tradition of Confucianism, however, most civil servants who completed their important government positions were expected to go back to their home towns to educate the next generation of young people for future government services. This social custom often prevented many aging yet physically active intellectuals from being permanently engaged in the capital city once they finished their administrative duties. As a result, Seoul was constantly filled with a flood of temporary residents, who not only wished to become a permanent fixture of the city, but who also willingly left for their home towns.

The opening of Korea's "Hermit Kingdom" to the outside world, followed by a period of Japanese colonial domination, signaled the beginning of the disruption of the well-preserved social balance. The Japanese colonial government forced many more cities to open and develop, particularly emphasizing infrastructure development such as railroads, highways, and harbors. Some of these newly developing cities took on a special meaning in the restructuring of urban space, becoming strategically important cities with connections to Japan and Manchuria, and subsequently provided opportunities for rural residents to relocate and participate in a more sophisticated urban lifestyle. When Japanese domination was ended in 1945, Seoul, along with the other major cities, became a haven for refugees and repatriates from Manchuria and Japan, due in a large part to the scarcity of land in their rural places of origin.

The devastating Korean War was an even greater catalyst for shifting and resettling the country's population. During the war the entire country and her fragile infrastructure were completely destroyed and, during one particular period in 1953, North Korean forces came very close to overtaking most of the land in South Korea. Immediately after the armistice agreement was reached in July 1953, a massive population exodus from rural areas to a number of larger urban cities occurred in South Korea, including those who had already fled North Korea during the war. Seoul absorbed a large number of migrants daily from rural areas and a major shift in population from rural to urban centers began to take place in South Korea.

When Korea's export-oriented economic development took a giant step forward during the late 1960s, yet another tremendous population surge from rural to urban centers occurred. As more jobs resulting from this robust economic growth were available in many large cities, many young men and women who were either unemployed or not satisfied with farm-related activities took part in this population shift. The entire country, under the new leadership of the military regime, was being spatially transformed in terms of identifying and developing new cities and regions for particular types of industrial development. For example, many cities in the southeastern and southern regions of the country were developed into special industrial zones producing heavy goods such as automobiles, steel, and ships, whereas other inland cities were targeted for light industries and high-tech industrial development.

Consequently, cities were able to attract workers to meet their required labor needs. At the same time, Seoul and other small and medium-sized cities immediately surrounding the capital were also fully participating in the vibrant economic growth cycle by attracting even larger numbers of new migrants. This influx of population was particularly acute as Seoul was still considered to be the center of the locus for financial capital, political power, bureaucratic and transportation networks, and abundant economic opportunities.

Urbanization

With an ever increasing rate of urbanization after the end of the Japanese colonial period, the influence of urban centers on Korea's spatial distribution has become an ever stronger force. In 1955, for example, the rate of urbanization for Korea was about 30.2% and this only increased to about 35.8% in 1960. However, with strong and constant economic growth beginning in the late 1960s, the trend towards larger urban cities for better employment opportunities and other amenities seems to have accelerated. During the next 20 years there were strong push factors in many of the rural areas that favored large urban cities providing better opportunities for jobs, education, family ties, and other attractions closely related to the quality of life. Indeed, Korea was changing from an agrarian society to a complex industrial society. Rates of urbanization showed substantial increases to 49.8, 68.7, and 75% in 1970, 1980 and 1990, respectively. According to a recent United Nations study, this rate of increase in urbanization during the last 30 years is one of the fastest in the world, even among other developing nations (Kang Dae Gi, 1987; City of Seoul, 1991).

Paralleling this impressive growth in urbanization, the dominance of Seoul in attracting new migrants as well as redefining the urban configuration in Korea has been substantial. Table 2.1 shows the growth

Table 2.1 Trends in population and number of households for Seoul and Korea

Year	Korea		Seoul					
	Population (000s): A	Increase (%)	Population: B	Increase (%)	B/A	Household	Increase (%)	Average number of people per household
1945	–	–	901 371	–	–	189 590	–	4.75
1950	–	–	1 693 224	13.44	–	318 673	10.95	5.31
1955	21 502	–	1 574 868	-1.44	7.3	259 660	-4.01	6.07
1960	24 594	2.72	2 445 402	9.2	9.6	446 874	11.47	5.47
1965	28 705	3.24	3 470 880	7.25	13.3	649 290	7.76	5.35
1970	31 435	1.83	5 525 262	9.74	17.6	1 096 871	11.06	5.04
1975	34 679	1.98	6 889 502	4.51	19.9	1 409 571	5.14	4.89
1980	37 419	1.53	8 364 379	3.96	22.8	1 842 239	5.5	4.54
1985	40 467	1.58	9 639 110	2.88	23.8	2 329 374	4.8	4.14
1988	41 975	1.24	10 286 503	2.19	24.5	2 658 371	4.5	3.87
1990	43 411	1.71	10 612 577	1.06	24.4	2 820 292	3.05	3.76
1992	43 663	0.3	10 969 862	1.68	25.1	3 383 169	9.98	3.24

Sources: Economic Planning Board, 1962–1994; City of Seoul (1961–1994); and Seoul Metropolis (1987–1993)

pattern in Seoul and Korea since 1945. As expected, the population increase for Seoul has been substantially higher than that of the nation as a whole. Although immediately following the civil war the total population in Seoul actually declined, the rate of increase for subsequent years was constantly high, with most of the growth taking place during the 1960s and 1970s. In 1955, the total population in Seoul was only about 7.3% of the country's total population, representing about 24.3% of the total population of cities with 20 000 or more people. In 1992, however, Seoul's share of the nation's population increased to 25.1%, whereas that of cities with 20 000 or more people jumped to more than 32%. In just over a 30-year period, the total population in Seoul mushroomed from a mere 900 000 in 1945 to almost 11 million in 1992, representing more than one-quarter of the country's total population.

This high rate of urbanization in Seoul had some serious consequences. With high expectations of a wide range of available employment opportunities, however seriously flawed at times, a large number of residents from rural and small towns migrated to Seoul without any realistic prospects for jobs or housing. As Seoul was very limited in its physical size, and had a very small supply of housing, many of the new migrants had to settle in the outskirts beyond the city boundary, thereby creating clusters of uncontrolled settlements. The growth of many squatter settlement areas was magnified by a series of chain migrations often seen in other underdeveloped countries. During earlier stages of urbanization, many of the squatter settlements were teeming, and crowded living situations persisted along with the lack of a much needed physical infrastructure, a degraded environment and high unemployment rates. Consequently, many newcomers had to rely on low-skilled menial jobs for employment. In an attempt to alleviate some of these urban ills, however loosely defined by government officials, many government-sponsored slum clearance projects were initiated. A vicious cycle of urban renewal projects found its roots and began spreading widely throughout the entire city.

Before Seoul became too large to manage, both in physical size and population, it was a small, lively, and integrated place; new migrants were able to assimilate themselves into the existing social and economic fabric of the capital. With the ever increasing size of the city, housing construction experienced a boom in Seoul, particularly in the mid-1970s. There was a conscious decision on the government's part to encourage private developers to construct many more high-rise apartment buildings with varied sizes and price structures. As Seoul expanded its physical growth to the south of the Han River, large-scale residential developments and dense commercial developments began to emerge. The surrounding infrastructure was based on the grid-street patterns of

Western countries. Most of the newly developed apartment buildings offered a modern heating system, a Western-style kitchen and bathroom, and other modern amenities, which appealed to an increasing number of residents who seriously considered them as alternatives to the traditional and inconvenient style of Korean housing. As many residents decided to experiment with the new and modern style of living, enjoying these new amenities in housing units in new high-rise apartment districts, it soon became fashionable for people to live in the newly created living quarters.

Urban slum-clearance projects, though initially intended to benefit their original low-income residents, often resulted in high-rise apartments for middle and upper middle income residents. Several residential areas suitable for higher income people were also continuously developed south of the Han River. As Seoul exhibited a high rate of residential mobility, it became clear that a new level of spatial rearrangement was taking place in many parts of the capital. Many more people were packed into large apartment complexes where the daily lives of the residents were boxed in, thus abandoning the traditional lifestyle of a close-knit neighborhood where their everyday activities were interwoven with other neighbors. Consequently, residential segregation along economic lines and social classes is only a very recent phenomenon.

Regional migration

There are various reasons why people participate in regional migration, even with the high costs associated with such a move: the high transportation costs of a long-distance move, uncertainty about the destination, the disruption of family life and the social network, and many other hidden and intangible factors. Frequently, however, employment opportunities do dictate the decision-making process for migrants, although a wide range of conditions at both the origin and destination may also be influential. It is unclear, however, how many potential migrants decide to make a regional move by first securing jobs at the destination. It has been shown that many migrants do come to a new place without the promise of new jobs and then search for employment opportunities.

Government policies favoring one region over another may be a strong factor in influencing the regional variations and fluctuations of their economic and political strength. In physical size alone, Korea is a very small country, but a strong regional variation has been in existence throughout her modern history.

This regional difference became even more acute in economic and political terms after the military coup of 1961. When President Park, Chung Hee, ex-general from the southeastern region of the country, was actively promoting Korea's new economic development plans, he and the power elites surrounding him made strong efforts to locate modern industrial development sites in the region from which they all originated: it made perfect political sense to them that they had to pit this region against other parts of the country, particularly the south-western region where Mr Park's political opposition leader maintained a strong and broad support. Since then this regional faction, however unreasonable and contentious it may seem, has become a part of daily political reality in Korea. The living standards of the southeastern region that the power elite represented continually outperform those of other regions by a substantial margin.

The enduring power of Seoul as the center of all political and econ-omic power has flourished and functioned as strong pull factors, while Korea's overall economy was still underdeveloped and rural areas suffered from a lack of available employment opportunities for the young. Since the end of the civil war, in-migrants to Seoul have con-tinuously increased at rates fluctuating by region and, until the early 1980s, represented a substantial portion of the city's total growth. Although the number and rate of in-migrants into Seoul has slowed in recent years, the total number of in-migrants in 1988, for example, was still about 960 000, whereas that of out-migrants was 770 000 (City of Seoul, 1989).

Of those who migrated into Seoul, about 41.8% of the total came from the neighboring Kyonggi-do Province, whereas the percentages from Chollanam-do Province, Chungchungnam-do Province, and Chollabuk-do Province were 8.7, 7.8, and 7.2%, respectively. Kyonggi-do Province received the most out-migrants from Seoul – about 54% of the total out-migrants. The city of Inchon had 8.9% of the total out-migrants from Seoul, whereas Chungchungnam-do Province and Chollanam-do Pro-vince took in 6.4 and 5.3%, respectively (City of Seoul, 1989; KRIHS, 1988). These patterns of movement have in recent years exhibited a clear indication for Seoul and its immediately surrounding region, Kyonggi-do Province, to dominate the movement of population. In other words, as almost half of the regional migration is concentrated in these two places, we must recognize the fact that they have recently developed substantially strong economic ties and will remain as the most powerful regional center, due in part to their very close physical proximity to each other.

According to two household surveys conducted for both long-term Seoul residents and the most recent migrants to Seoul, the most frequently mentioned factor for relocating to Seoul was economic reasons, regardless of their time of residence: 48.3% for long-term residents and 55.6% for recent migrants. Factors included as economic reasons were changes in the place of employment, company relocation, looking for jobs, and other employment-related motivations. For long-term Seoul residents, the next important factors for moving were family ties (20.8%) and better school districts for children (17.4%), whereas for recent migrants better school districts for children was the second most important factor (22.5%) (City of Seoul, 1961–1994; 1988; KRIHS, 1988). These results seem to confirm our expectation that chain migration might have served its useful function in the earlier stages of migration to Seoul, where existing family members were an important element in channeling and sorting out the necessary information or developing support networks in the new environment.

However, like many other Asian countries (e.g. Japan, China, Taiwan), educational aspiration under the influence of Confucianism is considered one of the most crucial elements in Korea. A proper path to the best high schools and universities, particularly in Seoul, is believed to lead to a successful career for Korean children and has resulted in one of the most fiercely competitive K-12 (kindergarten to high school) educational systems in the world. The curriculum is geared towards preparation for the university entrance examination. Therefore it is essential for parents to search for and locate the best school system that fits the need of their children, most preferably in notable secondary school districts in Seoul. A preference for better school systems, noted by both long-term residents and recent migrants, may be a clear indication that parents are willing to pay any cost, including the high cost of interregional migration, for an opportunity to send their children to better schools and universities in Seoul.

Residential mobility

More often than not, factors affecting residential mobility are very different from those of regional migration. Residential mobility is often associated with personal satisfaction with current residential services and the neighborhood environment and involves a shorter physical distance. For example, as families undergo a rapid change in the stage of the family life cycle by expanding their family size, they are faced with options. If they are fortunate enough to have financial means, they could exercise their options by either staying at their current residence or moving to a newer, roomier house to alleviate crowding. Many other factors such as distance to the place of employment, school system, neighborhood preference, marriage or divorce, home ownership, and psychological satisfaction with the current residence could be why people decide to make a local move.

Another reason for a high rate of residential mobility could be active participation in the local labor force, viewed as a strong and vital element of a certain community. On the other hand, residential stability could easily be threatened by this high rate of local mobility. A sense of belonging among friends and residents may no longer exist, and the ability to recognize familiar faces in the community may deteriorate – a defense mechanism which is an important element of urban living. Most of all, the social networks that follow a stable residential environment may also be shattered, thereby creating an urban environment where everyone becomes strangers to each other.

Accompanied by an ever increasing rate of urbanization, residential mobility in Seoul has been increasing. One study showed that more than 21% of the total residents in Seoul changed their place of residence in 1989 (*Choongang Daily*, 24 August 1990). Although detailed studies about residential mobility in Seoul are not readily available, a quick glimpse at the situation suggests that most people have made their moves based on their preferences: wanting to be closer to their place of employment or a shorter commuting time, wanting to be in a neighborhood of their own liking, or participating in real estate speculation. Many other residents, particularly those who did not own their own homes or who lacked financial resources, might have been forced to move out of their current residence. Many tenants are often faced with the unpleasant reality of an ever increasing rent, forcing them to look elsewhere for more affordable accommodation. It is a common phenomenon in Seoul's residential housing market that increasing numbers of people are not able to own their own homes due to escalating house prices in recent years. The rate of home ownership has been consistently below 50% and in 1990 fell below 40% for the first time in modern history (City of Seoul, 1990).

Another major factor for residential mobility in Seoul is the aspiration of most residents for a better school district. Some families may have become disenchanted with their current school district for their children and may choose to relocate to another school district where they believe their children could receive a better education. Presently, Seoul has eight school districts for K-12 education and it is obviously clear that many residents are making attempts to move into one of the better known districts, particularly those south of the Han River. The performance of a school district is generally measured by the percentage of high-school students who receive admission to a few highly selective universities in Seoul after taking a nationally conducted test. As competition for admission to these universities is fierce, any added incentive such as

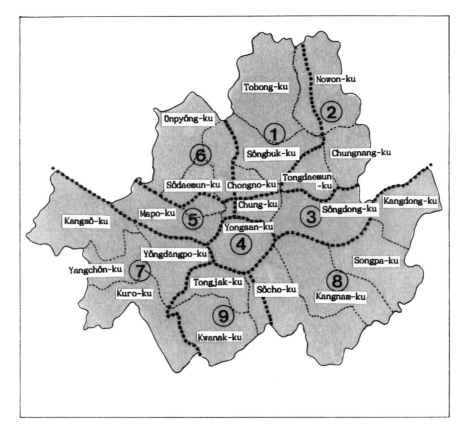

Figure 2.2 High school districts of Seoul

sending children to a better known school district that could offer a higher than average chance of attending one of the schools with a high rate university admission is considered a true bonus.

Because of severe shortages of available housing, national law prohibits residents in Korea from owning more than one home per head of household. As many residents in Seoul, who may exercise their option of moving to a better school district, often have their own homes, it creates a logistical problem for them to relocate to the desired school district without abandoning their current residence. Most people caught in this situation decide to lease their current residence and rent another home in the school district of their choice. Consequently, in one of the most highly coveted school districts south of the Han River, school district number eight in Figure 2.2, the cost of leasing a home is often higher than the actual selling price of the home.

Tiebout (1956) wrote in his seminal piece about consumers voting with their feet on the selection of a potential community to reside. Many studies based on his theoretical work have made attempts to quantify the variables influencing the decision-making process of consumers: property tax rates, population density, a better school system, distance to the city center, and others (Oates, 1969; Edel and Sclar, 1974). This unusually strong aspiration for a better school district, not only for Seoul residents but for most Koreans, may perhaps be the best available explanation for exemplifying Tiebout's theory, as many residents here are willing to make a residential choice at any cost without the consideration of all other prevailing factors: is this the fanatical nature of residents in Seoul or of all Koreans concerning their children's educational future? In any event, without a complete overhaul of the current educational system at the national level, this strong desire for better school districts, however ill-conceived, remains a forceful factor influencing residential mobility.

Spatial distribution

In 1945, Seoul had only eight districts (wards) with a very small population base, but has now expanded to 25 districts with a total of more than 11 million people. During the 1970s and 1980s, most development and growth took place south of the Han River and the population in all districts south of the Han River in relation to the total population in Seoul grew from 17.8% in 1966 to more than 50% in 1992 (City of Seoul, 1993).

During the early period of Seoul's growth, particularly until the late 1960s, Seoul could be characterized as a small city with one distinct central business district (CBD) where most important business and political activities took place. Although this old CBD maintains the symbolic and traditional importance of the city, houses City Hall and other key government offices such as the Presidential Mansion, and many business offices, Seoul today is a large metropolis with multiple CBDs scattered throughout the city. Over the years a clear density gradient from the CBD in terms of population distribution has not existed in Seoul. Some recent studies have indicated that most population growth has occurred in areas between 5 and 30 km away from the CBDs, with the most spectacular growth being in areas between 20 and 30 km from the CBDs (Kim An Jae, 1984; KRIHS, 1985).

With more global functions being introduced in Seoul, most CBDs were soon dominated by skyscrapers, hosting such activities as banking, information services, offices, hotels, restaurants, and other service-oriented business. Many more commercial development projects were created by clearing many of the existing older residential areas in the CBDs. The cost of land in and around the CBDs rapidly increased to a point where any type of conventional residential development was simply prohibitive. As a result, residents with enough financial resources were able to find new homes within the boundary of the city, whereas others who could not afford this ever increasing cost of housing had to look elsewhere, outside the city limit but within the boundary of the SMR.

Thus a new urban spatial fabric was born in Seoul, much like other cities in developed nations. Most residential functions are some distance away from the CBDs, separating the functions between the two, and CBDs concentrate business activities during normal business hours. More congested traffic is commonly seen during the rush hour, although the rush hour appears to be a permanent fixture from the early morning to the late evening.

Population and economic structure

Population structure

With Korea's rapid economic development and a success in population control measures since the 1960s, the general characteristics of the population resemble those of other advanced nations: a bell-shaped population graph indicating a significant decline in fertility and a substantial increase in life expectancy.

With almost a quarter of the country's total population residing in Seoul, the population distribution of Seoul, though heavily influenced by national policies, is still similar to that of the nation. A major difference between the two graphs is the greater proportion of people participating in the labor force in Seoul, as shown in Figure 2.3. This finding is not surprising as Seoul, the powerful center of economic activities, has attracted a larger proportion of the age cohorts between 15 and 50 years of age over the years.

Since 1940 the population structure for Korea has followed a unique characteristic of its own. Between 1940 and 1955, the painful recovery from both Japanese colonialism and the civil war contributed to a much lower total birth rate than previous years. In addition, as men were routinely forced to serve in the military and many of them were killed during these two tragic periods, the ensuing result was a lower proportional representation of surviving older men; a generally higher life expectancy for women is also responsible for this uneven distribution in the pyramid. Following this particular period, a baby boom began and lasted almost 10 years before it was curtailed by successful birth control policies that significantly reduced fertility rates. When Korea's economic development took off during the late 1960s and the early 1970s, another period of moderately high fertility followed. Owing to Korea's continuing national policies on birth control, coupled with the most recent fluctuations in both Korean and international economic growth, the total birth rate in Korea has been falling and has remained steadily low. It has now almost reached a stage of stable growth, with the total fertility rate among women of child-bearing age substantially reduced from 6.0 in 1960 to 1.6 in 1990 (City of Seoul, 1992). However, the traditional Korean custom of favoring boys over girls may explain why slightly higher rates of male births in the earlier age cohorts still exist. As more baby boomers go through their expected life cycle stages with marriages, the total population growth will continue to present a challenge to national policy-makers.

Clearly the population characteristics of Seoul have been affected by these unique national tendencies, along with intense regional migration and natural growth. Seoul now experiences a graying phenomenon where the total population is becoming older. For example, the distribution of the age cohort between 0 and 14 declined from 37.4% in 1961 to 28.3% in 1985, while that of the age cohorts over 60 years increased from 2.7 to 4.7% for the same years (City of Seoul, 1989). This graying phenomenon is due in a large part to strong national economic growth, an improvement in diet, a better health environment for the older generation, and a tremendous increase in the life expectancy of the general public.

Most recently, however, a tendency towards smaller family size has prevailed among the younger generation. The traditional Korean culture always emphasized a harmonious large family unit, with the eldest son taking care of his parents and younger siblings. Therefore it was fairly common that two or three generations of the family shared and lived in one household. As more Western-style culture was introduced through rapid economic development and an internationalization of Korean society, it was inevitable that the concept of the nuclear family became fashionable and grew as an acceptable social practice. Every young generation favoring and pursuing its own lifestyle, especially in Seoul and other major cities, has shown a preference to avoid the burden of caring for parents or siblings in one household. The steady decline in family size in Seoul may demonstrate this new phenomenon: the average family size (Table 2.1) was 6.07 people per household in 1955 and declined progressively over the years to 5.47 in 1960, 5.04 in 1970, 4.54 in 1980, and 3.24 in 1992.

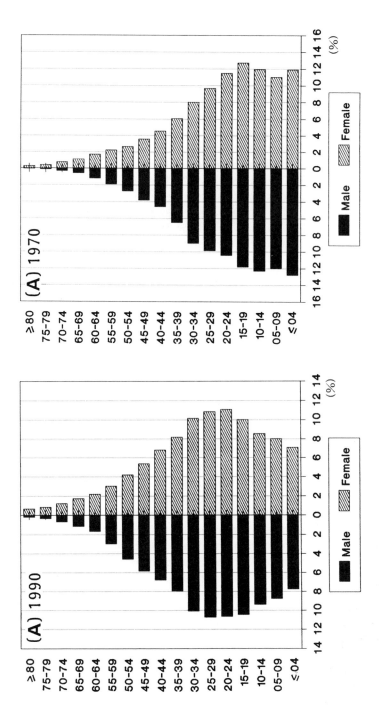

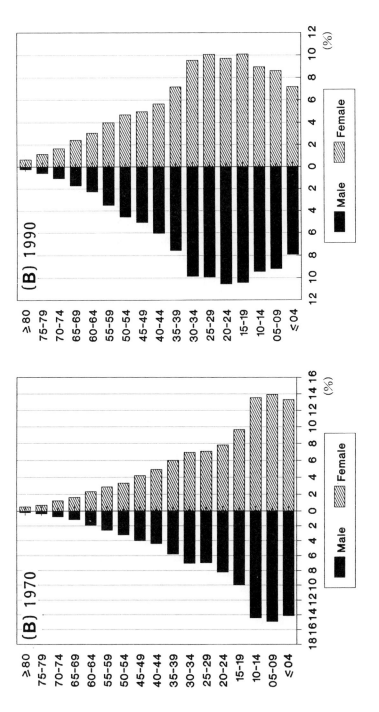

Figure 2.3 Population pyramids for (A) Seoul and (B) Korea, 1970 and 1990

Paralleling this trend towards a smaller family size, the number of one-person household units in Seoul has also been steadily increasing. In 1960, for example, only about 1.9% of the total number of households consisted of one person, increasing to 6.7% in 1985. In 1990, the national total for one-person households was more than 10% (City of Seoul, 1989; National Statistical Office, 1992). This new trend is largely attributed to the sudden opening of Korean society to Western lifestyles, an increase in the economic and social well-being from the country's successful economic development, a fluid social and population mobility, and changes in their cultural value system. Whatever the true reasons behind these movements, they raise some serious questions about traditional Korean family values as they are constantly challenged, reflected, and redefined. An immediate and practical issue facing these interesting, yet unsettling, trends is the supply of available housing with particular design criteria: the amount of physical space required for such smaller families may not be accommodated by the present housing market.

Economic structure

As Seoul became a locus of urban growth, its overall economic activities expanded accordingly. Table 2.2 illustrates Seoul's economic growth and position in relation to its national share since 1960.

Using the 1980 Korean won as a constant value ($1.00 equals about 800 Korean won), the growth rate of gross regional product (GRP) for Seoul has been significantly higher than that of the nation's gross national product (GNP) at the beginning of national development. Since the late 1980s, the growth rate for Seoul slowed compared with that for the nation.[1] As expected, in the earlier stages of urbanization, when most urban cities provided much of the nation's economic and employment activities, Seoul's per capita GRP was about twice the nation's per capita GNP, but over the years the difference has significantly narrowed; by 1991 they had become almost identical, a clear indication of the improvement in economic strength of non-urban areas. Although the rate of increase for Seoul's portion of the nation's GNP has slowed in recent years, Seoul still commands almost one-quarter of the nation's GNP, a substantial concentration for a small country such as Korea.

---

[1] The exchange rate between Korean won and U.S. $ fluctuates. A rate of 800 won for $1.00 is used throughout the book. The growth rate after 1986 in Table 2.2 should be viewed with caution, since time periods are much shorter than the previous years.

Table 2.2 Changes in GNP and GRP with time for Seoul and Korea

	Nation (A)						Seoul (B)						B/A (%)		
	GNP			Per capita (a)			GNP			Per capita GRP (b)					
	Population (000s)	Current price*	1980 price	Current price†	US $	1980 price	Population (000s)	Current price*	1980 price	Current price†	US $	1980 price	Seoul/ Nation population	GRP/ GNP	b/a
1960	24 989	245	7054	10	94	282	2445	46	1337	19	180	547	9.8	19	194
1970	32 241	2684	15 777	83	243	489	5525	699	4108	127	371	744	17.1	26	152
1980	38 124	34 321	34 321	900	1481	900	8367	9825	9825	1174	1931	1174	22	29	130
1986	41 569	90 598	88 173	2207	2505	1497	9799	22 800	17 275	2611	2962	2000	23.6	28.8	133
1989	42 449	141 794	119 577‡	3353	4494	2816‡	10 334	35 265	29 044	3412	5081	2810‡	24.3	24.9	102
1991	43 268	206 026	141 602	4767	6498	3273‡	10 597	51 102	34 218	4822	6573	3229‡	24.5	24.8	101
Ave. rate of change (%)															
1960–70	2.6	27	8.4	10	10	5.7	8.5	31.3	11.9	20.9	7.5	3.1	–	–	–
1970–80	1.7	28.5	8.2	26.4	18.9	6.4	4.2	30	9	24.7	17.1	4.6	–	–	–
1980–86	1.5	16.7	10.1	15.1	7.6	8.9	2.7	16.8	9.9	14.3	7.4	9.3	–	–	–
1986–89	0.7	21.2	31.9	17.3	19	29.4	1.9	18.2	12.7	10.2	23.8	13.5	–	–	–
1989–91	0.96	22.6	9.2	21.3	15.3	8.11	1.3	22.5	8.9	20.6	14.7	7.5	–	–	–

* In billion won.
† In thousand won.
‡ 1985 price.

Source: Bank of Korea, 1983; Economic Planning Board, 1978–1986; Seoul Metropolis, 1984b; City of Seoul, 1961–1994; and Korea Urban Administration Institute, 1994.

With the rapid expansion of the country's economic development came an improved standard of living for most people. As shown in Table 2.2, Korea's per capita GNP in 1960 was only $94, whereas Seoul's per capita GRP was only about $180. Over the years, however, both measures have shown a remarkable increase to about $6498 for per capita GNP and $6573 for per capita GRP in 1991. As long as Seoul maintains its dominance over general economic and political affairs, the standard of living for Seoul will continue to be higher than that of most regions of the country. However, it is expected that the gap between Seoul and the rest of the country may not widen as much in the future as the quality of life in Seoul continues to deteriorate and other regions of the country progressively improve their economic activities and overall living standards.

Throughout the economic progress Korea has maintained, the distribution of income among the general public has also improved. The Gini Index for Korea has been steadily improving and was about 0.3355 in 1988, an indication that the distribution of income may be reaching a more equitable position (City of Seoul, 1989). Because Korea has always emphasized and adopted economic development policies based on absolute growth, yet ignored many serious social consequences, very few policies and programs about social distribution have been introduced. As a result, Seoul, following the national trend, has shown a pattern of not having any significant social programs and has an uneven distribution of income that has not been critically addressed.

With intense competition for daily survival, an increasing number of households began falling below the poverty level. According to an official study conducted by the City of Seoul, about 3% of Seoul's population was considered welfare-dependent (City of Seoul, 1989). Among these about 65 000 families or 212 000 individuals were welfare recipients falling below the level of urban poverty. An average monthly income for most families was below 46 000 won and they did not hold reliable, permanent employment. An additional 12 500 households or 17 300 people were considered as handicapped. In general, many of the handicapped people had chronic mental illness or permanent physical disabilities. The remaining figures applied to those who could not actively participate in the labor force due to their age limitations (over 65 years or below 18 years of age) or to other health-related problems (City of Seoul, 1989).

The same study further surveyed a residential development area, originally a squatter settlement area but later expanded as a heavily populated locale consisting of low-income households. The results indicated that almost 44% of the residents had a monthly income less than 300 000 won ($1.00 equals about 800 won), which falls well under the official guideline of urban poverty. More than 72% of the total respondents said that their monthly income was so low that their daily needs outstripped any possibility of savings every month. These studies again indicate that economic growth does not automatically equate to a better distribution of income, particularly for a rapidly growing and urbanizing city such as Seoul. More government policies and programs addressing social issues must be developed so that any social ills stemming from a potentially widening gap between "haves" and "have-nots" can be effectively minimized.

As the development of Seoul closely followed the economic growth of Korea, the economic structure of Seoul has been largely influenced by the restructuring of Korea's industrial development (Cha, 1986). Tables 2.3 and 2.4 chronicle the historical emergence of different industries and illustrate an employment distribution for the nation and for Seoul. As illustrated in Table 2.3 for 1960, the proportion of the nation's primary industry, measured as a share of Korea's GDP, was about 44.3%, whereas that of secondary industry was only about 10.1%. The overall trend in Korea's agriculturally based economy being increasingly trans-formed into a more complex heavy and light industrial based economy bolstered by aggressive national economic development plans is seen in the continuing decrease in the primary industrial sector for both Seoul and the nation over the years. Indeed, Korea exhibits more economic activities in secondary and tertiary industries, especially in the high-tech and service industries.

This trend has been a major factor contributing to the growth patterns of Seoul's industrial sectors. Although primary industry in Seoul has never been a significant part of the overall industry (2.6% in 1960 and 0.5% in 1991), it has now become almost non-existent and has yielded to other types of industrial activities such as the fast-rising secondary industry. Over the years, as more and more agricultural land and other green areas have been developed into part of the new urban landscape in Seoul, most of the people who were once engaged in the agriculture and forestry sector have had to change their jobs. Furthermore, as the more recent industrial policies for Seoul have discouraged permits for new manufacturing firms and also encouraged the relocation of many existing manufacturing factories with high pollution problems, heavy industrial operations, or antiquated equipment to outside the city limits, a gradual decrease in secondary industry has also been seen over time. Table 2.4 confirms this historical trend. Manufacturing and service related employment have dominated the overall picture and there has been no indication that this pattern of employment structure will change in the near future.

Table 2.3 Changing nature of industrial structure for Seoul and Korea. Values given are percentages of the total

Year	Primary industry		Secondary industry		Tertiary industry	
	Nation	Seoul	Nation	Seoul	Nation	Seoul
1960	44.3	2.6	10.1	22.1	45.6	75.3
1965	37.6	–	19.9	–	42.5	–
1970	26.8	2.6	22.3	26.5	51	70.9
1975	24.9	1.4	28	27.3	47.1	71.3
1980	16.9	1.1	30.7	24	55.1	74.9
1985	13.5	0.9	29.6	28.7	56.9	70.4
1987	11.4	0.6	31.5	29.6	57.1	69.8
1992	0.5	0.5	51.3	27.3	48.1	72.3

Sources: Economic Planning Board, 1978–1986; City of Seoul, 1984; City of Seoul, 1961–1994; and Ministry of Labour, 1993.

Table 2.4 Employment by industrial sector. Values given are percentages of the total

Year	Agriculture, forestry and fisheries		Mining and manufacturing		SOC* and other services	
	Nation	Seoul	Nation	Seoul	Nation	Seoul
1966	57.2	3	13.2	27	29.7	70
1970	50.8	2	15.2	28.7	34	69.3
1975	45.9	2	19.2	34.4	35	63.5
1980	34	0.9	22.6	32.5	43.4	66.5
1985	24.9	0.9	24.4	28.7	50.6	70.4
1987	21.9	0.6	28.1	29.6	50	69.8
1991	16.7	0.5	26.9	34.3	56.4	65.3

* Social overhead capital (secondary capital improvement projects).

Sources: Economic Planning Board, 1962–1994; and City of Seoul, 1961–1994.

The total labor force in Seoul has also shown a tremendous growth over the years. Table 2.5 shows an enormous increase in its total labor force from 1.26 million in 1970 to 4.8 million in 1992. This impressive rate of increase exceeds the rate of increase for the economically active population for the same period. Although the labor force participation rate has remained consistent, fluctuating between 47.7 and 49.7%, for 1970 and 1987, it has been significantly increased to 60.1% since 1990, perhaps an indication of the continuing economic expansion. More importantly, the unemployment rate has decreased substantially from 13% in 1970 to about 3% in 1992. Not only does this indicate a possible

Table 2.5 Economically active population of Seoul

Year	Population 15 years old and over (000s)	Economically active population					Non-economically active population (000s)
		Economically active population (000s)	Activity rate (%)	Employed (000s)	Unemployed (000s)	Unemployment rate (%)	
1970	3039	1450	47.7	1257	193	13.3	1589
1975	–	2248	–	1998	250	11.1	–
1980	5847	2665	45.6	2391	274	10.3	3182
1985	6855	3202	46.8	2926	277	8.6	3652
1987	7337	3468	49.7	3404	244	6.7	3689
1990	7803	4691	60.1	4505	186	4	3112
1992	8217	4966	60.4	4804	162	3.3	3251

Sources: City of Seoul, 1961–1994; and Korea Urban Administration Institute, 1994.

shortage of workers in some sectors of the economy for Seoul, an expected benefit from a robust economic growth since the early 1960s, but it also partially explains why there are so many foreigners from Southeast Asian countries working in various service sector jobs.

The occupational distribution of the total labor force in Seoul is shown in Table 2.6. An overall pattern of the distribution for all occupational categories does not seem to vary very much over time, except for some of the obvious sectors previously discussed: agriculture, fishery and forestry, and manufacturing, transport and storage.

With Seoul's growth as the center of economic and political activities, a steady growth of professionals and clerical workers was evident, as expected, from 19% in 1966 to 32% in 1987. Employment for administration and government did not expand much as a very strict civil service examination system still dictates almost all the available employment opportunities for young people. This might explain a consistently low rate of 3% or below for this particular occupational group. Although the distribution for both sales and service sector workers remained largely unchanged over time, these two sectors may generate more employment opportunities in the future as Seoul follows the pattern of more advanced nations and becomes an integral part of the international economy, thereby attracting more consumer and information oriented economic sectors.

Our discussions in this section have concentrated on the formal sector of economic activities. Seoul, like many other major cities in the world, also has a large informal sector. Full employment is far from a realistic goal for the economy, largely due to the interrelationship between a rapid rate of urbanization and the ability to absorb a rapidly growing labor pool from national economic expansion. As a result, some have argued that the informal economy is a necessary condition of a modern city. Holand (1976) presented an analysis of surplus labor, whereas Berry (1981) linked it to a street economy, with residual economic activities outside the regulated labor force. The informal sector of the economy is represented by small-scale businesses, characterized by a low intensity of capital, and operative outside the boundary of state-regulated economic activities. However, according to a recent study the informal economy is not viewed as a set of survival activities performed by destitute people on the margins of society, but instead is systematically related to the activities of the formal economy (Portes et al., 1989).

The informal economy consists of various economic activities often associated with a lower status of labor, unpreferred conditions of work environment, and some illegal activities (Portes et al., 1989). Street vendors as one part of the informal economy have always been an

Table 2.6 Occupational structure in Seoul. Values given are numbers in thousands (percentages)

	1966		1970		1980		1987		1992	
All occupations	884	(100)	1622	(100)	2391	(100)	3404	(100)	4777	(100)
Professional and technical	53	(5.9)	98	(6)	153	(6)	280	(8.2)	–	
Administrators	30	(3.4)	47	(2.9)	31	(1.3)	110	(3.2)	1700*	(35.6)
Office and clerical	122	(13.8)	237	(14.6)	564	(23.6)	814	(23.9)	–	
Sales	199	(22.5)	334	(20.6)	654	(27.3)	736	(21.6)	–	
Service	120	(13.6)	231	(14.2)	247	(10.3)	431	(12.7)	1539†	(32.2)
Agriculture, forestry and others	25	(2.8)	31	(1.9)	20	(0.8)	15	(0.4)	22	(0.5)
Production and equipment operators	336	(38)	621	(30.3)	723	(30.3)	1017	(29.9)	1516	(31.7)

* Total for professional and technical, administrators and clerical.
† Total for sales and service.

Source: City of Seoul, 1961–1994.

integral part of the total economic structure in Seoul. Casual observers strolling the streets of Seoul have probably encountered a diverse nature of goods and services provided by the street vendors who sell ice cream, clothes, food, small merchandise, unusual books, oriental medicines, and other products. Most of them are not registered with the proper authorities of the municipal government and thus their activities are often illegal. Although many of these entrepreneurs lack the necessary capital to expand their business activities beyond what they presently barter, they are mobile in a sense that they can quickly change their business whenever it is needed.

The City of Seoul has always recognized the importance of the street vendors and only when officials believe that their presence has harmed public health and safety do they institute the procedures to clean up illegal activities. The total number of people participating in the informal sector economy in Seoul fluctuates, depending on the goodwill of local officials or the clean-up policies following such national events as the 1988 Summer Olympics. According to a study conducted by the City of Seoul in 1989, the total number of street vendors increased from 9300 in 1984 to over 20 300 in 1989 (City of Seoul, 1989). Among the street vendors surveyed, about 29% earned less than 300 000 won per month, whereas a monthly income between 300 000 won and 500 000 won was earned by more than 67%. The findings confirmed that most people engaged in the informal sector appear to earn a low monthly income. This study, however, did not include those street vendors who use small trucks, whose activities are generally conducted in small alleys in residential areas, and who move constantly from one location to another. The total number could have been severely underrepresented. There has not been a systematic study examining the impact of the informal economy on Seoul's total economic activity. However, according to a national study on the informal economy, their activities represented about 35% of the nation's economy, implying an even higher magnitude for Seoul (Pae, 1985).

The informal sector in Seoul is expected to grow and continues to be an integral part of the total economy. The expanding nature of this sector might bring some positive effects: jobs for low-skilled people, business opportunities for people with very limited venture capital, a market flow of low-price goods, close personal services, outlets for some second-quality, defective merchandise, and an eventual entry into some aspects of the formal economy. However, there is always a high risk of these people being socially marginalized by the institutionalized power, particularly as most of them are not under the protection of the nation's labor law. It might be important for the local authorities to recognize the critical issues facing people in the informal economy and to develop practical plans to improve their social welfare and allow their eventual integration into the formal economy.

Emergence of Seoul Metropolitan Region

With the explosive growth Seoul has experienced over the last 30 years, coupled with its near absolute dominance of the nation's economic, cultural, and political scenes, it is not surprising that Seoul has become a large metropolis with a towering influence over Korea. Metropolitan Seoul, officially defined as the SMR, includes the city of Seoul itself, and other surrounding satellite towns and cities in Kyonggi-do Province. As a result of its dominance over other parts of country, the SMR is often referred to as the SMR Republic. This cynical reference to the SMR is due in part to the lack of policy recommendations concerning a balanced regional development over the years, particularly during the military regimes. Until a solution is found to break up the SMR Republic and encourage an orderly development of all regions in Korea, policy-makers will be left with a great challenge in their lifetime.

As shown in Figure 2.4 and Table 2.7, the physical size of the SMR is relatively small in proportion to the country's total land area, only about 11.5%, yet its current estimated population of 17 million people represents approximately 39% of the total population of Korea. Table 2.7 further illustrates the dominance of the SMR in many aspects of national affairs. Almost half of the nation's employees and more than 60% of the bank deposits are found in the SMR. According to the most recent estimates, and also partially verified in Table 2.7, the SMR is home to 59% of the nation's manufacturing sector, 50% of the service sector, 42% of the hospitals, 52% of the public service offices, and 41% of the college students (*Hankook Daily*, 1993). Furthermore, about 47% of the nation's GNP and 41% of the GRP are generated in the SMR, while approximately 57% of the nation's business establishments along with the total loans are located in the SMR (*Hankook Daily*, 1993; Economic Planning Board, 1993). In addition, almost half of the total vehicles are operated in the SMR.

Clearly this heavy concentration of various businesses and civic activities in the SMR has been a major obstacle to a more even and balanced regional spatial development, preventing other regions of the country from exploring and establishing diverse fields of economic development that might actually complement that of the SMR. The supremacy of the SMR in economic, political, cultural, social, and many other aspects of Korean affairs over other parts of the country is indeed difficult to comprehend, even in comparison with other developing nations.

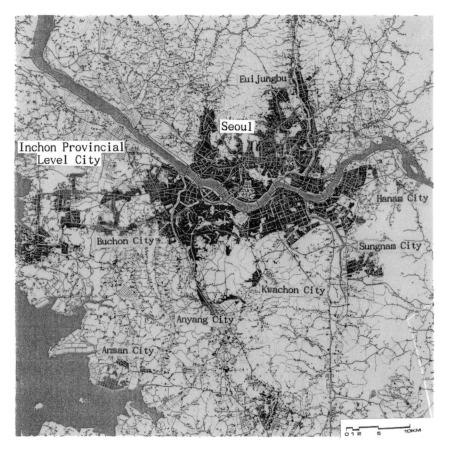

Figure 2.4 Growth of Seoul Metropolitan Region. Reproduced from Seoul Metropolis (1990a) by permission of Seoul Metropolitan Government

Development stages of Seoul Metropolitan Region

As previously mentioned, under the heavily centralized government system in Korea it might have been a logical outcome for their urban fabric to give birth to the SMR. The formation of the SMR, however, did not happen over night and, in fact, took more than 30 years, at times abetted by natural growth forces, but too often guided by government policies. As explained in the previous sections, most growth in the satellite cities and towns was at the mercy of the rapidly expanding, powerful Seoul until the early 1980s. Overpopulated Seoul was not in a position to absorb all the potential in-migrants, given the capital's very limited physical size, and consequently some people had to settle for the

Table 2.7 Degrees of concentration for Seoul and Seoul Metropolitan Region (SMR)

	Nation (A)	SMR (B)	Seoul (C)	Concentration (%)	
				B/A	C/A
Area (km²)*	99 313.66	11 379.35	605.36	11.5	0.6
Population (000s)†	43 410	16 782	10 612	38.7	24.4
GRP (billion won)	207 397.10	84 801.10	51 102.40	40.9	24.6
Total industry					
No. of establishments	2 118 247	944 812	581 092	44.6	27.4
No. of employees (000s)	11 356	5772	3629	50.8	32
Secondary industry					
No. of establishments	301 143	136.74	90 509	45.4	30.1
No. of employees (000s)	4294	2270	1136	52.9	26.5
Tertiary industry					
No. of establishments	1 815 984	793 864	490 496	43.7	27.1
No. of employees (000s)	7036	3493	2486	41.9	35.3
No. of undergradutes (000s)	1052	400	285	38	27.1
No. of hospitals*	27 008	11 293	8189	41.9	30.3
Banking					
Deposits (billion won)	98 507.90	60 828.50	51 983.40	61.7	52.8
Loans and discounts (billion won)	89 415.60	52 671.90	45 605.60	58.9	51
No. of offices for public services	12 657	6571	2048	51.9	16.2
No. of vehicles	4 247 816	1 984 845	1 374 677	46.7	32.4

* 1992.
† 1990.

Sources: Ministry of Labour, 1993; Economic Planning Board, 1962–1994; City of Seoul, 1961–1994; Seoul Metropolis, 1991, 1992–1993; and Korean Statistical Association, 1991.

second best option of locating in the surrounding cities and towns that were still close enough to the boundary of Seoul to provide them with much needed daily conveniences.

After Seoul adopted a greenbelt policy in 1971 to manage the rapidly sprawling urban areas and to encourage an orderly development of land use within the city limits, most population growth, particularly during the 1980s, continued to take place in cities and towns in Kyonggi-do Province, which were adjacent to many of the designated greenbelt areas. This unexpected growth was a logical progression in terms of population movement because many of these rapidly growing places were also close to public transportation systems and to places of employment in Seoul. Many more new cities with a large population base were developed and some of the existing older towns gained enough population to be reclassified as cities. In an attempt to alleviate the ever increasing pressures from the continual population and physical growth of Seoul, the central government has initiated and has just finished developing two new cities with more than 700 000 planned inhabitants. No doubt increased congestion in the SMR will come with this projected expansion of residents into the region.

Although the physical proximity between most places in Kyonggi-do Province and Seoul was very close, the potential for a symbiotic relationship between the two did not materialize until recently, when Kyonggi-do Province was drawing a significant portion of its business activities and active labor force from Seoul and the rest of the country. It soon established itself as an important actor in the national economy. By virtue of emerging from the shadow of powerful Seoul, yet simultaneously creating a systematically close relationship with Seoul, Kyonggi-do Province has established itself as an integral part of the SMR.

Table 2.8 illustrates the growth rates and a proportional relationship among Seoul, the SMR, and Kyonggi-do Province in relation to the nation's total population since 1960. As expected, the dominance of Seoul with respect to a relative share of the nation's total population has remained strong; in fact, the only time it fell behind Kyonggi-do Province was in 1960, just about the time it began its explosive population growth (9.8 versus 11.0%). However, the relative strength of Kyonggi-do Province has been stable and the rate of population growth, beginning in 1980, has outweighed that of Seoul, becoming a vital component of the SMR. An estimate of the population growth for Kyonggi-do Province in 1993 appears to be slightly falling, however. In any event, combining these two strong forces, the total distribution of the SMR in relation to Korea's total population seems to be beyond the reach of other parts of the country; it was only about 20.8% in 1960, but

Table 2.8 Population estimates and distribution in the Seoul Metropolitan Region (SMR). Numbers are in thousands

	1960	1966	1970	1975	1980	1985	1988	1993
SMR (A)	5194	6913	8894	10 924	13 302	15 807	17 168	17 383
Seoul (B)	2445	3805	5536	6889	8367	9629	10 310	11 305
Kyonggi-do Province (C)	2749	3108	3358	4035	4935	6178	6858	6079
Nation (D)	24 989	29 193	31 435	34 681	37 445	40 432	41 975	44 040
A/D	20.8	23.7	28.3	31.5	35.7	39.1	40.9	39.5
B/D	9.8	13	17.6	19.9	22.3	23.8	24.6	25.7
C/D	11	10.6	10.7	11.6	13.2	15.3	16.3	13.8

Sources: Economic Planning Board, 1962–1994; City of Seoul, 1961–1994; and Economic Planning Board, 1960–1990.

mushroomed to 39.5% in 1993. According to a recent estimate, if the present trend continues, it is expected that by the year 2000 almost half of the nation's total population will reside in the SMR (Economic Planning Board, 1993).

Closely following the expansion of the nation's economy, the total growth of the manufacturing sector in the SMR has been impressive for the total number of both manufacturing firms and employment. As shown in Table 2.9, the relative strength of the SMR in relation to the nation's total number of firms and employees in the manufacturing sector was rather small, 26.7 and 34.8% in 1960, but its growth continued to 59.8 and 47.3% by 1985, respectively. However, the total share of the SMR began declining slightly in 1988 and continued to decline until 1991 (50.6 and 39.2%), perhaps indicating a national trend of industrial relocation where manufacturing firms have positioned themselves to explore new locations with better physical and business environments. Moreover, the national government in recent years has introduced new policies encouraging broader industrial developments in the southwestern region of the country, which had been neglected for political reasons.

The new trend for industrial relocation is even more self-evident when we examine the relative distribution of Seoul over time. In 1960 the dominance of Seoul within the SMR was 63.6% for manufacturing firms and 70.1% for total employees, but by 1991 Seoul's position was drastically reduced to 47.7 and 36.3% for the same categories. Although a relatively large proportion of the total employees (almost 30%) declined, only about 17% of the total firms moved out of Seoul during this period. One reason for this unusual occurrence is that a large number of small firms have always started their businesses and decided to stay in Seoul, whenever they could, as they have had constant access to financial capital and human resources, and gained information about more advanced technologies resulting from the research and development of other major companies.

The decision of smaller manufacturing firms to remain in Seoul was again reflected by the amount of changes reported in the sum of total revenues minus the cost of products purchased from other firms. When the value-added amount was calculated over time, its share with respect to the nation's total was about 31% in 1960, but it was continually reduced to 16% in 1991. This is a clear indication that those firms which have remained in Seoul have become smaller since 1960 (City of Seoul, 1992).

Figure 2.5 further indicates the overall structure of manufacturing firms that have recently undergone some key changes. Although a key change towards light and high-tech manufacturing activities has occurred during the late 1970s and continued into the 1980s and

Table 2.9 Changes in the manufacturing sector. Values given are numbers in thousands (percentage)

Year	No. of establishments				No. of workers			
	Nation	SMR*	Seoul†	Kyonggi-do Province†	Nation	SMR*	Seoul†	Kyonggi-do Province†
1960	15 204	4062 (26.7)	2585 (63.6)	1477 (26.4)	250	87 (34.8)	610 (70.1)	26 (29.9)
1970	24 114	7916 (32.8)	5708 (72.1)	2208 (27.9)	861	396 (46.0)	292 (73.7)	104 (26.3)
1980	30 823	13 332 (43.3)	7652 (57.4)	5680 (42.6)	2015	924 (45.7)	445 (48.2)	479 (51.8)
1985	44 307	26 498 (59.8)	13 627 (51.4)	12 861 (48.6)	2438	1154 (47.3)	483 (41.9)	671 (58.1)
1988	59 947	34 810 (58.1)	17 125 (49.2)	17 685 (50.8)	3122	1337 (42.8)	553 (41.4)	784 (58.6)
1991	72 213	36 548 (50.6)	17 418 (47.7)	19 130 (52.3)	2918	1145 (39.2)	416 (36.3)	729 (63.7)

* Values in parentheses are percentage share of the nation's total.
† Values in parentheses are percentage share of the SMR for each year.

Source: National Statistical Office, 1992.

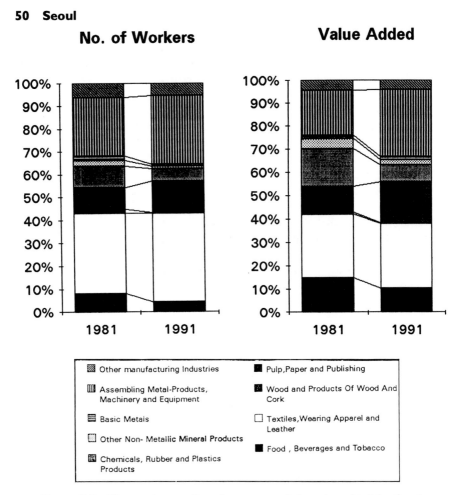

No. of Workers   **Value Added**

Figure 2.5 Changes in manufacturing sector and the value added for Seoul

beyond, a significant change emerged, as expected, between 1981 and 1991. The three most dominant manufacturing sectors measured by the total number of workers were represented by textiles and leather, paper and publishing, and assembling metal products in 1981 and appeared to have expanded their dominance over other sectors by 1991. In 1991, although the proportional strength of textiles and leather and assembling metal products continued its increase over others, firms in paper and printing emerged as a third important manufacturing activity. Although this new trend was also closely followed by the value added, the amount for metal products was slightly higher than that for textiles, perhaps illustrating the stronger economic activities of the high-tech related products. From this, however, it can be clearly seen that Seoul is increasingly dominated by high-fashioned clothes and high-tech related industries, forcing other manufacturing activities with heavy industrial pollution or unattractive manufacturing companies to relocate either in the SMR or other regions of the country.

Kyonggi-do Province has improved its representation of manufacturing firms steadily since 1960, and in 1988, for the first time, its proportional share was more than that of Seoul (Table 2.9). By 1991 the difference between Seoul and Kyonggi-do Province was widened, a more drastic change occurring in the number of total workers (36% for Seoul and 64% for Kyonggi-do Province). As already discussed in our earlier sections, this phenomenon was believed to be caused by the industrial relocation decision, when many of the larger firms in Seoul decided to relocate their factories to nearby Kyonggi-do Province or other less urbanized areas with an easy transportation access and low land cost. This process was accelerated by the policies made by the local authorities in Seoul for implementing more stringent air pollution controls, new regulations for safety, and other measures dictating the operation of their factories.

During the earlier development stage of the SMR, Kyonggi-do Province attracted a variety of industries or economic activities whose functions were less desirable: a cemetery, squatter settlements resulting from urban slum clearance in Seoul, and factories not meeting the regulations required for Seoul. Although this trend has continued, though with much reduced magnitude, there has been a drastic shift in the patterns of development activities in recent years, particularly in the areas of higher education, research and development centers, and other education-related functions. This has been particularly true since the early 1980s, when the central government policy-makers made an attempt to disperse the population of Seoul by granting branch campuses for major universities located in Seoul. As a result there are now full-fledged branch campuses for nine major Seoul universities, four small colleges, 17 junior colleges, 12 divinity colleges, and two special colleges, all totaling more than 115 000 students attending in the area (Kyonggi-do Province, 1985; Ministry of Labour, 1993). Paralleling this new trend of development, more than 81% of the high-tech industries are now located in the SMR and it is expected that this concentration will continue.

One of the unfortunate aspects of this newly expanding population and economic activities in the SMR is that instead of dispersing the population in Seoul, it aggravated the congestion for commuting in both directions as more and more residents in Seoul, many who serve in the newly developing high-tech industries, nine branch campuses, or other education-related institutions, decided to keep their roots in Seoul. Daily, they commute to their new places of employment in the region (Park, Sam Ok, 1989a, 1989b).

Table 2.10 Summary of government decentralization policies for Seoul Metropolitan Region (SMR)

Year	Policies
1964	Cabinet's resolution against population concentration in large cities
1969	Established Presidential Advisory Committee for SMR problems and deconcentration measures for population and facilities
1972	Announcement of the guidelines for SMR decentralization policies
1973	Announcement of SMR decentralization policies
1975	Promulgated population dispersal plan for Seoul
1976	Created Minister-level office in charge of SMR decentralization policies
1977	Finalized master plan for population redistribution of SMR
1982	Introduced development control of government offices and large-scale building construction
1982	Enacted the SMR redevelopment planning law
1984	Promulgated SMR redevelopment plan
1989	Drafted basic guidelines for balanced regional development
1993	Revised the SMR redevelopment planning law: physical control to economic disincentive (congestion charge) system

Source: City of Seoul, 1961–1994.

Government policies

At present, the SMR has grown to a gigantic metropolis with one special city, Seoul, one provincial status city, Inchon, 12 cities and 33 towns from one special city, Seoul, two cities and nine towns in 1960. The rate of urbanization of the SMR has been extremely high over the years and it reached over 91% in 1992 (City of Seoul, 1993).

As previously discussed, this rapid expansion of the SMR was aided by continuing government policies, though most were simply used as a window dressing to be effectively used as a guiding tool. As summarized in Table 2.10, the central government initially introduced a policy for controlling the growth of major cities in 1964, particularly targeting Seoul, and established a presidential advisory committee for looking at potential growth problems facing the SMR. However, the rapid countrywide economic development in the late 1960s accelerated intense growth and development of the population, as well as industrial activities in most large cities. In an attempt to accommodate more growth, Seoul and other major cities expanded their physical sizes by allowing more aggressive annexation policies, which in turn caused a spiral of unpleasant real estate speculations. In 1971 the greenbelt policy was passed to slow the rapid growth and to promote an orderly growth of Seoul; in reality, this was largely responsible for the beginning of the leap-frog type of growth and development around Seoul.

In 1972 the central government introduced the first national development plan to prevent Seoul from becoming an overpopulated and ungovernable city. In addition, a number of priority cities and towns for growth, particularly close to major cities around the country, were identified to promote a balanced and equitable regional development. Guidelines for decentralization policies were announced for the SMR. In Seoul, college enrolments were strictly regulated, urban slum clearance projects were initiated, and a new property tax system was introduced. At the same time, central government began campaigning for what was then known as the "new village movement" (*Saemaul Undong*). The main purpose of the new village movement was to develop rural areas by providing modern amenities to the residents so that the existing gap between urban and rural areas could be narrowed.

As central government tightened its dictatorial grip, which was exacerbated by a worsening political and military relationship with North Korea, the policies for controlling the growth of Seoul were speeded up even further. Plans for relocating Seoul to the central part of Korea for strategic reasons and redistributing the capital's general population were introduced in 1976 and 1977, but could not be implemented. At the same time a ministry level office was created not only to be responsible for the SMR decentralization policies, but also to oversee the development of a master plan for such efforts.

None of these government policies was successful in curtailing the explosive growth of Seoul and the SMR. In 1979, with the assassination of President Park, Chung Hee, an iron-fisted dictator for over 28 years, a political turmoil ensued until the next successor, an ex-general named Mr Chun, Doo Hwan, was sworn in as the President of Korea. Most plans for the dispersion of the SMR were forgotten by the policy-makers and when the International Olympic Committee awarded the 1988 Summer Olympics to Seoul in 1982, President Chun's government put enormous emphasis on the preparation of the Olympics by giving Seoul an artificial face lift and allowing more people and industries to locate not only in Seoul, but also in the SMR. For them, a successful staging of the Olympics was needed not only to establish their political legitimacy, but also to boost Korea's image as an emerging international member. With a peaceful transfer of power from President Chun, Doo Hwan to another ex-general President Rho, Tae Woo in 1989, this new government returned its attention to the never-ending problem of the rapidly expanding SMR. Although the central government introduced plans to deal with growth controls and balanced regional development in 1989, the plans again failed to limit the growth of the SMR. In addition, the government initiated the development of five new towns in

Kyonggi-do Province, which added another agony by contributing to the overcrowding situation already facing the SMR.

With President Rho's term coming to an end, there was yet another peaceful transition of power in Korea's modern political history. After more than 30 years of military rule, a civilian government was established in March 1993 under the leadership of President Kim, Yong Sam, once a leading opposition leader who later joined the ruling party of President Rho. Most recently, President Kim's government announced a new policy guiding the development of the SMR. This new policy is yet another attempt by the new administration to respond to another layer of the unsuccessful history of regional development policies surrounding Seoul and the SMR.

As shown in Table 2.11, the national policy-makers made a serious attempt to develop regional industrial sites based on a well-balanced regional growth and to steer the growth of the SMR in a more manageable way. Both industrial location and structuring legislative plans were introduced from 1964, emphasizing site development for export-oriented manufacturing industries. The main policy tools relied on an indirect positive incentive such as the preferential treatment of public land with essential support from the administration. In 1970, more active measures based on positive financial incentives to attract some industries to designated areas were introduced through the Local Industrial Development Law. Tax exemptions and reductions for a certain period of time were awarded to firms relocating out of the SMR, but it was widely believed that the total amount of tax exemption was not sufficient to offset the total cost involved in the relocation.

The enactment of the Industrial Distribution Law in 1977 was another intervention by the government for the development of regional industrial relocation policies. This particular law adopted new national industrial zoning and allowed a reduction of corporate income tax by 10% of the relocation building cost if firms decided to move to a properly designated industrial zoning area. Furthermore, a relocation reserve fund was also made available to industries to offset a 10% loss from the total corporate profits. Various other tax incentives were structured into the law, making the relocation decision more attractive. Additional government controls were also included in the law so that any attempts of expansion by undesirable manufacturing companies in the SMR could be severely restricted, particularly those firms producing heavy pollution (Choe and Song, 1984).

As the robust growth of Seoul and the SMR continued, the SMR Redevelopment Planning Law – the basic relocation plan – was introduced in 1982 to curtail the further development of industries in the region as well as to aid the relocation of heavily polluting existing

Table 2.11 Legislative actions and major policy instruments

Year	Legislative actions	Major policy instruments
1964	Export Industrial Estate Development Promotion Law	Preferential sale of publicly owned land Provision of basic infrastructure Administrative endorsement
1970	Local Industrial Development Law	Tax exemption and reduction Provision of basic infrastructure
1973	Industrial Site and Water Resource Development Law	Creation of the government corporation in charge of industrial estate development Land price freeze for compensation of the proposed site for industrial estate
1977	Industrial Distribution Law	Adoption of national industrial zoning Reduction of corporate income tax (10% of building cost for relocated plant into inducement zone and 5% in other zones) Accounting 10% loss for the purpose of relocation reserve Exemption of capital gains tax of corporation for the sale of land and buildings occupied by relocated firms from dispersal zone Higher basic exemption rate of capital gains tax for the sale of individual premises Exemption of acquisition and registration tax for relocated worker's housing initially for one year Accelerated depreciation rate
1982	Seoul Metropolitan Region Redevelopment Planning Law	Delineated SMR into five sub-categories by intensity of development control Introduction of development permits for new location and expansion of industrial plant and facilities Strengthened land use control
1993	Seoul Metropolitan Region Redevelopment Planning Law (revised)	Changes from physical control to economic disincentive (congestion charge) Redelineation of SMR into three sub-categories by intensity of development control

Sources: Choe, Sang Chuel and Song, Byung Nak, 1984; City of Seoul, 1993.

industries from the region. It delineated the SMR into five sub-regions according to various intensities of development control. New industrial development was encouraged in the southwestern portions of the SMR, whereas areas close to the present Demilitarized Zone in the north were restricted in growth.

Under the revised law of 1993, however, the existing SMR, which was divided into five sub-regions, has been simplified and reorganized into three sub-regions. Its aim has shifted from physical development controls to economic disincentives by assessing congestion charges, thereby prohibiting large industrial developments of any sort to the already congested, over-developed central region while promoting an orderly, managed development of various industries and preserving the natural environment in other areas (*Hankook Daily*, 3 June 1993).

As shown in Figure 2.6, the region that has been allowed an orderly development is concentrated in the seashore areas of the southwestern section of the SMR, while most areas in the region north of the Han River, which had originally been identified as a strategic location for military targets, have been relaxed for growth and have since been identified as the growth management region. New policies under the new administration appear to be determined to continue plans to limit the expansion of the SMR, however flexible it may seem, particularly those industries which do not follow their national economic plan, and further to encourage a strategic location of new industrial activities throughout the country.

Where do they go from here?

Based on what has happened, what other roads should the government take? It seems clear that most government programs that promoted balanced regional growth and the orderly development of Seoul and the SMR over the last 30 years have not had any major success.

One of the main reasons for failing to meet their initial goals was that most policy-makers believed population decentralization and limiting the growth of Seoul with legal coercion was the best available means, and that they truly thought that was possible and within their reach. Secondly, as shown in Tables 2.10 and 2.11, most plans and policies did not come from one government agency that had a vested interest in the success of programs. As more agencies were involved in both the plan-making and the decision-making processes, it was inevitable that most of the plans failed in the implementation stage as more coherent and straightforward plans were not formulated and forthcoming from the agencies involved. Central government was neither interested in

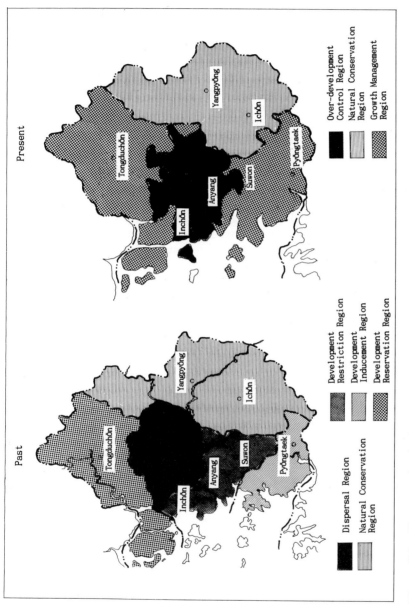

Figure 2.6 Changes in the development and management regions of the Seoul Metropolitan Region. Reproduced by permission of the Ministry of Construction (1982, 1987)

forcefully carrying out the plans nor possessed the skills needed for systematically coordinating the plans. Finally, central government did not provide enough financial resources for most of the proposed plans. Under the centralized government system, it was even more critical that a well-balanced regional development should be guided with strong financial support from the central government. As most government officials have given only lip service to these policies since the early 1960s, the agencies involved in the process of introducing plans began producing policies of their own without much substance, only to concentrate on how good they look on the surface, however utopian and unrealistic their plans may be.

The problems facing the SMR are not just limited to the SMR itself, and, as a result, solutions cannot be found only by looking at the issues in the SMR. It is unusual that the SMR in Korea has heavily dominated all aspects of Korea: political, cultural, economic, social, and many other areas. Consequently, all other regions in Korea were under the shadow of the SMR and the wide gap between the two will undoubtedly worsen unless some drastic government measures are introduced soon. Not only has there been an unequal distribution of regional growth, but the gigantic SMR has created a high degree of inefficiency in the daily life of people, thereby lowering the quality of life of its residents.

What is needed now in Korea is foresight into new perspectives on balanced and equitable spatial development. Korea is rapidly abandoning the Cold War rhetoric after the dismantling of Eastern Europe and the former Soviet Union. With the country adjusting to a new world order by embracing the former communist countries for political ties and economic trade, Korea must critically assess its present spatial development and explore a more meaningful arrangement for all regions of the country. For example, more active trading with China may require several port cities in the western region that are strategically closer to China, whereas a major development of other port cities in the eastern region may be needed for the anticipated open trade with Russia. As the capital of Korea, Seoul will continue to be an important city, an evolving international city, but the previous growth patterns of Seoul and the SMR and their complete dominance of most aspects of Korean affairs is neither desirable nor healthy for the future of Korea. This is particularly true as a large chunk of the national budget is needed to maintain the current spatial arrangement with this extremely skewed and unbalanced regional development.

The present concentration of the SMR has been a contributing factor to the presence of regional factions in Korea. As the central government moves towards revitalizing local government control, it becomes even more critical that regional favoritism disappears from the political scene.

Accelerated decentralization and local government control cannot be achieved unless these local units are given complete political independence, coupled with the local control of economic resources. With constant encouragement for local government autonomy from central government, it will then be possible for these units to develop their own unique political, economic, social, cultural, and other identities, thereby contributing to the well-balanced regional development and curtailing the accelerated growth of Seoul and the SMR.

Finally, with the opening of international communities, including the former communist countries and North Korea, it may be sooner than expected that the two Koreas are united. Any future plans for national development should consider this possible reunification and encourage a well-balanced regional development incorporating all the important aspects of local governments. Within the context of a unified Korea, the decision about industrial location and a dispersal of the existing industries has to be carefully evaluated and planned. Furthermore, the position and importance of Seoul and the SMR could well be changed, thus making a very different urban fabric possible.

3

Urban land use and transportation

Visitors on their maiden flight to present day Seoul may encounter an aerial view of an impressive cityscape that is intertwined with and surrounded by a river, rolling hills, and mountains. The city appears to be a mosaic collection of mixed residential development of single-detached and medium height dwellings in many different sections, widely dispersed but densely developed modern commercial sky-scrapers along its wide streets, and unvarying, monotonous high-rise apartment buildings along the Han River. However, Seoul's massive and complex physical form seems to follow a sense of order and calmness.

A jolting reality awaits most visitors, however, on their cab ride from the airport to various downtown destinations: endless queues of cars crowding many city streets that create and add to the interminable traffic jams, the resulting air and noise pollution, and an enormous volume of people crammed into commercial development areas and on narrow residential streets. Perhaps, for the visitors unfamiliar with Seoul, this chaotic environment may generate a spectrum of experience ranging from a sense of excitement to a feeling of alienation. In any event, if we wish to better understand the current state of land use patterns and transportation systems of Seoul, it is essential to begin with a review of the unique historical development of the city.

Internal structure of Seoul

Changing historical patterns of urban land use

As previously discussed, when Seoul was born as the capital of the Yi Dynasty in 1394, the main characteristic of the city was a walled-in city (castled city). The main purpose of its traditional city structure was to provide and protect most of the functional needs of the royal palace.

The original growth of the city rested on a basic understanding of, and enormous respect for, such natural elements as the location of mountains, the availability and duration of sunlight, the wind direction, the use of native building materials, and the presence of rivers. With most of the arable land in the country reserved for agricultural use, particularly for rice production, the city structure in and around Seoul was indeed very simple. Its continuous layout of largely single-story homes based on traditional Korean architectural styles was intermixed with some scattered flat land for rice production, narrow streets, and limited open space for occasional markets. In an attempt to create the main accesses to the city, four main (east, west, north, and south) gates were erected and they, in turn, determined the scope and size of the city for future development.

For example, the physical size of Seoul until 1910 was only 6 km in diameter, populated by approximately 230 000 residents. As most people conducted their daily activities on foot, rather than any other type of public transportation then available, Seoul was a very small city with most trade and commerce occurring within the confined areas of the four main gates. The present primary core of the city north of the Han River is about equal to the physical size of the old walled-in city, though the area now includes major government offices and several very concentrated commercial and business districts. Even during the Japanese domination from 1909 to 1945, the main character of the city did not show signs of drastic change. In 1920, however, railroad lines for steam-engine trains, connecting Seoul and Pusan, and Seoul and Inchon, were introduced. At the same time, public transportation using electric streetcars was developed in Seoul and some segments of the walls along the four main gates had to be torn down to make room for the streetcar lines. Not surprisingly, the city grew along these newly developed transportation lines, though in a scattered pattern, and some businesses, including limited industrial activities, consequently began locating outside the four main gates.

Following the liberation from Japanese rule in 1945 and through the late 1950s, Seoul was flooded with a rapid stream of people migrating from all parts of the country. As the city's very limited housing stock offered severely confined physical spaces for newcomers, it was inevitable that Seoul was inundated with shanty housing sites. Most of these housing units were developed without proper housing permits and often resulted in densely populated urban squatter settlements located along the banks of streams, hilltops, and at various edges of the city, particularly outside the four main gates. During this explosive period of population growth, which was a driving force for Seoul's unexpected and unplanned physical expansion, the city's public transportation system remained primitive, relying primarily on buses and electric streetcars on the very few existing lines.

Urban sprawl became a dominant phenomenon in terms of reshaping the physical features of the city, but the city officials were unprepared for presenting an orderly development plan for the city and instead busily expanded existing bus services and introduced new bus lines to areas outside the four main gates, populated largely by residents whose daily commuting needs to the inner city were not adequately met. Generally, the extension and meandering of bus lines were inspired by the combined interest of private bus companies and land speculators to open up and continue new land development in the urban fringes. By the mid-1960s, electric streetcar lines, one of the most important instruments in mapping out new urban spatial patterns in Seoul, were completely replaced by the newly developing and expanding bus lines.

During the 1960s the city faced continuing population surges and thus ever increasing pressure for its physical expansion. To meet the challenge, city officials initiated unlimited annexation policies, urban slum clearance projects, and large-scale public infrastructure improvements. Based on the aggressive attitude of city officials towards expansion, pro-growth plans continued and the settlement pattern of Seoul's population shifted and accelerated to outside the four main gates and the urban fringe areas, closely paralleling the extension of bus lines and areas inundated by uncontrolled land speculation. With an increasing number of single-family housing units being developed, either attached or detached, the city officials responded to the escalating demand by simply clearing more land for urban land development projects. Opportunities to develop land in an orderly pattern decreased. Consequently, the haphazard layout gave way to problems aggravated by the unanticipated growth in and around the city: traffic bottle-necks were becoming commonplace.

Recognizing the limitation of the pro-growth development plans, city officials announced a land-use concept plan in 1966 that included a basic transportation network system which consisted of four ring roads and 13 radial arterial roads. The 1966 development plan was Seoul's first comprehensive effort in planning. As shown in Figure 3.1, it promoted a major ring road surrounding the primary core of the inner city area within the four main gates, and three other ring roads serving other sections of the city. Areas where major radial arterials met the ring roads were designated as secondary core areas of the city. The four newly created secondary core areas were scattered around the city, evenly representing all sections of the city, and it was expected that approximately

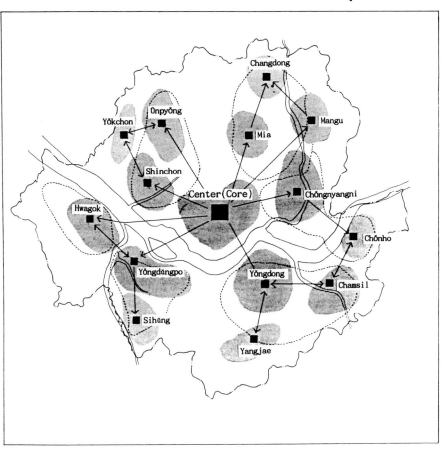

Figure 3.1   First comprehensive development plan of 1966

21 small, well-planned, self-contained communities surrounding these four areas would be created (Seoul Metropolis, 1972, 1977).

However, the unabated rate of population growth and the city's physical expansion, following the Korean civil war, thwarted the successful implementation of the 1966 comprehensive development plan. Uncontrolled urban sprawl, coupled with the very rapid growth of satellite cities surrounding Seoul, continually pushed the outer limits of the capital city further, repeatedly threatening valuable agricultural land. In addition, city officials made the city physically even larger by annexing a number of newly created districts. Located south of the Han River, some of the districts housed mainly relocated residents from the urban slum clearance project areas in the central city. All these development pressures beginning in the 1960s fueled the metropolitanization of Seoul, yet made the city increasingly ungovernable. Undesirable land speculation escalated and the newly developing areas of the city lacked adequate transportation access to the city center. To encourage balanced growth between urban and rural areas, particularly for the orderly development of urban land use, the national government introduced a comprehensive national land development plan in 1971. The 1971 plan included the designation of greenbelts around major cities and had a tremendous impact on the growth of Seoul, especially on the future residential land use patterns.

No development was permitted in the areas designated as the greenbelt around the edges of Seoul, though a large proportion was owned by private individuals. As shown in Figure 3.2, the greenbelt law of 1971 contributed to the escalation of infill development pressure in the central city, but at the same time added to uncontrolled leap-frog development patterns beyond the greenbelt areas. The leap-frog development stemmed from the often poorly designed activities of land speculators. As a result, land prices became prohibitively expensive and the land available for residential development rapidly dwindled in the central city.

After many years of soul-searching, it became clear to many local government officials that they needed to revise the existing 1966 plan, which was never seriously implemented to better meet the rapidly expanding needs of the city. The need for a revised plan was especially acute as the national government, under pressure from a possible military attack from North Korea, however unrealistic it had been, had strongly endorsed another plan to disperse the population of Seoul and to relocate various government functions to south of the Han River, particularly to some distant cities in Choongchung-do Province. Although the decentralization plan for moving government functions away from Seoul did not successfully materialize, the development plan for south of the Han River moved very quickly, perhaps without adequate attention to proper and efficient implementation.

Increasing amounts of farmland and open space south of the Han River were rapidly developed and acquired a steadily expanding population base. Meanwhile, neither practical nor conceptual plans issued by the city's leadership called for effective growth management and a limitation of the city's huge physical size.

In the 1970s, the existing bus lines did not adequately serve the commuting needs of most residents in Seoul on both sides of the Han River. The first serious attempt at alleviating worsening urban commuting congestion was the completion of the first subway line in 1973. Approximately 9.5 km in total distance, the subway line linked Seoul Railway Station in the primary core area of the inner city and

1960s

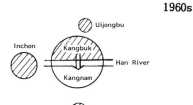

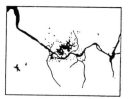

From Kangbuk to Kangnam
Urban sprawl and explosion

1970s

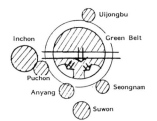

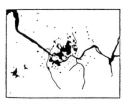

Infilling of Kangnam

1980s

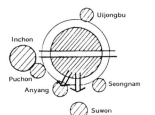

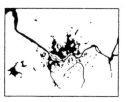

Designation of Green Belt
Increased overall density

1990s

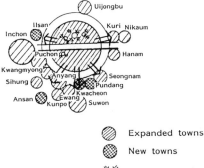

Expansion beyond Green Belt
Planned new town development

⬚ Expanded towns

⬚ New towns

⬚ Urban renewal

Figure 3.2 Schematic diagrams showing development phases of Seoul

Chongrangri, which was at the center of the secondary core area in the eastern portion of the city. At the same time, the construction of two rapid transit lines, between Seoul and Inchon and between Seoul and Suwon, was completed to further relieve the commuting pains of residents in the rapidly developing satellite cities in Kyonggi-do Province.

The combination of subways, rapid transit lines, and existing bus lines by the late 1970s assisted Seoul's emergence as a city with a modern mass transportation system, however unsophisticated it might have been. Unfortunately, systematically well planned urban restructuring, based on the newly created urban mass transportation system, did not follow. The distressful commuting situation for most residents in Seoul and in the immediately surrounding satellite cities continued. Compounding the existing traffic nightmare, city officials followed pro-growth policies and developed the island of Youido, which had been used as an airport for small airplanes. Youido, then some distance from the boundaries of congested and densely populated Seoul, could have been reserved for open space and developed as a much-desired urban park for Seoul residents, much like Central Park in New York City. Instead, the entire island was developed with a large number of high-rise apartment buildings for middle and upper-middle income families, supermarkets, elementary and secondary schools, and a tall skyline of office and commercial buildings. A new building of modern design for the National Assembly was also constructed. Youido Square, similar to Tiananmen Square in Beijing, China, occupied an enormous physical space in the middle of the island. Planned for ceremonial occasions, it gave the finishing touch to this highly developed urban pattern of Seoul (see Figure 3.3 for the original Youido master plan).

Encouraged by the Youido development, hailed by some as an important success story in Seoul's modern urban development, the next major development plan for the city was carried out south of the Han River. It affected approximately 10×10^6 m^2 of undeveloped land occupied by 250 000 residents in Jamsil district, located in the southeastern part of Seoul. Given the massive size of the development, it was much like creating a new town, except that all the necessary elements required for a new town were not carefully considered. For example, as city officials put the development of residential sectors as the single most important criterion for Jamsil district, thereby creating a greater spatial separation between the places of employment and residence, most residents in this newly created district had to commute to the primary core area of the inner city, which still dominated all aspects of the city, including cultural, business, and employment activities.

Paralleling the Jamsil district development in the 1970s, city officials were also actively engaged in the process of making decisions about

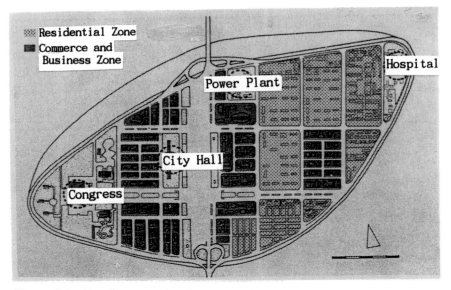

Figure 3.3 Youido master plan. Reproduced from Seoul Metropolis (1971) by permission of Seoul Metropolitan Government

how and where they should put a second subway line to provide more effective transportation services for all residents, particularly for those in the rapidly growing areas south of the Han River. Perhaps these simultaneous events signaled a conceptual framework for a multiple-nuclei city, with three major core areas representing the entire city, as shown in Figure 3.4. Announced in 1974, the multiple-core concept plan emphasized the provision of an efficient transportation network and effective land use for Seoul. A second subway line connecting the proposed two new major secondary core areas – one in the southeastern part of the city, the other the southwestern section – was supplemented by a major urban highway system surrounding the outer rings of all three major core areas. Furthermore, it was recommended that major railroad lines serving the city would be relocated outside the greenbelt areas.

By the late 1970s, the second subway line encircling all three major core areas was completed as originally planned. Although urban commuting for most residents in and around Seoul was still a major struggle, the construction of two major subway lines did alleviate some of the commuting burdens carried mainly by existing bus services. By the early 1980s, the overall cityscape and function of the city shifted towards the newly developing districts of the city, mainly south of the Han River. Major department stores, trendy stores, restaurants, and

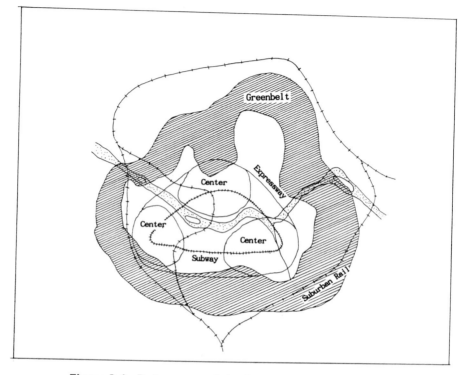

Figure 3.4   Basic concept of the three major area plan of 1974

other consumer-oriented stores began relocating to other major core areas, south of the Han River, away from the primary core area of the inner city where their dominance had been of historical importance. Offices that were directly connected with the stock exchanges and other businesses and commercial activities located in the island of Youido. More significantly, a large volume of high-rise apartment buildings mushroomed in the wide plains south of the Han River, adding to the constantly changing cityscape. By 1990, for example, approximately 33% of all households in Seoul resided in one of the apartment complexes rapidly developing throughout the entire city (City of Seoul, 1991).

High-rise apartment living was alien to most people in Korea. Until the late 1960s, for example, there were only about 30 apartment buildings nationwide, accommodating approximately 1000 households (Seoul Metropolis, 1983). Most people were accustomed to single-family dwelling units, either detached or attached, with a small area serving as an inner courtyard. In fact, this traditional land use pattern was mainly responsible for creating social networks and a unique sense of neighborhood. When city officials were heavily involved in urban slum clearance projects in the 1960s, the construction of apartment buildings, mostly medium-rise, was dramatically increased and their use was largely reserved for low income households. Based on a mixed land use concept, an increasing number of the slum clearance projects produced medium-rise apartment buildings where the lower floors were reserved for business and commercial activities.

Most low and moderate income families living in the apartments neither had the financial resources to own the business establishments below, nor worked there, as most of the businesses were family-owned and small scale in nature. As a result, the continuing separation between the places of residence and work was widened again. A number of projects, massive in their physical scale, cut across many city blocks in the primary core area of the inner city, often destroying an already existing harmonious physical and social environment, and leaving a hazardous working and living atmosphere in their wake. In retrospect, many experts now believe that these mixed land use projects in the primary core area (known as the Sewoonsangka) should never have been built as they are a living dinosaur which the city has to painfully deal with in the near future.

Though the campaign for newly created medium- to high-rise modern apartment living was actively promoted by city officials, most middle and upper-middle income families shied away from this unfamiliar environment. To make matters worse, a number of apartment buildings collapsed in the 1960s due to either a lack of building technology or poor workmanship. However, given the explosive population growth and limited land for residential use in Seoul, city officials continued to push towards the construction of high-rise apartments, as shown in Table 3.1. In 1974, for example, there were 1405 apartment buildings constructed, housing about 57 100 households. During the 1980s, the size of apartment construction projects became larger, as evidenced by the total number of households occupying such projects, approximately 69 000 households and 944 buildings in 1990, for example.

The 1971 greenbelt law, coupled with the 1973 and 1979 world fuel price increases, was probably another leading force in shifting and encouraging land use from single family dwellings to high-rise apartment buildings in Seoul. The maintenance costs for single family homes skyrocketed, while developers and speculators constantly looked for cheaper parcels of land away from the inner city for higher density housing development. Land readjustment procedures that were used to consolidate land in both rural and urban areas also contributed to this important shift in residential land use. Land readjustment procedures generally involve both the public and private sectors, with land contributions made by the private sector, while land servicing, such as

Table 3.1   Apartment house construction in Seoul

Year	No. of buildings	No. of households
1974	1405	57 105
1976	2748	11 874
1978	629	37 232
1980	233	24 573
1982	394	23 321
1984	333	22 261
1986	325	30 917
1988	836	77 532
1990	944	68 804

Source: City of Seoul, 1961–1994.

roads and other public uses, was developed by the public sector (Doebele, 1982; Kim, Joochul, 1991). Aided by newly developed high-rise apartment buildings on the island of Youido, which were warmly embraced by middle and upper-middle income families as their long sought-after living style with modern amenities, the perception towards this unfamiliar surrounding of high-rise living showed a significant change in the 1970s. It was indeed an extraordinary turnaround towards positive attitudes among residents in a very short period of time.

Following this high-rise apartment boom closely, land readjustment projects and residential land development projects, involving both the public and private sectors, comprised approximately 78×10^6 m^2 in 1980. Assuming a density of 200 people per hectare of land, these enormous housing projects housed about 1.6 million residents. Many of these projects were originally guided by the Residential Land Development Promotion Law 1980 and were carried out to meet the goal of the national government for providing five million more houses in Seoul. Although this ambitious government goal was hardly met by the projects completed during the 1980s, a significant majority of the housing developments was actually located south of the Han River, resulting in a variety of available housing types ranging from single family dwelling units to high-rise apartments for middle and upper-middle income families.

As more and more undeveloped land south of the Han River was occupied by huge, high-rise apartment complexes, less and less land became available for similarly sized potential development projects; most existing land packages were too small to meet the legal require-ments for such developments. In an effort to sell off these small and often irregular-sized parcels of the land, developers and speculators created a market for three- to five-story row or town houses, generally small in scale and providing more privacy than the existing apartment complexes. These homes were quickly sold off as garden houses, villas or town houses, and became a popular status symbol among upper-income families who valued their privacy and less crowded living environment. Meanwhile, the only alternative left for large apartment developments for middle and upper-middle income families was for city officials to revisit urban slum clearance projects of the 1960s and 1970s, however controversial it became politically. In any event, this concentrated development effort was a momentous beginning of an era during which the area south of the Han River dominated the city's growth and became an integral part of Seoul's overall development strategies.

This remarkable growth south of the Han River was magnified by an increasing population base. In 1966, for example, the distribution of population between north and south of the Han River was 82.2 and 17.8%. With more intense development occurring south of the Han River, the population difference between the two areas narrowed. In 1976 it was 67.1% in the north and 32.9% in the south; by 1986, however, the gap closed to 53.2 and 46.8%. It was expected that most of the population would be found south of the Han River by the mid-1990s (City of Seoul, 1989).

Although this shift in population continued between the two areas, the major employment centers and financial districts were still concentrated in the primary core area of the inner city. As a result, most residents south of the Han River still had to contend with difficult commuting to the north. Since the mid-1980s, two more subway lines connecting the existing two lines have been completed and four additional lines covering most areas of the city have been either planned or constructed to ease the strain of urban commuting. During the last 30 years of urban development in Seoul, an effective transportation system linking the places of residence and employment on both sides of the Han River has never been fully delivered. The latest challenge to the never-ending urban commuting battle is the tremendous increase in the use of private automobiles that has resulted from the successful national economic boom of the last two decades. In recent years, due to a rapid increase in the number of cars and the limited carrying capacity of almost all urban highways and narrow local streets, the urban expressways and all major arterial roads have frequently resembled huge parking lots. Automobiles on roadways have actually been crawling for hours.

Since the late 1970s and well into the early 1990s, the internal structure of Seoul changed, transforming from one primary core based monocentric city to one with multiple-core centers. The satellite cities immediately surrounding Seoul such as Euijongbu, Kwachon, Buchon, and Sungnam have mushroomed and expressed their desire to grow even more. Clearly the 1974 multiple-core concept plan did not antici-pate this surging growth of the city and, as a result, the pressure of growth simply overtook the plan, thwarting orderly, successful imple-mentation. Recognizing this, city officials in 1984 recommended yet another concept plan that was finally adopted by the city government in 1989. The 1989 concept plan called for one primary core area in the inner city, three secondary core areas evenly distributed south of the Han River, consisting of 17 city districts, and 50 neighborhood centers (City of Seoul, 1990). This plan also emphasized the dispersion of the major employment base of the primary core area of the inner city to other targeted areas south of the Han River, not only to develop an orderly process of decentralized employment centers, but also to soothe escalating urban commuting pains for all the residents of Seoul. A major difference between this plan and other previously attempted plans was that the latest plan anticipated a politico-administrative reform of introducing local autonomy and decentralized government structure, encouraging a flexible plan that would provide local districts with more freedom to respond to their changing needs.

Obviously, the current cityscape of Seoul is a culmination of the past 600 years of growth and development, although most of the intense growth has occurred during the last three decades. As many develop-ments occurred without the city's direct control and guidelines, it is not surprising to observe that the city still exhibits a dual nature of land use. For example, modern skyscrapers command their spatial dominance next to single-story residential houses, while pre-industrial sectors coexist with modern high-tech industrial sectors. The result is that throughout the massive plain of Seoul, the current cityscape of non-conforming land use is pervasive. No matter how long the latest plan has been in place to guide and implement the future growth of the city, Seoul's existing land use patterns will persist: highly mixed land uses, crowded and dense business development located on small parcels of land, and uncoordinated and environmentally hazardous strip develop-ment, not only in major streets, but also in residential districts. Rooted in a unique history, Seoul will require meaningful long-term solutions to remedy its fractious urban environment.

Development of land use and zoning laws

During most periods of Seoul's spatial expansion and growth, the concept of modern land use controls and regulations in Korea was unfamiliar territory. Until 1962, Korea did not have nationwide land use regulations that could successfully control and guide urban land uses. Although the present cityscape does include some modern city structures, depicting a closer representation of the advanced international development technologies and strategies, a current dualistic character of land use, as discussed in the preceding section, may explain the widely sprawling, accidental nature of city growth due to the lack of a comprehensive land use control system.

With the opening up of the castled city, the Japanese colonial government in 1936 first introduced a plan for the development of city's legal boundaries by incorporating 135.9 km^2 of available land in Seoul. After Korea's liberation, the legal boundary for Seoul expanded continuously outwards through annexation and by redefining the city's administrative area, actions prompted by Seoul's increasing population. In August 1949, for example, the city's administrative area was again expanded. The Ministry of Home Affairs, in December 1949, annexed more land, closely following the newly proposed administrative area. Subsequently, the total area within the city limits was increased to 269.8 km^2, nearly doubling from its original physical size of 135.9 km^2. Much of the expansion took place, not in direct and well-positioned anticipation to the future needs of the city, but rather in passive, often abrupt, responses to the tremendous population surge, striving to house approximately two million people within this redefined physical space. As discussed earlier, the population grew geometrically from the late 1940s to the 1960s. By 1963, with additional land, the total city boundary was expanded to 595.6 km^2 to accommodate the rapidly growing small towns and villages immediately surrounding the city. The historical change in the city boundary since 1936 is summarized in Figure 3.5.

Although the city boundaries continued to move outwards, the size of the population grew larger and the urban infrastructure development intensified, the development of land use regulations lagged far behind actual urban growth. For example, the development of zoning ordinances for the 1949 city boundaries was finalized in 1964, whereas that for the 1963 expanded area was completed in 1969. These lengthy time lags created huge problems in terms of controlling land uses, developing and conforming to proper building codes, and actively guiding potentially complex urban projects. In addition, concerns for the invasion of the private property rights of individuals were raised, as the exchange of properties had to be curtailed until the final land use laws were put together in 1969.

There appeared to be three major reasons why the development of zoning ordinances was slow in coming. The tragic civil war required concentrated government efforts in physically rebuilding the hopelessly

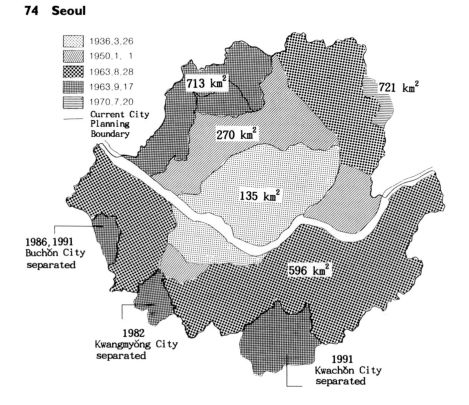

Figure 3.5 Changes in city planning boundaries. Reproduced with permission from Seoul Development Institute (1994)

destroyed capital city; when faced with reconstructing the urban infrastructure, the development of land use regulations was perceived as a luxury item. A lack of knowledge of modern land use issues and policies among the decision-makers in Korea was another obstacle. Soon after being liberated from Japanese colonialism, most Koreans simply did not have ample opportunity to become familiar with any modern concepts dealing with urban land controls. Finally, a long delayed bureaucratic response to organizing a proper bureau to handle zoning issues was an additional hindrance to this effort. Without a proper organizational structure, the implementation and enforcement of zoning ordinances was indeed a difficult task.

Perhaps the challenges facing any city government in terms of planning and developing a city along a well-ordered spatial arrangement with services being provided would be an impossible assignment, even when presented with vacant land and unlimited financial resources. Throughout the growth periods of Seoul, with her unique history, there appear to have been two golden opportunities lost in terms of developing an attractive, world-class city. The period immediately following the Japanese domination presented such a chance, when the restructuring stages of society were in a fluid state and needed guidance and leadership that could have been installed without too much societal pain and upheaval. The second opportunity was the period succeeding the tragic Korean civil war, when most of the city was completely devastated. Again, active leadership and societal guidance could have reshaped the city into a more harmonious configuration of the classic city. These lost opportunities were particularly painful when compared with two world-class cities that were successfully rebuilt even from unforeseen natural disasters. London survived and was rejuvenated after the 1666 fire, whereas Tokyo was mostly reconstructed after the 1923 Kanto earthquake.

Instead, over the years, the growth and expansion strategies for Seoul have not encouraged the orderly development of a capital city where a mix of contrasting city structures which preserves ancient traditions, introduces modernity, presents a human-scale spatial arrangement, and highlights the importance of livable urban space is fully realized and appreciated. It was clear that when well-thought out growth and management plans were critically needed, the city grew aimlessly with never-ending urban sprawl. When a remedy for major surgery for certain development sites was required, city officials proceeded with minor cosmetic improvements, hoping that the most critical issues would retreat and dissipate. When a small-scale, human solution to many of the urban slum clearance projects was called for, city officials aggressively brought in a method of bulldozing with that they could clear the entire site for a massive, high-density commercial and residential development without an understanding of an appropriate scale for such projects. Much of the unplanned and uncontrolled urban development occurred during periods when necessary land uses and zoning laws were not officially in place and enforced.

At present, the total area of the city that was officially redrawn by the Ministry of Construction in 1982 remains at 721 km^2, as previously shown in Figure 3.5. Although most of Seoul's city boundaries coincide with the city's administrative area, some portions of the city stretch beyond this. Given the current system where the city is under the strict control of the centralized national government, inter-jurisdictional problems may not pose a serious problem for growth and development. However, when a fully-fledged local autonomous government system is fully enacted some time in the very near future, these areas could become ripe for disputing which local jurisdiction controls and governs their future development.

As mentioned earlier, the use of zoning ordinances was not a commonly understood concept in Korea. When it was first introduced in 1934 by the Japanese colonial government, four major classifications for general land use were initially recommended: residential, commercial, industrial, and unspecified areas. In an attempt to satisfy the special needs of many cities and towns, however, additional classifications for four special land use districts were also added: scenery, beauty, fire hazard, and social action districts. These special use districts were specific to their area in that their own unique historical and natural settings determined what types of special districts cities and towns should institute. For example, major port cities such as Inchon and Pusan have maintained harbor districts, whereas Seoul has several special districts that encourage the preservation and enhancement of the traditional Korean architectural housing stock. From the onset, these special districts were heavily influenced by local and national political pressures, relaxing some districts for non-conforming uses and consequently deviating from the original intention of preserving locally specific characteristics. In 1993, Seoul still maintained 11 special use districts, totaling a land area of 517 km^2, as shown in Table 3.2. Of the total area, a special use for parking lots for vehicles was the largest, approximately 292 km^2, highlighting the emerging and increasing use of private automobiles.

The original intent of the zoning ordinances, which included both general and special land use districts, was to promote an orderly physical growth, to protect the safety and welfare of the public, and to enforce proper building codes within the city's legal boundaries. In 1936, under the first-ever legally adopted zoning ordinances, the distribution of the total land area of 135.6 km^2 was 92.1 km^2 (68%) for residential uses, 6.0 km^2 (3.4%) for commercial uses, 6.7 km^2 (5.0%) for industrial activities, and 30.6 km^2 (22.6%) for unspecified uses (Seoul Metropolis, 1962). Residential areas were designated in most sections of the city, whereas most commercial activities were concentrated within the areas of the present primary core of the inner city, where a large majority of the Japanese population resided during the colonial period. Paralleling most land use decisions during this particular time, additional commercial areas and industrial uses closely followed the existing and proposed railroad and streetcar lines, and were intensified in areas near major train stations; in particular, a number of major collecting streetcar stations were at each end of the lines. Though the initial purpose of the unspecified uses was to preserve some land for future use, a significant portion began to drift to mixed uses that eventually contributed to some of the chaotic, unattractive urban patterns throughout the city. The overall internal structure of the city exhibited a discontinuous, linear

Table 3.2 Special land use districts in Seoul, 1993

Land use districts	Number	Area (km²)
Total	439	517
Nature landscape districts	24	16.6
Aesthetic districts	243	22.3
High land districts	8	69
Apartment districts	15	12.7
Fire protection districts*	111	3.5
Preservation districts	1	5.3
Airport districts†	1	51.5
Parking improvement districts	–	292
Urban design districts	12	9.4
Disaster prevention districts	20	27.5
Institution protection districts	4	7.2

* 1992.
† 1991.

Source: Seoul Development Institute, 1993b.

pattern of development along streetcar and bus lines, particularly in areas outside the four main gates.

Following the liberation and subsequent expansion of the city through the annexation of four additional areas contiguous to the existing city boundaries in 1949, the revised zoning ordinances of 1952 based on Article 23 of the Ministry of Home Affairs were introduced. The revised ordinances reflected only the marginal alteration of some of the existing zoning laws of the colonial government. The unspecified uses were reclassified as mixed and green areas. This minor modification did not meet the new challenges facing the rapidly expanding city, but became an unintended tool for accommodating much of the unplanned and accelerated urban development.

As shown in Table 3.3, the distribution of most other land uses in 1952 was maintained at approximately the same level as in 1939. With more intense pressures from both population growth and urban development, city officials eliminated the land use category for mixed use in 1962 and introduced another category for quasi-industrial use areas throughout the entire city in 1963. Most of the quasi-industrial use areas, however, came from previously designated mixed use areas, particularly at various locations north of the Han River, and represented about 18.6% of the total land area in Seoul.

Over the years, four major categories of general land use (residential, commercial, industrial, and green areas) emerged and have been in use ever since 1966. One striking phenomenon concerning the changing distribution of the four major categories is a drastic reduction in

Table 3.3 Changes in general land use. Values given are area in hectares (%)

Year	Residential		Commercial		Industrial		Green		Mixed		Total
1939	9213.2	(68.0)	599.1	(4.4)	665.8	(4.9)	3057.4	(22.7)	–		13 535.5
1952	8764.8	(64.6)	636.3	(4.6)	668	(5.1)	590.4	(4.4)	2887	(21.3)	13 664.4
1964	13 872.7	(49.3)	751	(2.7)	617	(2.2)	7651.6	(27.2)	5222.3	(18.6)*	28 114.6
1966	33 922	(47.6)	886	(1.2)	9354	(13.1)	27 126	(38.1)	–		71 324
1976	28 630	(39.7)	1736	(2.4)	3292	(4.6)	38 429	(53.3)	–		72 087
1988	29 708	(41.8)	2179	(3.1)	3088	(4.4)	35 864	(50.6)	–		70 839
1993	30 124	(45.2)	2148	(3.2)	2908	(4.4)	31 418	(47.2)	–		66 598

* Quasi-industrial.

Sources: Economic Planning Board, 1962–1994; City of Seoul, 1961–1994; and Seoul Metropolis, 1987–1993.

residential use over time, decreasing from 68% in 1939 to 45.2% in 1993. With an explosive population increase, coupled with the ever-expanding physical space of Seoul, this substantial decline was indeed incomprehensible. It is no wonder then that the prevailing high density residential development is an inevitable outcome of urban growth as less and less land became available for residential development. It is even more extraordinary as the vast land south of the Han River was rapidly being developed under the guidelines of the newly revised zoning ordinances from the late 1960s. Although it was originally planned to accommodate more residential use in most areas south of the Han River, the ensuing result was impressively similar to the overall historical distribution of the entire city; about 47.6% was designated for residential use, whereas more commercial and industrial uses were encouraged.

Resulting probably from the greenbelt law of 1971, more land has been increasingly designated for green areas since 1966. Though city officials in 1976 reclassified the greenbelt as natural green and agricultural green areas and some of the existing land use regulations underwent minor modifications, the basic structure of the zoning ordinances did not deviate too much from the 1976 citywide land use regulations. The existing zoning ordinances, accompanied by historically inconsistent enforcement practices, did not prevent Seoul from creating many of her undesirable land uses and urban growth patterns. Perhaps extremely intense development pressures from all sectors of the economy, including tremendous population growth in such a short period of time, could have contributed to her present urban form, however unimaginable they may seem. Given the current pressure for easing the greenbelt law of 1971 for more urban development and the completion of several new satellite towns surrounding Seoul, a relaxation of the greenbelt areas and open space will clearly change future land use patterns of the city and in the SMR.

Growth and expansion of various functions of the city

In the previous sections we showed that the internal structure of Seoul has been transformed from a very simple, monocentric city to one that is multiple-core, supplying a much more complex variety of functions as a modern and international city. Although most functions of the city, providing simple to complex activities, were closely linked with various stages of structural development in her 600 years of history, the most dramatic shift and growth has occurred during the last 30 years when enormous economic and population growth took place. Not only have the spatial patterns of the city increased in size and complexity, but simultaneously other social and cultural fabrics have also accompanied the intense expansion over the years.

Historically, several studies have made attempts to understand the emerging functions of the city at various stages of growth and development as well as their interaction with spatial structure (Lynch and Rodwin, 1958; Foley, 1964; Webber, 1964; Bourne, 1982; Castells, 1983, 1990). Clearly, the functions of a city are fluid and varied, yet location-specific in that space, urban form, and certain activities are closely intertwined. At different stages of development, some key functions do change or shift, much like the rise and fall of particular types of spatial arrangements: the locational shift in some central business district activities, the flow and density of population, or the intensity of cultural activities. Although some functions can be easily explained, the combination and concentration of such elements as daily activities, work, leisure, and networks often determine the city's spatial configuration (Geddes, 1949; Chapin, 1974). Most recently, however, with the development of the information age, along with the capital flow of multinational corporations, some city functions seem to be floating without any permanent spatial attachment.

To understand and describe the complex nature of functionality for Seoul, the following attempt was made to explain the widely available current activities by specific spatial order. The entire city was identified and grouped by the physical areas of core, district center (sub-centers), and neighborhood center. The core areas were further classified into primary and secondary core areas, while population size was used to better define district centers and neighborhood centers. In addition, the availability of employment and the daily functional needs of residents were considered for a more refined description. Based on this concept, Seoul was seen to have one primary core, three secondary cores, 13 district centers, and 49 neighborhood centers, representing both sides of the Han River, as shown in Figures 3.6 and 3.7.

The city functions are closely related to their spatial areas of influence as well as to their specific order of space, as described earlier. For example, most functions that largely rely on international clientele are found in the core areas and can be described by the presence of such activities as international tourist hotels, duty-free shops, international schools, foreign trade offices, international telephone and telegraph offices, and offices for various international organizations. On the other hand, other functions such as convenience stores, neighborhood movie theaters, and small inns seem to be frequently located in neighborhood centers. Clearly, there are some functions that seem to duplicate themselves when classified by certain locational configurations, but in general they appear to preserve their own unique characteristics in terms of the

Figure 3.6 Urban spatial systems and hierarchies for Seoul

functionality of the city. Undoubtedly, as Seoul advances through additional phases of development and enhances its standing as an international city, various functions will either shift their locations or be permanently replaced by new ones.

Transportation

Just a few days before a highly celebrated national holiday period in September 1993, most connecting roads and bridges serving the primary core area north of the Han River became so heavily congested that daily traffic flows often came to a complete stop. Most commuters who were caught in the unusual traffic jams wondered what caused their plight. Apparently, three major department stores located in the heart of the primary core area decided to have one of their annual sales with the

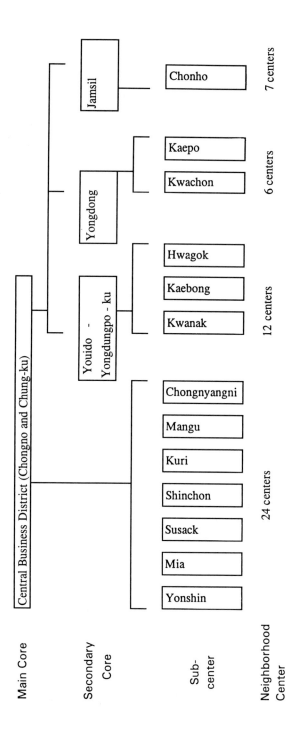

Figure 3.7 Urban spatial structure and hierarchies

year's biggest price reduction to celebrate the national holiday. Because many middle and upper-middle income customers drove their private automobiles to shop at the big sales, the existing roads could not handle this unexpected increase.

National media and some government officials scolded the three major department stores for not coordinating and staggering their sale date to minimize the impact of the increased traffic volume. This episode, however unrealistic it may seem, illustrates how serious the traffic problems in Seoul have become in recent years. With the enormous increase in private automobile ownership, coupled with an insufficient transportation system, it is very unlikely that any plausible solutions to Seoul's transportation crisis will come anytime soon. In this section, we explore how the current transportation situation has evolved into what it is today.

Development of the transportation street system

One unique characteristic of a castled city was that most activities were exclusively reserved for serving the royal palace. Most roads and other public infrastructure evolved around the palace. The main focus of the transportation system was to cater to the needs of those who served the palace, as exemplified by major roads between the palace and the places of residence of most civil servants. Historically, because the main mode of transportation was by foot in Seoul, most roads were developed with very narrow widths, attesting to the importance of pedestrian movement. The average width of the major boulevards, for example, was only about 17 m, whereas those of the main roads and small secondary local streets were 5 and 3.3 m, respectively. In many residential areas the common width of many local streets and alleyways connecting various neighborhood sections was less than 2 m, unthinkable by today's modern city standards that address automobile traffic. The street system that was built around pedestrian and other primitive modes of transportation pre-dated the introduction of automobiles and was maintained for over 500 years of Seoul's history. In the period of Japanese domination, the colonial government neglected to improve the existing street system within the city and instead decided to emphasize the development of connecting roads between Seoul and other strategically located major cities throughout the country for military purposes.

The most notable development of the transportation street system has occurred since the mid-1960s, when Korea's economic development took a giant step forward. Indeed, it was the beginning of the modern transportation street system that still exists in its present form. For areas

—— Urban Expressways
■■■■ Limited Expressways
—— Arterial Roads

0   2   4   6Km

Figure 3.8 Road expansion plan. Reproduced with permission from Seoul Development Institute (1994)

within a 5 km radius of the primary core area, the existing street network that was originally developed by the colonial government was improved by constructing a number of secondary and arterial roads connecting to the center of the city. Since the development of the expanding areas south of the Han River did not begin until the late 1960s, only three bridges connecting both sides of the Han River served the entire city. Beginning in the early 1970s, the internal structure of the city changed rapidly, particularly with the intense development of the areas south of the Han River. As shown in Figure 3.8, the infrastructure for transportation experienced a dramatic increase, providing new arterial and circular roads, urban expressways, a modern subway system, more buses, and substantially more bridges linking both sides of the Han River.

The main emphasis for most arterial roads was to improve the existing north–south transportation network and also to provide for efficient connections to major east–west traffic flows. Three major ring roads were constructed to provide easy access to various city districts within the city boundaries. For example, the first ring road encircled the edges of both the primary and secondary core areas and the most densely developed city districts. The second ring road connected various city districts within a radius of 5 km, whereas the third ring road encompassed the periphery of the city outside the radius of 15 km. The third ring road was also used as a physical boundary to enforce the greenbelt law that prohibited urban development. A fourth ring road that connects various satellite cities and towns within the SMR and Kyonggi-do Province is currently under construction.

For the preparation of both the 1986 Asian Games and the 1988 World Summer Olympics, a major expressway serving as an efficient gateway to the east–west traffic flow for most districts in the area south of the Han River was constructed by the mid-1980s. It was named the 88 urban expressway to celebrate the 1988 Olympics in Seoul. Although this newly introduced expressway was hailed as one of the newest highway systems built to alleviate most traffic bottle-necks and enhance efficient traffic flows, particularly linking most districts south of the Han River to the north, it soon became obsolete because traffic, caused by the ubiquitous presence of automobiles, buses, and trucks, was frequently delayed with numerous bottle-neck points along the expressway. The roads soon resembled giant parking lots. During the same period in which Seoul prepared for the Olympics, urban slum clearance projects in various sections of the city were intensified to beautify many deteriorated areas of the city. In the process, a significant number of very narrow neighborhood streets and alleyways less than 2 m wide – unique to Korean tradition and culture – were quickly replaced by major streets that accommodated automobiles. The preservation of traditional Korean customs fell by the wayside to modernization, a concept routinely connected to human 'progress' and prosperity, that escapes much-needed critical assessment.

Perhaps many of the present transportation problems may have inevitably resulted from the city experiencing one of the fastest population growths in modern history. More bridges linking both sides of the Han River have been constructed, many more arterial roads and circular roads have been created to alleviate unpleasant traffic jams, and urban expressways have been developed to speed up east–west traffic flow. Even with all these developments, it seems that as long as the main focus of the existing streets serves to provide more immediate access to the primary core area north of the Han River, an insufficient transportation network will persist with a much less than adequate carrying capacity. This remains true despite the unsuccessful efforts of city officials to decentralize some government and commercial functions of the city.

With more and more private cars being introduced, it appears that Seoul has already reached another critical level of diverse and intense traffic demands such as commuting, leisure activities, and business. Without an adequate road system within the primary and secondary core areas of the city that connects to many of the rapidly developing city districts, the overflow from the existing road network will pose a serious threat to the present and future transportation system. Recent government plans to expand the existing road network, over 1000 km in total additional length, and to build double-decker urban expressways, could be seen as another desperate response to the present crisis (*Hankook Daily*, 1993).

Growth of transportation volumes and trips

In Seoul, daily activity patterns in relation to the mode of transportation have undergone a profound change. Until the early 1960s, most residents transported themselves on foot, as the public transportation system was very limited, consisting mainly of streetcars, buses, and taxis. With the city's rapidly expanding population and physical size, the customary reliance on foot for their daily activities became an almost impossible task for most residents in Seoul. The pace of life became faster, the functions of the city became more diverse and, consequently, the purpose of daily trips took on a more heterogeneous character. As a result, the closer proximity to a mode of convenient transportation became an important factor for deciding where to locate for most residents and businesses.

As mentioned earlier, the total population in Seoul currently exceeds 11 million, a five-fold increase in less than 30 years. With the increasing complexity of the social, economic, and leisure activities of individuals, the average number of trips per person per day has also been increasing. For example, as shown in Table 3.4, the total number of daily trips in 1978 was 11.6 million, representing about 1.48 trips per person per day. By 1988, the total number of trips and average daily trips increased to 18.6 million and 1.80, respectively. However, in a short period of only three years, the total number of trips escalated to 27.7 million, while the average trip went up to 2.62 per person per day in 1991, a truly remarkable increase. It was also estimated that, by the year 2000, the average number of trips per person per day may reach 3.0 trips. Between 1978 and 1991, the annual rate of increase of the total number of trips generated was about twice that for population growth. This is an indication that the lifestyles of residents have become more elaborate. The total number of automobiles had tremendously increased during the

Table 3.4 Volumes for trip generation between 1978 and 1991

	1978 (A)	1983	1988	1991 (B)	B/A	Rate of increase (%)
Population (000s)	7823	9024	10 287	10 580	1.35	2.7
Total trips (000s)	11 578	15 437	18 517	27 715	2.39	10.7
Trips/person	1.48	1.68	1.8	2.62	1.77	5.9
Automobiles (000s)	167	315	779	1375	8.23	55.6
Road ratio	14.4	15.66	17.82	18.4	1.28	2.2

Source: City of Seoul, 1961–1994.

same period, and the escalation will probably intensify for some time to come (City of Seoul, 1992).

When we look more closely at the purpose of the trips generated, the changing nature of the daily trips become apparent. Table 3.5, for example, summarizes four major purposes for daily trips for Seoul residents since 1977. The most significant change among the four categories was associated with noncommuting-related activities. By 1991, this particular category grew consistently over the years, while the commuting trips declined slightly. This gives clear evidence of how diverse daily trips have become over time. As residents continually strive to improve their standard of living, the growth of trips such as those for social, leisure, shopping, and business purposes will undoubtedly accelerate. Because most of these trips do take place at randomly selected time periods, including the business hours, not only could they contribute to the current traffic jams, but they could also generate new types of traffic congestion that persist throughout most of the day. Still, the sheer volume and complicated nature of the total number of commuting trips present a major challenge in dealing with the transportation problems facing Seoul and the SMR.

The present trend in automobile ownership seems to further compound the current transportation crisis. In 1975, the total number of cars in Seoul was only about 100 000, a modest number considering a city size of about 7 million people. As the standard of living for city dwellers, particularly in Seoul, has improved dramatically since the mid-1970s, their desire for better material goods, including private automobiles, has also grown. Table 3.6 illustrates a recent phenomenon in automobile ownership in Seoul. The total number of private automobiles increased the most during a relatively short period of time, between 1980 and 1990. In fact, by 1990 more than one million cars were on the streets, approximately 70% of which belonged to private

Table 3.5 Number (%) of daily trips by purpose

Type of trip	1977 (%)	1982		1986		1991	
Morning commute							
School	19.1	2 529 764	(16.3)	2 632 754	(16.9)	3 005 891	(13.6)
Business	22.3	3 119 529	(20.1)	2 838 262	(18.2)	3 689 786	(16.8)
Evening commute	46.8	7 527 222	(48.5)	6 652 718	(42.8)	9 170 300	(41.5)
Others	11.8	2 343 531	(15.1)	3 437 661	(22.1)	6 230 743	(28.1)
Total	100.0	15 520 046	(100.0)	15 561 395	(100.0)	22 096 720	(100.0)

Sources: Korea Transport Research Institute, 1987; and Seoul Development Institute, 1993a.

Table 3.6 Increase in automobiles in Seoul between 1980 and 1990

	1980	1985	1990	Rate of increase (%)	
				1980–85	1985–90
Automobiles (A)	206 778	445 807	1 064 026	16.6	19
Private passenger cars	99 544	256 327	726 592	20.8	23.2
A/1000 Population	24.7	46.2	97.6	13.3	16.1
A/1000 Households	111.8	190.5	34.6	11.2	14.5

Source: Seoul Metropolis, 1990b.

individuals. With the presence of a strong automobile industry in Korea, it is expected that this current trend in private automobile ownership will accelerate.

One of the most striking phenomena resulting from the rapid growth in the ownership of private automobiles is the unusual, often theatrical, scenes played out in the parking lots at most high-rise apartments. As a large majority of high-rise apartment buildings were constructed before the automobile boom, the area designated for resident's parking was exceedingly limited as the available land for such large-scale construction was always scarce. When the residents return home from their daily jobs or other social engagements, they quickly exhaust the available space. Residents who arrive home later, however, locate parking spaces in between the rows of already parked cars, usually by parallel parking. Once their car is parked and locked, the residents must remember not to engage their emergency parking gear, so that early risers the next morning can maneuver themselves out of their hemmed-in parking space by pushing and pulling their neighbor's cars that are temporarily blocking their path. It is one of the most intriguing sights to behold, an example of the impact that the lack of parking spaces and the over-abundance of private automobiles can have!

With this seemingly unlimited growth in transportation demand, accompanied by inadequate roadways, it is hardly surprising that we now see the worst traffic jams, bottle-necks, and clogged streets in Seoul's modern history. According to a recent study, the average speed of automobiles on roadways decreased from 31 km/h in 1980 to 16.5 km/h in 1990 (Korea Transport Research Institute, 1990). Also speculated in the study was the projection that, by the year 2000, the average speed of automobiles on the roads would be further reduced to a mere 8 km/h, unless some drastic measures resolving the current traffic problems are instituted by city officials.

Emergence of public transportation

Following the explosive growth of Seoul's population and automobiles during the last 30 years, the current transportation problems in Seoul have become so critical that most politicians and city officials have constantly been searching for possible answers. In this section we will examine the expansion of the existing public transportation network along with new mass transportation developments and how they shape the transportation debate facing the city today.

Ironically, electric streetcars introduced by the Japanese in May 1899 were Seoul's first public transportation system. By 1910 there were five service routes with 37 streetcars covering a total of approximately 22.2 km. During most of the colonial period, the streetcar service was the first and most widely available public transportation system and the service area was continually extended to almost 40 km served by 257 streetcars by 1945. Although the concept of public transportation was slowly understood and accepted by most residents during the colonial period, ridership grew from a mere 7000 in 1909 to almost half a million by 1945. By this time, more than 50% of the residents became accustomed to, and dependent on, various available routes in the streetcar system (Lim, 1984). Although streetcars remained the most important mode of transportation during the 1950s and 1960s, the impressive growth of automobile use and buses began competing for space in the narrow streets of the city. Most streets became extremely crowded with buses, cars, streetcars, bicycles, and people, often threatening the safety of the public. When streetcars, with their inherent inflexibility of the fixed rails, could not provide the speed they needed to compete with cars and buses, city officials quickly decided to eliminate streetcar services and covered the existing rails with new pavements, thus ending one of the most dependable public transportation elements in Seoul's early public transportation history.

Bus services were first introduced in 1928 during the colonial era. A service was provided by only about 30 buses. Although the service initially consisted of two bus routes covering the heart of the inner city, most residents were unfamiliar with the newly created motorized bus service and instead continued to rely on the streetcar system. In the late 1950s, however, bus services began emerging as the most dominant public transportation system. Most people found the bus service convenient, dependable, and flexible. By the mid-1970s, approximately 60–70% of the total public transportation services provided in the city were carried by buses. As the service was constantly expanded, not only did buses begin providing efficient connections between the primary core area and other districts in the city's periphery, but they also instituted services extending to several outlying areas of the city (see Figure 3.9). Although serious attempts were made to decentralize service lines throughout the entire city, the main emphasis for most bus routes still remained making connections to the primary core area of the city. Perhaps this was one of the major causes for creating extremely overcrowded traffic congestion in inner city areas.

As bus ridership escalated steadily in the late 1950s, it became apparent that they could not handle the rapidly increasing passenger demands. The carrying capacity for buses soon began to deteriorate rather quickly. By the mid-1970s, buses became extremely overcrowded, worsening rapidly, and provided inconvenient, often hazardous services

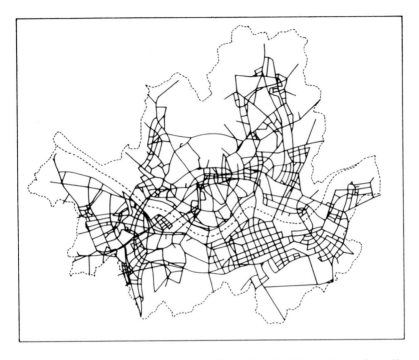

Figure 3.9 Summary of bus service lines. Reproduced with permission from Korea Transport Research Institute (1990)

to most residents. The increasing use of private automobiles made most roads even more congested in such a way that providing efficient bus services became a very difficult task. Furthermore, as most bus companies were privately owned and operated, competition for better routes, particularly for efficient and profitable connections to the city center, became fierce. Services to some of the outlying areas of the city were gradually discontinued by some bus companies. When some bus routes were arbitrarily reduced for profit-related reasons and without concern for passengers' convenience, the overcrowding conditions for bus passengers worsened.

When the dependability of the existing public transportation system was frequently questioned and perceived as deteriorating rapidly, the pressure for a complete, modern mass transit system was intensified. The development of a new subway and rapid transit system in 1974 was intended to address Seoul's transportation woes. The main purpose of the rapid transit system was to provide an efficient commuting opportunity for the rapidly growing satellite cities, particularly two outlying cities, Inchon and Suwon in the SMR. The newly developed subway system in Seoul was to provide adequate connections to two rapid transit lines so that the primary core area north of the Han River as well as many peripheral cities in the SMR could be effectively linked. Within 10 years from the time the first subway line was introduced, three more subway lines were added, covering a large physical area of the city: one encircling the primary core and secondary core areas on both sides of the Han River, and two others making direct north–south connections within the city limits. In the meantime, three additional rapid transit lines were constructed to serve a larger segment of the residents in the SMR. This combined system of rapid transit and subway lines has become an integral part of the modern mass transit system in Seoul.

Table 3.7 and Figure 3.10 show either the proposed or already developed combined system of subways and transit lines serving the city and the SMR. According to a ridership study, the total daily ridership capacity of the system was estimated at 11 million for the transit lines and five million for the subways (Korea Transport Research Institute, 1990). The daily ridership for both systems rose very quickly. When the first subway was introduced, the total daily ridership was only about 230 000. With the completion of three other subways providing more than 100 stations, however, the daily ridership increased to approximately 2.5 million. According to the same study, it was expected that in a few years the total demand would exceed well over three million per day, representing approximately 20% of the total daily ridership of the entire mass transit system (Korea Transport Research Institute, 1990). At the same time, the growth of the population in nearby satellite cities intensified with the development of five transit lines. As more and more residents in the SMR relied on the existing transit lines for their morning and evening commutes, the overall carrying capacity failed to keep pace with the increasing ridership; trains became extremely overcrowded and the safety of passengers was increasingly threatened. As expected, though hardly desired, the rush-hour traffic volume on the subway system led to the rapid deterioration of the carrying capacity, thereby contributing to yet another overcrowding crisis in the mass transit system.

In an attempt to alleviate the system-wide oversaturation of the daily ridership projected by the year 2000, five more subway lines have been proposed, making a total of 12 available lines for the region. The additional lines would add 184 km of service to the existing network. An additional 70 km of transit line extension intended to serve satellite cities and new towns in the SMR is also planned (City of Seoul, 1961–1994).

Although some segment of the planned subway construction had already been completed by the early 1990s, the overcrowding condition

Table 3.7   Development of subways and transit lines for Seoul and SMR

Service line	Service area	Distance (km)	Year of service
Kyonggi line	Seoul–Suwon	41.5	1974
Kyongin line	Kuro–Inchon	27	1974
Kyongwon line	Chongnyangri–Euijongbu	18.6	1986
Chungang line	Chongnyangri–Yangpyong	84.5	1973
Ansan line	Ansan–Keumjong	20.4	1988
Seoul Subway			
Line No. 1	Seoul Station–Chongnyangri	9.5	1974
Line No. 2	City Hall–Ulchiro 1ga	54.3	1984
Line No. 3	Chi ch'uk–Susoe	36.9	1985 (93)
Line No. 4	Tang Kogae–Namtaeryoung	34.3	1985 (94)
Line No. 5	Kimpo Airport–Goduk, Guyou	52	1994
Line No. 7	Sanggae–Hwayang	16	1994
Line No. 8	Chamsil–Songnam	15.5	1994
Line No. 6	Yokchon–Sinnae	31	1997*
Line No. 7	Hwayang–Onsu	26	1997*
Line No. 8	Chamsil–Amsa	4.5	1997*
Line No. 9	Kimp Airport–Dunchon	38	1999*
Line No. 10	Shihung–Myunmok	35	1999*
Line No. 11	Yangjae–Sinwol	35	1999*
Line No. 12	Wangsipri–Songbuk	9	1999*

( ) Additional services added in this year.
* Planned year

Source: Bureau of National Rail Service, 1988; Seoul Metropolis, *Seoul Administration*, 1993.

during the rush-hour periods has not significantly improved. Moreover, frequently unexpected breakdowns of the most recently constructed subway lines have contributed to a growing anxiety on the part of many residents and commuters concerned with the overall quality of the mass transit system in Seoul and the SMR. However, the dependence on the transit and subway lines has consistently been increasing. In contrast, bus ridership had drastically decreased from 70% in the 1970s to less than 50% by the early 1990s. The huge expansion in the ownership of private automobiles accounts for about 20% of the daily commutes. Although this newly created trend is expected to continue, city officials have constantly emphasized that the combined system of transit and subway lines should remain the most important elements of the mass transit system, a policy aimed at relieving the burden currently pre-vailing on the surface transportation network such as buses, taxis, and private automobiles. Nonetheless, the existing road network is ill-equipped to carry even a small increase in transportation demand.

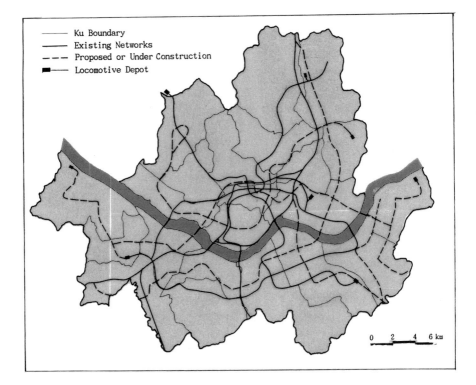

Key:
- Ku Boundary
- Existing Networks
- Proposed or Under Construction
- Locomotive Depot

0 2 4 6 km

Figure 3.10 Existing and planned subway networks. Reproduced with permission from Seoul Development Institute (1994)

Transportation problems and policies

Even before the population of the SMR grew to account for almost 40% of Korea's total population, it might have been possible to foresee the magnitude and devastating effects of the current transportation crisis on the city and the SMR. With very limited buildable land available anywhere in the country, the excessive population growth was indeed an essential factor in inducing a wide range of newly created problems such as transportation, housing, and improper land use. One of the most urgent issues facing city officials is to treat transportation problems not as an isolated incident, but to understand the various factors contributing to the existing problems and to develop sensible policies to deal with the current and projected future problems.

Steady increases in daily ridership for the mass transit system have not significantly reduced the constant presence of traffic jams and bottlenecks. The existing subway system has been perceived as providing an efficient, convenient, and safe service to most residents and visitors to the city. However, due to a limited number of trains in operation during the rush hours, the overcrowding situation has persisted, thereby creating unpleasant and inconvenient commuting for most riders. When the proposed subway extension providing a total of eight lines and covering most areas of the city is completed, its share of the total ridership from the mass transit system is expected to reach about 47% (Seoul Metropolis, 1986–1994). Perhaps overcrowded conditions could then be eliminated. Until this becomes a reality, city officials must continue to explore elsewhere for possible remedies.

In searching for possible solutions, the present use of buses has been carefully evaluated. Although its share of the total ridership in the mass transit system has been steadily decreasing, some of the bus lines serving outlying areas, where no subway services are available to either the primary or secondary core area, have maintained a noticeable increase in ridership. Furthermore, existing bus lines connecting to various subway stations in the peripheral areas have also enjoyed a substantial increase in ridership, though overcrowding conditions for commuters have been persistent. Once the expanded network of the subway system is completed, bus services could be changed within the context of an integrated mass transit system. Instead of providing long distance services between many of the outlying areas and the primary and secondary core areas of the city, which often overburden the surface street network, bus services could be used as short distance feeder links between some districts and various subway stations in the outlying areas. More minibus services could also be provided for commuters traveling between their homes and the nearest subway stations. In fact, several minibus lines connecting some subway stations and selected business districts or large apartment complexes at various city locations have already begun their successful services during the morning and evening rush hours.

Taxi services are widely used for commuting and other business and social trips. Their share of the total ridership has been consistently high, approaching almost 18% of the entire mass transit system (City of Seoul, 1991). However, as taxi fares in Seoul are one of the cheapest in the large metropolitan cities of the world, it is often a struggle to hire a taxi, especially during rush hours. Taxi drivers frequently refuse to be hired for a long distance trip, a shared ride among passengers is commonly accepted, and traffic laws are habitually broken by aggressive and busy taxi drivers. Despite one of the worst taxi services known among international cities, the taxi service has been an important dimension in the existing mass transit system. However, there has been a deliberate movement towards making the taxi service, not a commuting arm for

Table 3.8 Distribution of street system

	Length		Area	
	km	%	km^2	%
Paths	6042	79.9	31.35	43.42
Roads	720.3	9.52	11.67	16.16
Streets	572.9	7.58	16.72	23.16
Avenues	226.4	3	10.12	14.02
Squares (No.)	76	–	2.34	3.24
Total	7561.40	100	72.2	100

Source: Seoul Metropolis, *Seoul Administration*, 1993.

the general public, but a fleet tailored for special purposes. Substantially increased fares with a fast, courteous, and convenient service would gear the service to busy business people. Beginning in the early 1990s, Seoul introduced a deluxe taxi service with such an intention. With a remarkable increase in service, these deluxe taxis have been a welcome addition to the existing mass transit system, though the basic fare is set about three times higher than a regular taxi.

As we previously mentioned, most roads in Seoul were developed for pedestrian use. Table 3.8 shows the distribution of roads based on their width. For example, the secondary neighborhood streets with some widths narrower than 10 m (paths) represent about 80% of the total road length and about 43% of the total area occupied by the street system, a truly inefficient road structure for a rapidly expanding city such as Seoul. Combined, major arterial streets and avenues occupied less than 11% of the total length, and approximately 37% of the street system's total area. As the number of private automobiles grew by 379% between 1983 and 1990, coupled with dwindling public expenditure on roads and other essential urban infrastructure, it is reasonable to assume that the existing roads and streets will not be able to meet the increased demand, thereby causing inefficient traffic flows (Seoul Metropolis, 1990b). The resulting traffic delays, high vehicle emissions, and additional fuel consumption clearly contribute to the increased social costs that not only city officials but all residents in Seoul must encounter.

With incredibly limited space for parking despite the growing number of vehicles over the years, the provision of parking space for private automobiles has been one of the most critical transportation issues facing the city. The parking problem is so widespread in the city that not only are the areas of the inner city, but also many districts and apartment complexes in the peripheral areas, beset with a parking crisis. The practice of illegal parking such as parking in no parking zones and double parking is pervasive throughout the entire city and seriously threatens public welfare. Emergency vehicles, ambulances, and police cars often cannot respond efficiently to calls due to impassable road conditions stemming from illegal parking along roadways. Serious attempts have been made to increase the available space for parking: the encouragement of underground parking, the essential provision of parking spaces for newly constructed office buildings, and curb-side parking. However, the increasing use of private automobiles for commuting and other business activities has made the parking situation almost impossible, particularly in the primary core area of the inner city. The daily use of private automobiles has continued to rise, currently representing more than 44% of the total vehicles on the road and contributing to worsening road congestion and traffic jams (City of Seoul, 1991).

Unpleasant traffic jams and inefficient traffic flows seem to have been a daily occurrence in recent years, and the outlook for improved traffic conditions does not appear promising. The expansion of existing roads and new street developments have not been aggressive enough to surpass the explosive growth in automobiles, buses, and other vehicles. As a result, traffic flows are extremely slow in both directions along the urban expressways and major boulevards at all times, beginning early morning to late night. A sudden collapse of a bridge (Sungsoo Bridge) connecting both sides of the Han River on 27 October 1994 amplified how grave the traffic situation has become in Seoul. As other existing bridges could not handle the additional traffic flows stemming from loss of the Sungsoo Bridge, its effect was felt everywhere in the city. Moreover, long overdue inspections of many of the existing bridges have additionally contributed to the already existing traffic delays.

The average vehicle speed in the inner city area and densely developed city districts was estimated at 20 km/h in 1990. This is not an attractive speed for efficient traffic flows, though hardly as bad as 10–12 km/h for Paris and 15–19 km/h for Tokyo. Following the collapse of Sungsoo Bridge, the current traffic conditions have worsened. It is further expected that, if the current trend continues, the average speed will become much worse than Paris or Tokyo and decrease to about 8 km/h by the year 2000 (City of Seoul, 1991).

By now, it will be clear that any solution to Seoul's transportation problems will not come easily. The aggressive physical expansion of the road and street network may be able to relieve some pressures from the current situation, but the city needs more far-reaching solutions. Concerted efforts in developing effective policies discouraging the concentration of the population in Seoul and the surrounding cities and new towns in the SMR are remedies that require careful implementation.

An understanding of the newly created automobile culture is also needed. Car pools, flexitime, staggered work hours, and other behavioral programs must also be considered and instituted if the current crisis is to be successfully managed and solved. The politics of the real transportation costs of providing and subsidizing the public transportation system, diseconomies resulting from unbearable traffic jams and vehicle emissions, and the power of automobile industries and their desire to serve the domestic market should also be publicly debated. Above all, a true understanding of the relationship between land use patterns and the transportation infrastructure is essential to the development of a more sensible spatial arrangement in Seoul.

4

Housing, urban growth, and urban redevelopment

In previous chapters we examined the existing patterns of land use and put in context the historical factors that contributed to the current mosaic of urban growth. Many of the factors that were largely responsible for the urban spatial expansion of Seoul were also closely linked to the city's residential development: an extremely high rate of migration from rural areas, improved and more economic and employment opportunities, explosive population growth, and the limited supply of land for development.

Over a relatively short 20 year span that began in the early 1960s, Seoul's physical capacity for growth deteriorated rapidly. Presented with ever-shrinking amounts of land available for development within and immediately surrounding the city boundary, the pressure for urban redevelopment grew immensely, thereby producing an uneven and highly dense development of spatial structures in various sections of the city. Unattractive urban physical settlement patterns ensued, consisting of non-conforming land uses and chaotically developed housing now widely seen throughout Seoul.

Historically, more often than not, the dominant political ideologies of government that drove the national priorities and agenda dictated how and what types of urban development should take place through various government programs and incentives. They ultimately shaped the outcome of urban spatial structures, without providing a forum for any meaningful discussion and participation from the general population. During the last 30 years, successive governments in Korea have emphasized economic growth at any cost and placed minuscule importance on social justice and political freedom for all citizens. This was the case particularly before the inauguration of the civilian government in 1993, which was a break from the previous military dictatorships. Industrial development and employment-generating activities were a major driving force for the national economy. Subsequently, the attention given to the national investment in housing was secondary and inadequate until housing problems, especially in Seoul, reached a major crisis level.

Housing shortages were widespread for all segments of the population. However, when there was a call for more affordable housing to be made available to lower and middle income households, the military governments sponsored slum clearance projects that were often implemented along popular ideals that supported continuous physical expansion and economic prosperity for middle and upper-middle income households. Not only were these projects completed without a thorough understanding of how urban squatter settlements resulted from a lack of affordable housing, but the governments also displaced households from slum areas without due consideration for decent housing. Social inequalities and conflicts have inevitably arisen due to this particular relationship between the heavy-handed government policy-making and the subsequent spatial arrangement.

In this chapter, we will look closely at the current housing situation in Seoul and explain how housing development has evolved over time. How various government policies affected housing, urban growth, and urban redevelopment processes in the capital city will also be explored.

Housing

In most societies, home ownership is regarded as the single most important dream for people. A comfortable, ideal home is where household members can relax and enjoy their privacy. Even in a socialist country such as China where housing is provided almost free to most citizens, particularly to urban residents, the aspiration for a private, two- or three-room apartment is frequently a life-long dream that is difficult to fulfil.

The treatment of housing is hardly universal. In a market economy, housing is an important part of national economic development strategies, often left to private entrepreneurial initiatives and closely tied to the performance of the national economy. In a socialist economy, housing is considered a nonproductive consumption factor in a nation's economic development and the national government decides what proportion of the GNP should be used for housing construction. Unlike many capitalist countries where housing is not only a market commodity, but also one of the most important investment decisions a homeowner will make, housing in socialist countries is accepted as a social welfare right. It is a socialist government's responsibility to determine the distribution of housing for the general public. In China, for example, urban housing reform has accelerated since 1984. Although housing is still regulated and provided by the state and work units, the recent economic reform policies encourage a commercialization of housing in many of the urban cities such as Beijing, Shanghai, and Guangzhou. Some individuals who have benefited from their economic activities do indeed purchase a two- or three-room apartment as their living quarters, but to most urban residents home ownership is an unattainable dream. Under the current wage and housing distribution system, neither incentives nor the ability to buy a house exists for most urban dwellers.

The main issues facing Korea are housing affordability and home ownership, whereas in China a speedy elimination of crowded housing conditions and the provision of sufficient funds to maintain the existing and rapidly aging housing stock are the critical concerns.

A tremendous surge of in-migration to large, urban cities does exert heavy pressures on a limited housing supply. Regardless of the different political ideologies among countries, split-off family situations such as the marriage of young couples and routine changes in a family's life cycle often compound the persistent housing shortage. Housing shortages commonly precipitate a sudden escalation in home prices as well as a steady decline in housing tenure. Providing decent housing for all residents has become an essential challenge facing most governments, including Korea.

Housing construction and the desire for home ownership

Housing problems in Seoul are indeed serious and the future prospects for a brighter housing outlook appear to be grim. In Korea, home ownership had historically been the most sought-after dream of many residents. Most people buy homes not only to satisfy their investment decisions, but also to derive locational benefits such as desirable school districts, quality neighborhoods, and physical and social amenities. For many years Seoul was perceived as the best city in providing most of these amenities to residents.

As previously discussed, one of the main reasons for the tremendous housing shortage facing Seoul is the stream of people migrating into the capital city. Seoul has always attracted in-migration because it offered more employment opportunities, better school districts, stronger political connections, and other cultural amenities that were simply not available to residents in rural areas and small cities. A change in Korean family structure also contributed to the housing crisis. As the nuclear family as a model for households gained a wider acceptance with the younger generation in Korean society, a deviation from the extended family network of old, this led to the creation of many new small-sized households.

With accelerated economic growth and a steady improvement in living standards for many residents, the demand for better housing stock and amenities received far greater attention. Subsequently, more housing construction with some variations in living space and price was provided, although the supply of housing in Seoul has consistently been inadequate. Even though Korea does not allow the owning of more than one home for the same head of household, housing speculation became a norm. A spiral of inflationary pressure that brought a never-ending escalation in housing prices followed.

It is difficult to determine the exact number of prospective home-buying households who have the sufficient financial means to do so. This is particularly true as the concept of mortgage finance is still not firmly rooted in Korea's current housing system and most residents pay a large sum of cash when purchasing a home. As home prices have substantially increased in recent years, many families have found it next to impossible to generate the large sum of cash for a home purchase, which averages over $250 000 for a three- or four-bedroom apartment in Seoul. It has become customary for prospective home buyers to open savings accounts primarily reserved for future home purchasing. According to a study completed in 1989, it was estimated that more than 860 000 households carried such savings accounts, waiting for the right moment to purchase their dream home. Considering the fact that there were about 1.4 million existing homes and more than 2.4 million households in the entire city, the combination of the aspiration for home ownership and a limited housing supply clearly demonstrates the magnitude of the housing problems in Seoul (Kim Hyung Gook, 1989).

Therefore it is not surprising that house prices have continuously escalated. Accompanied by constant speculation for urban growth, they increased faster than the consumer price index (CPI) until the central government instituted strong policy measures to curb the run-away housing and land prices in the early 1990s. Table 4.1 shows recent trends in the relevant prices of the housing market with respect to the CPI. Based on the 1990 price as a constant index of 100, the increase in the CPI from 1985 to 1993 did not fluctuate widely, whereas the index for housing indicated a significant increase, showing a substantial jump to 16.7% in 1989 and 24% in 1990. Since 1991, however, the housing price index has shown a steady decline, perhaps resulting from the

Table 4.1   Changes in housing price index and CPI

	1985	1986	1987	1988	1989	1990	1991	1992	1993
Housing price index	64.9	62	63.3	69	80.5	100	97.8	92.5	89.6
Increase (%)	–	−4.47	2.1	9	16.67	24.22	−2.2	−5.42	−3.14
Seoul CPI	76.8	78.8	81.4	87	91.9	100	109.7	115.9	121.7
Increase (%)	–	2.6	3.3	6.9	5.6	8.8	9.7	5.7	5

Source: Korea Housing Bank, 1985–1993.

government policies of regulating land speculation and higher property taxation. Although the general inflationary pressure during the mid-1980s partially accounts for some of the sudden rise in the costs, persistent speculative housing purchases and soaring land costs have been considered largely responsible for the upsurge in prices.

Although there was much rhetoric about the need for more housing construction, the Seoul municipal government did not receive enough financial resources from the national government to accomplish its goals in providing adequate housing for rapidly growing, diverse households. For a dominant city such as Seoul, the housing crisis was even more severe as the city grew to control most aspects of the national scene, not only in terms of population size but also in social, cultural, and political influences.

In addition, the tragic civil war between 1950 and 1953 both interrupted a fragile transitional effort in creating Korea's own national development and further devastated the rebuilding effort of the capital city for many years to come. As a result, the provision of housing for all citizens could not be actively pursued, due in a large part to the lack of financial means. Rather, it was often left to private citizens to satisfy their housing needs; some individuals, equipped with strong financial means, were able to find their dream homes in the private market place, while others, financially less fortunate, had to constantly struggle even to rent a marginally suitable place for their family.

The rate of the available housing is often used in assessing the situation of housing shortage. This rate is derived simply by dividing total number of existing housing units by the total number of house-holds: it tells us the proportion of homes that could be occupied by the number of available households at given time. Under the national policy of one house for one household, this rate is generally accepted as one of the best alternatives in measuring the fluctuation in housing shortage.

Table 4.2 compares the rate of available housing in Seoul and the nation as a whole. Although it clearly shows that the available housing

Table 4.2 Changes in rates of available housing for Seoul and Korea

	1960	1970	1980	1988	1990	Increase between 1960 and 1990 (%)
Nation						
Population (000s)	24 989.00	30 852.00	37 406.80	41 975	43 520	74
Households (000s)	4262.80	5576.30	7469.50	9612	11 357	125
Houses (000s)	3588.60	4360.00	5318.90	6670	7374	86
Ratio of supply	84.2	78.2	71.2	69.4	75.1	–
Seoul						
Population (000s)	2445.40	5422.70	8350.60	10 286.50	10 627.80	335
Households (000s)	433.4	1029.50	1754.40	2347.30	2817.30	550
Houses (000s)	267.9	583.6	968.1	1397.60	1463.10	446
Ratio of supply	61.8	56.7	55.2	59.5	50.6	–

Sources: Korea Housing Bank, 1989–1991; and Seoul Metropolis, *Seoul Administration*, 1989.

decreased over time for both, the rate is considerably lower for the city of Seoul, perhaps indicating the hardship that many residents experience in finding suitable housing. One of the telling points for Seoul is that even if the percentage changes between 1960 and 1990 for population, housing, and households all exhibited an explosive growth, the rate of available housing decreased consistently and remained at about 50.6% in 1990. Though not as severe as the situation facing Seoul, the rate of available housing for the nation has not been promising either, although there was a slight increase between 1988 and 1990. Considering that the magnitude of decline experienced from 84.2% in 1960 to 69.4% in 1988 was even more drastic than that of Seoul, the hard reality of the nation's housing crisis will not disappear unless more drastic and broader housing policies are instituted in the near future.

Clearly, housing construction in Korea has not kept up with an ever-increasing number of households, and the situation seems to be worsening. When faced with an escalating housing shortage, many residents are left with not being able to own their dream house. The rapid increase in housing prices in recent years has made the ideal of home ownership even more impossible, particularly for young couples newly entering the housing market.

The rate of available housing does not necessarily translate into home ownership, however. In fact, in 1980, only about 44.5% of Seoul's households owned their homes, while the rest had to rent their living space. By 1985 the percentage of home-owners dropped even further to 40.9% (Seoul Metropolis, 1989a, 1989b). According to most housing specialists in Seoul, it is expected that the situation will worsen in the future. This may explain the most recent phenomenon of the rising cost of rental housing, while the selling price of apartments has been consistently falling in Seoul (*Hankook Daily*, 8 August 1994). This trend is distressing to the Seoul municipal government, as their sponsored housing programs that were supposed to help low and moderate income families to become owner-occupiers do not appear to have been successfully implemented. Instead, most residents who happened to be owners seem to have relied on the private sector housing market in Seoul.

Housing types and standards

Traditional housing in Korea was exemplified by a small-scale, single-story detached dwelling unit for one family with an inside courtyard. All rooms were built around the inner courtyard, with most daily activities taking place around the courtyard. There were no specific functional divisions within the living space. For example, without a separate dining room, eating generally took place in the parents' room. Although this room was considered the main room for all family members, it did not preclude others from sometimes eating in the other rooms. Since the early 1970s, however, this traditional housing type has been quickly replaced by high-rise apartments. Promoted heavily by the government, this change was one of the most powerful examples of the shift in housing form and the functional use of housing for the general public. No longer was there a mix of functional uses within the living space. Instead, the new, Western-style living quarters were completely enclosed without any open yard. Most activities were assigned to well-defined areas in the apartment: living room, dining room, indoor bathroom, kitchen, and bedrooms.

Until 1970, single-story family dwelling units dominated the distribution of all housing types in Seoul, approximately 88.4%, illustrating the horizontal lay of land use development. By 1990, however, it dramatically decreased to only about 46.1% of the total housing stock, and even more construction in the form of high-rise apartment homes is anticipated. This substantial increase in the form of apartments is truly remarkable in that while only 4.1% were represented by this type of housing development in 1970, its share among all housing types was drastically increased to 35.1% by 1990. This vertical development pattern might be an inevitable outcome for Seoul given that available land has become scarce and that escalating housing prices, coupled with a very high population density, limit the opportunities for the development of spacious single-story family units. Although some owners have expressed concerns about the negative effect of high-rise apartment living on children, particularly the psychological impact from the lack of natural open areas, others prefer the distinctively western-style modern amenities, however enclosed their living space might be. Table 4.3 illustrates the changing composition of housing types since 1970.

The spatial distribution of housing types has depended upon the historical development cycles of the areas within Seoul. As shown in Figure 4.1, most older areas north of the Han River, including areas surrounding the original city center, are still dominated by single family dwellings in the traditional Korean architectural style. Massive high-rise apartments in other recently developed or newly developing areas south of the Han River seem to dominate the urban landscape. Because development sites will continue to become more limited with the increasing population, it is anticipated that future housing development, new or redevelopment projects, will increasingly rely on high-rise apartments in all areas of the city.

Compared with Japan, where the size of housing is generally small and tidy, most Koreans prefer large and spacious living areas. Table 4.4

Table 4.3   Trends in housing types between 1970 and 1990. Number of houses in thousands

	1970		1980		1988		1990	
	No.	%	No.	%	No.	%	No.	%
Detached dwelling	515.9	88.4	684.1	70.7	735.9	52.7	659.6	46.1
Apartment	24	4.1	183.8	19	455.8	32.6	502.5	35.1
Row house	34.4	5.9	68.9	7.1	205.9	14.7	181.2	12.7
Others	9.3	1.6	31.3	3.2	–	–	87.8	6.1
Total	583.6	100	968.1	100	1397.60	100	1431	100

Sources: Korea Housing Corporation, 1989; and Seoul Metropolis, *Seoul Administration*, 1989–1991.

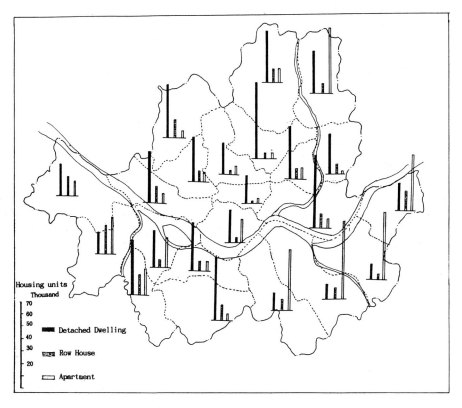

Figure 4.1   Distribution of housing types in Seoul

Table 4.4 Trends in housing size

Area (m²)	1975		1980		1985		1990	
	No.	%	No.	%	No.	%	No.	%
Under 33	112 518	15.1	78 725	8.1	45 834	3.9	46 027	3.2
33–49	152 043	20.4	170 575	17.6	142 237	12.1	195 692	13.7
50–66	171 084	23	205 537	21.2	215 305	18.3	284 973	19.9
67–99	189 811	25.5	277 720	28.7	360 457	30.6	424 952	29.7
100–132	57 939	7.8	106 207	11	184 341	15.7	196 767	13.8
133–165	30 283	4.1	62 578	6.5	93 434	7.9	104 410	7.3
Over 165	30 569	4.1	66 591	6.9	134 554	11.4	178 160	12.4
Total	744 247	100	968 133	100	1 176 162	100	1 430 981	100

Sources: Economic Planning Board, 1975–1990; and City of Seoul (1961–1994).

indicates how the physical size of housing has changed in recent years. Clearly most housing (about 84% of the total) had less than 100 m² of living space in 1975; only about 4.1% of all houses were larger than 165 m². In 1975, approximately 35.5% of households occupied a living space of less than 50 m², a very crowded condition for an average family size of five or six.

This pattern has changed considerably over the years, however. It seems clear that more residents favor larger living spaces, and this trend was borne out both in 1985 and in 1990. Over one-third of the total housing stock was larger than 100 m², a significant change from the previous years. In contrast, housing with less than 50 m² of living space decreased to only about 16.9% in 1990. There has been some criticism about the size of houses becoming larger; most arguments rest on the limited land for housing development, the continuing housing shortage, and the lack of improvement in home ownership among lower income families. Although the arguments indicate the present inefficiency and inequity in Korea's housing system, this pattern of change may not be all negative in that the quality of life as measured in the amount of living space has been progressively enlarged and could be regarded as the single most important factor in contributing to the decline in crowded housing conditions. It is essential, however, that more programs directed towards the housing needs of lower income families are provided.

It is often cited that housing conditions are directly related to the social and psychological well-being of residents in a modern society (Park, Moon Bae, 1989). As society becomes more complex and specialized in the mode of production, the availability of less crowded living spaces is a critical element in the enhancement of the quality of life of

Table 4.5   Trends in housing standards

	1970	1975	1980	1985	1990	1992
Persons/household	5.04	4.89	4.54	4.14	3.8	3.2
Pyong/household	–	11.42	13.16	14.93	14.67	19.23
No. of rooms/dwelling unit	1.79	1.87	2.03	2.12	2.48	2.68
Average persons/room	2.8	2.6	2.2	1.9	1.5	1.2
Average living floor space (m^2)	–	2.33	2.9	3.61	3.92	5.89

Sources: Economic Planning Board, *Population Housing Census*, 1970–1991; City of Seoul, 1961–1994; and Korea Urban Administration Institute, 1994.

residents who seek respite from daily workplace stress and a dense urban environment. Of course, the circumstances of crowding may vary depending on culture, economic strength, and various national priorities. In China, for example, crowded housing conditions are a very serious problem in that sometimes two or three generations of a family share a one-room living space, while in the USA each person in a family generally enjoys his or her own private room in a very spacious setting.

In developing countries, the definition of crowded housing conditions is often used as a measurement for improved housing standards for the general population. In China, one of the main goals of government policies is to advance housing standards by providing more living space for individual family members, thereby reducing already extremely crowded housing conditions. Although the crowded housing situation in Korea is also serious, though not as severe as that in China, it has not been used or adopted as a policy tool in assessing existing housing standards. Table 4.5 summarizes the trends in the crowded housing conditions measured by various aspects of living space beginning in the year 1970.

As previously mentioned, the continuing trend in Korean households is towards a nuclear family structure, thus reducing the requirement that a number of immediate family members live together. When crowding is measured by persons per household or by living space in pyong (one pyong is about 3.3 m^2) per household, the results in Table 4.5 clearly showed a decline in the total number of persons per household and a consistent increase in living space per household. Together, these statistics indicate a shrinking household size. When the number of available rooms per household or the total number of occupants per room is assessed, a positive gain over time is indicated: more rooms and less crowded occupancy per family. However, a large number of families remain who are accustomed to and practice the concept of the extended family. This may explain why, on average, nearly two people still occupied one room in 1992. Although policy-makers in Korea knew that most developed Western countries have enjoyed a one person per room density since the early 1960s, a goal the Korean Government wanted to achieve through various housing programs, it may require more financial resources and strategic initiatives to realize such a goal in the near future.

A measurement of living space in pyong per person has also gained significant ground since 1975, advancing from 2.33 pyong in 1975 to 5.89 pyong in 1992. As long as a lower fertility rate and the trend towards smaller family sizes among the younger generation remains, it is expected that this consistent enhancement of the living space will continue. Moreover, the modernization of housing has also followed and enriched not only the existing housing standards, but also the quality of life in general. For example, more than 70% of homes, most of them either newly constructed apartments or renovated traditional Korean houses, now have modern kitchen facilities with sinks. In addition, almost 80% of the homes have acquired Western-style bathrooms with a shower and combined hot and cold water facilities (Korea Research Institute for Human Settlements, 1986; Economic Planning Board, 1962–1994; Korea Urban Administration Institute, 1994).

What is not clear from this analysis is how much of the improvement in housing standards actually benefited lower and moderate income families, particularly those urban dwellers who were not fortunate enough to own their own homes. The current trends in the escalation of rental housing costs along with the aspiration for homes with larger living spaces appear to indicate that most enhancements in housing are not broadly appreciated by all segments of Seoul's population. The future facing most tenants who fall within the category of lower income families indeed seems to be grim.

Urban squatter settlements

During periods of rapid urbanization, housing is one of the most critical factors affecting the lives of new migrants. As the housing shortage intensifies, and the population growth becomes too difficult to control, urban squatter settlements become one inevitable outcome. Most often, housing in squatter settlements is sub-standard and, consequently, the entire area deteriorates into an urban slum. Nevertheless, residents in many of the settlements rely on the district for daily social networking and find employment opportunities through acquaintances there. This particular type of networking is often efficient, as most of the residents are not highly trained professional workers and have similar socio-economic characteristics. Usually stressful concerns about occupying sub-standard housing give away to their immediate need for daily survival as well as to the rise in the vitality of social interaction with other squatter settlers. This is one of the many reasons why urban slum clearance projects have been very difficult to carry out, largely ignoring the meaning of the targeted area's social mosaic.

A quick glance at the patterns of squatter settlement in Seoul reveals a unique development process, though most sites physically resemble other settlements seen in many underdeveloped countries. To understand how the settlement process began, we must go back to the beginning of Japanese domination in Korea's modern history. Under the colonial policy of exploitation, most farmers became financially bankrupt and were forced to relocate to either other major cities such as Seoul, or to various regions of Manchuria in China. Thus began the exodus, often forced, of many farmers in Korea, which ultimately led to their own unique settlement patterns. During this particular period, most farmers who migrated to Seoul built underground earth shelters for much-needed housing. This unusual, yet sub-standard, housing type was widely practised until after liberation in 1945 (Kang Hong Bin, 1986; Kim Hyung Gook, 1989).

After the liberation Korea faced the very difficult task of rebuilding the country – then the tragic civil war tore the country apart, resulting in even more squatter settlements in the capital city. Farmers, expatriates, and refugees from North Korea assembled their makeshift homes along canals, river banks, parks, and on hilltops or small mountains. During this period, living quarters were constructed using wooden structures or tents, deviating from the primitive housing style of the underground earth shelter. In the 1960s and 1970s, a large majority of settlers were farmers leaving rural areas to look for better employment opportunities. The squatter settlements had mostly grown in already existing areas, but by this period long-term residents started improving or renovating their existing homes using cement or concrete topped with traditional Korean clay roofs (Kim Won, 1983). Once completed, many of these houses looked much like the other homes built outside the settlement areas. The only difference was that most homes in the settlements were located on government land and constructed without proper housing permits, whereas those in the regular districts were built with permits and were allowed to be freely exchanged on the open market.

Since the late 1970s, however, government-sponsored urban slum clearance projects took hold in many settlement areas and displaced all the residents to other geographical locations that were farther away from the city center. As expected, many of the newly found displacement sites were near the edges of the city boundary and lacked many essential city services such as transportation, water, and sanitation. The lack of housing in particular was another important reason squatter settlements persisted, as many of the displaced settlers were forced to reconstruct what they had to survive. As before, their housing, after relocation, continued to be mostly sub-standard and built without proper housing permits.

In the mean time, the settlers inside the city limit who were not yet affected by the clearance projects, and who were lucky enough to have the financial means, began renovating or expanding existing structures to meet their growing family needs. In these areas, the exchange of houses actively took place as if they had been on the open market: most buyers fully understood that they were purchasing houses without proper permits and which, without warning, city officials could come in and seize without compensation. However, the alternatives available to most residents were not particularly attractive either. With limited financial resources, it was almost impossible to purchase houses with proper permits in other districts. Indeed, the risk appeared to be worth taking as the housing shortage in Seoul was becoming more acute. The risk was further emphasized when the Seoul municipal government introduced urban redevelopment programs, however reluctantly, that converted the ownership of homes on government land to long-term residents in the settlements, thereby legally allowing claims on properties occupied by squatters.

There are now numerous settlement areas that can be categorized as mixed settlement districts. In many of these districts, housing turns over regularly. Although there are some "old-timers" with sufficient financial means who are able to improve their existing homes, there are many newly arriving families who lack the financial ability even to consider renting marginally enhanced housing and must instead occupy sub-standard structures. The socio-economic characteristics of the residents also vary. The families who have struggled over the years and eventually overcome the initial hardships by achieving some sense of financial stability have reached middle-class status for all practical purposes. Others who still rely on temporary employment sectors such as carpentry, construction, and clothes-making constantly move from one job to another for survival. As a result, many of these mixed areas are recognized as "Daldongne, the village of moon" or "Sandongne, the village of small mountain." Although both references carry some sort of stigma in terms of social status, most of these settlement areas are indeed vibrant, proud communities, providing the necessary social and cultural networks to all residents.

The spread of settlement areas is induced to some extent by government policies directed towards lower income families. Recognizing that a housing crisis existed for most lower income families, the Seoul municipal government made numerous attempts to alleviate the crisis. During the early 1950s, an initial attempt was made to construct lower income public housing projects, primarily for refugees from the Korean War, expatriates, and some rural farmers. When most of the earlier housing projects rapidly deteriorated, additional housing programs were introduced in the late 1950s to promote self-help housing, intended for those who had been displaced by urban slum clearance projects. For displaced residents, the Seoul municipal government provided seven to ten pyong of land to each family so that they could build their own housing.

Beginning in 1969, an additional housing program was introduced to further relieve the housing shortage for lower income families. Owing to a lack of available land for less dense single family units, high-rise and high-density apartment buildings were constructed. Unlike other high-rise apartment buildings that were geared towards middle- and upper-middle income families, the quality of the high-rise projects suffered: sites were selected on higher ground without adequate soil analysis, construction costs were intentionally cut due to widely practised political and bureaucratic corruption, and construction workmanship was extremely poor. Indeed, most were flimsy constructions from inception. Consequently, at least one of the apartment complexes collapsed in 1970. (The collapse of the "Wawoo" apartment building resulted in 32 deaths and 38 wounded. This was one of a series of accidents involving low-income public housing projects in Seoul.)

After the terrible accident, the Seoul municipal government shied away from similar public housing projects and made repeated attempts to provide housing contracts to private developers based on a quota system. For a certain number of housing projects, a proportion of the units was reserved for lower income housing, while the remaining units could be sold. Unfortunately, a world-wide recession in the construction industry quickly thwarted this effort. Moreover, most of the previously practised programs were insensitive to the financial needs of most lower income families and the officials administrating such programs also lacked an understanding of their limited financial capacity for self-help housing projects. Most settlers became disenchanted with the existing programs and the city officials had to abandon many of the programs of the 1970s. This was especially true after the 1971 Gwangju incident in the province of Kyonggi-do, where riots erupted because of a lack of government support for their housing projects.

During the 1980s the concept of housing redevelopment took a radical turn: not only was the Seoul municipal government building more high-rise apartments on previously urban slum areas, but they began grading new construction sites such as wetland areas and vast open spaces surrounding newer settlement areas at the city periphery for immense housing projects that resembled new towns. Developed and operated under government guidelines, the main intent of these projects was to reserve and lease new housing to low and moderate income families, an incentive for them to gradually own a house without a large deposit. This leasing program, combined with the general improvement in apartment construction quality since the 1970s, became an integral ingredient for the overall acceptance of high-rise apartment living by the general public.

Although many of the newly developed renewal projects contributed to an increase in home ownership for moderate income families who had enough financial resources to occupy the units, there were no guidelines or program considerations for tenants in the settlement areas. As a result, many settlement areas plunged into turmoil and brought in more urban unrest, organized primarily by tenants. Most tenants demanded more humane treatment of their plight and asked for compensatory relocation. City officials, reasoning that they had no legal obligations to meet these demands, often moved ahead with the projects, discounting the social and economic concerns raised by the tenants. More and more tenants were forcefully displaced from their original place of residence to settlement areas outside the city boundary. The uncompromising stance taken by the government in dealing with renewal projects led to social turmoil and contributed to an urban social movement organized by the affected tenants and other social activists, however crudely organized the protests might have been initially. In the meantime, the original intent of most renewal projects shifted because of housing speculation and attracted more middle and upper middle income families into the projects. The shift negated the original purpose of the program.

Housing programs for low income families had to overcome built-in obstacles. The physical deterioration of existing apartments, such as inadequate plumbing, water lines, and walls, became very serious and threatened the safety of the residents. Although most of these families experienced a steady rise in rent, there was neither an effective rent control mechanism nor a general subsidy program to protect low income households from rapidly escalating inflation. With very limited governmental subsidies to support housing needs, the financial burden overwhelmed most families and their daily struggle for survival continued. There were about 188 000 sub-standard homes in 1970 and this number decreased to approximately 154 000 houses by 1980 (City of Seoul, 1961–1994). With ongoing government programs for urban clearance projects, it is anticipated that the total number of housing units will continue to decrease. However, without a significant revision of the existing housing programs and a substantial increase in the housing supply targeted for low and moderate income families, a meaningful reduction in the total number of sub-standard housing units will not be easily attained.

Development of housing policies and the housing supply

When the function of local government is not independent from that of central government, most local policies are dictated by central government. The budgetary priorities of the local government often do not represent the interests of the local residents. Seoul's housing supply has not received adequate attention from the Korean national government over the years. Housing simply was not considered an important factor in the overall economic development strategies at the national level. The development of the industrial sector, ranging from heavy to light industry, was instead the national priority. The export economy also drove national economic growth. The total housing investment with respect to GNP has been always dismal, consistently falling below 5.3%. It is not clear, however, whether the total housing investment will ever be higher than the present rate of 5.2–5.3% (City of Seoul, 1992). Perhaps this lack of national housing investment explains the current housing crisis facing Seoul.

As shown in Figure 4.2, the total housing supply for the capital city did not show a constant growth over the years. Although it was expected that total housing production would fall reasonably below the absolute growth of households, the housing supply fluctuated widely between 1962 and 1990. This effectively widened the gap between the available housing and the total number of households. In fact, only twice during this period, in 1977 and 1987, did the total housing production surpass the growth of households. The uneven growth pattern for housing production is closely related to the cycle experienced in the private housing industry in Korea. As the country's housing supply was largely dependent on the private housing industry, the unstable housing cycle was partially responsible for not being able to provide a steady supply of housing.

In fact, when we examine the distribution of Seoul's housing supply, more than two-thirds have been provided by the private housing industry. In 1975 the distribution consisted of three major providers of the housing supply: the private housing industry (67%), the Korea Housing Corporation (KHC) – a government-invested organization concentrating on the production of housing (26.4%), and the Seoul

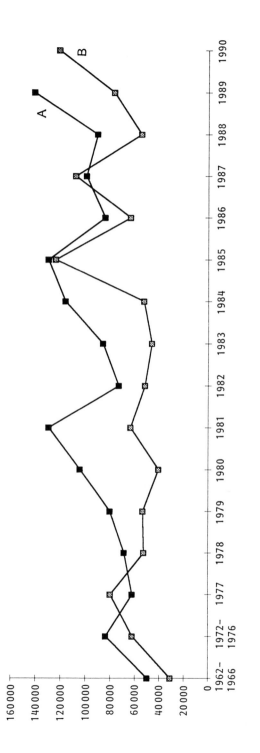

Figure 4.2 Growth in housing supply and total number of households. (A) Households; and (B) housing construction

municipal government (6.6%). In 1980, however, the distribution had changed to 79.9, 10.5, and 9.6%, respectively. By 1988, the share was 63.5, 26.9, and 9.6%. Although the increasing proportion provided by the municipal government over the years may not seem too significant, from 6.6 to 9.6%, this trend could continue as the municipal government renews its active role in providing housing for low and moderate income families (City of Seoul, 1989). This newly activated initiative occurred, not because of an increased awareness of or change in the philosophical outlook on housing, but rather as a political response to the outcry from middle-class families facing a housing crisis. National politicians did not wish to face a possible erosion from this solid political support base for the upcoming general elections.

In the following section we explore more fully the development of housing policies since 1945. A modern housing program was created under the Japanese colonial government in 1941. The colonial government opened a housing construction office and built about 12 000 housing units, mostly for laborers and some middle income families, between 1941 and 1945 (Choo Jong Won, 1986). After liberation, most housing policies were handled by various government agencies, but effective housing programs were not successfully developed, mainly due to the lack of national financial resources. With almost 600 000 houses destroyed during the civil war, essential housing programs relied mainly on foreign aid money to provide necessary housing for those families who most needed shelters (Korean Housing Corporation, 1979).

The year 1957 brought a new meaning to Korea's housing policy. Instead of providing free housing for the needy, government programs shifted radically by asking households to pay for their own housing. In an attempt to reduce the escalating financial burden on low income families for housing, a housing finance system based on long-term leasing was created. Between 1957 and 1961, almost 400 000 homes were constructed and the rate of available housing reached more than 82%. In 1962 this national housing policy became an integral part of the first five-year national economic development plan (1962–1966). In addition, there were new laws dealing with national land development planning and construction. The KHC, a non-profit, quasi-governmental organization, was also established to consolidate all housing-related projects. Although the expectation for the success of these housing policies and programs was initially high, most national investment decisions were allocated to industrial development, thereby reducing the nation's budget for housing. Between 1957 and 1966, the total housing investment was between 1.5 and 1.7% of the GNP, nominal figures at best. Foreign aid for housing also decreased, while the escalation of inflation, including construction costs, persisted during this period. Consequently,

the housing supply worsened and the rate of available housing subsequently dropped to 74.5% nationwide (Choo, 1986).

During the period of the second five-year national economic development plan (1967–1971), the private housing industry continued to drive
national housing policies. Most housing construction was developed by
private industry and the central government provided additional
incentives for more private housing funds by creating Korea Housing
Bank in 1969. The policy of one house for one family was officially
adopted and promoted, while high-rise apartment complexes were
developed on sites created by clearing urban slums. In addition, the
renovation of traditional Korean thatched roofs popular for housing in
rural areas was encouraged. Housing policies during the third five-year
national economic development plan (1972–1976) emphasized increased
funding for public housing investment; the share of public housing
increased to nearly 30% of the total housing construction. In an attempt
to expand the housing supply, the Housing Construction Promotion
Law was implemented in 1972. Meanwhile, efforts to improve the
standard of housing quality were prioritized. Housing improvement and
renovation programs targeted at rural villages were also instituted
during this period.

The fourth five-year national development plan period (1977–1981)
brought the most notable change in housing development. Although a
well-balanced housing construction among all regions of the country
was promoted, most public housing development encouraged the use of
smaller scale housing design. During this period, the total housing
investment increased to 5.3% of the GNP, with more than one million
houses built. This remarkable achievement was further strengthened by
an additional increase in the share of public housing to approximately
44.6% of the total housing investment (Korea Housing Corporation,
1989). In an attempt to provide suitable sites for housing development,
the Korea Land Development Corporation, another quasi-governmental
organization, was created in 1978. Policies for new town development
and the development of satellite cities surrounding the capital city were
also encouraged. Also promoted was the continuation of the accelerated
designation of large apartment districts for future development.

Housing policies during the period of the fifth national economic
development plan (1982–1986) adopted more of the same programs
from the preceding period. The improvement in housing conditions was
emphasized and housing speculation strongly curtailed. As housing
improvement became a continuing slogan, more and more urban
renewal projects were carried out. During this period, the city beautification movement was used to justify large-scale urban slum clearance.
However, one hidden motivation was to prepare for the upcoming 1988

Summer Olympics. As expected, more social turmoil developed following most urban renewal projects, as the government officials did not consider the social and economic hardship on tenants. In the meantime, more funds continued to be invested in the public housing sector, which amounted to approximately 47.6% of total housing investment (Korea Housing Corporation, 1989).

When the sixth Republic was inaugurated in 1988, Korean national politics underwent some changes. Although the new government under the presidency of Mr Rho could be seen as another extension of the continuing military rule since 1961, it was the first free election in almost 30 years. However imperfectly the election might have been processed, it selected the first balloted president in Korea's modern history. As the new government faced rapidly increasing inflation, rising housing and land costs, and spiraling land speculation, it had to respond to the newly heightened housing crisis, which by then threatened even the economic stability of the middle class. The housing programs in the sixth national development plan period (1987–1991) emphasized smaller scale housing development. As a result, the available units for more families were increased. The government also overhauled the existing housing financing programs to assist more lower and middle income households. Land costs for housing construction were kept to a minimum, while the existing programs for leased housing were significantly enhanced.

In recent years, as the uneasiness about the housing crisis grew among the general public, most government policies focused on new town development, the increase in the supply of affordable housing for middle-class families, housing programs for long-term leases, and concerted efforts in developing more housing for laborers. As Korean society has become even more diverse, and existing national resources increasingly pulled into different directions, the central government was hard pressed to heed any real or perceived housing crisis in the capital city. Clearly, policy decisions affecting the capital city have long been under the shadow of central government, particularly during the last 30 years when the national government exercised almost absolute rule.

In recent years, however, the political tide has shifted. New political movement towards a decentralized government structure rapidly emerged and has been implemented since the beginning of the civilian government in 1993. In 1995 there was a direct mayoral election for all cities, including Seoul, marking a turning point in the shift of political power from central government to some of the powerful local governments. However, we must still wait and see how this newly adopted decentralized government structure will change the national agenda relative to local affairs. Until then we can only speculate about the dynamics of, and interrelationship between, responsive local and national politics.

Urban growth

This section provides an in-depth look at how the urban growth took place during the enormous physical expansion of the capital city. The effects are also described of the various stages of government programs on general urban growth and development, and the impact of such growth on the social welfare of certain segments of the population is assessed.

As we discussed previously, the physical development of Seoul and its present spatial arrangement resulted more from accidental growth than rational, forward-looking political plans and decisions. Although there have been continuous government attempts to control and guide the process of growth, the overall growth of the city was largely based on the accumulated growth of many districts, sprawling one at a time. This stemmed, in part, from the lack of effective comprehensive planning and strong political pressures from the development community.

Over the last 30 years the rapid population and physical growth surpassed the carrying capacity of land that it was possible to develop. As a result, the SMR continued to expand, as it does now, while the growth and pressure for an increasingly dense, in-filled development at various city centers accelerated. Perhaps these combined factors explain the drastic increases in the recent phenomena of the urban redevelopment process that began in the early 1980s, and which will remain as a contributing factor towards an even higher urban density.

There are numerous laws relating to different types of development projects, but their applications tend to vary depending on particular land uses, project sizes, zoning, and degrees of significance with respect to the public interest. The existing development laws, however, have affected various development processes and have influenced the overall pattern of city growth.

In general, development projects such as large-scale apartment complexes or urban renewal projects have been left to a number of major private development companies. They were required to comply with relevant development laws such as the City Planning Law, the Housing Construction Promotion Law, the Land Readjustment Law, and the Residential Land Redevelopment Law. Although intended to benefit the public, most of these projects relied heavily on private funds and subsequently generated benefits to individuals who were fortunate enough to occupy the available housing units at such development sites.

However, if potential benefits were expected to accrue to the general public through certain projects, more often than not government, either central or local, has exercised complete control of such projects by applying more stringent and complicated development laws, including eminent domain. In most instances, these projects have been reviewed under a stricter form of control by the government from inception to completion.

However, even with the latter case, private companies were sometimes invited to participate in certain stages of the projects, such as the development of initial planning and design, and the eventual construction phase. It was clearly understood by all parties that the government, if needed, would intervene during the entire development process and make the necessary decisions for the projects. Such heavy-handed government intervention is currently undergoing a significant change, as the political movement for the decentralization of central government has gained strong momentum and has also been approved by the general public. It is expected that more deregulation of housing and the construction industry will follow the mayoral elections in all major cities during 1995, thereby bringing in more participation from the private development community as well as requiring more flexibility or eventual changes in existing development laws. It may be some time before the impact of these changes in housing and development laws can be assessed in the context of public welfare.

Urban land development methods

Like many other developed cities in the world, the City of Seoul has been through various stages of growth, from a very small pedestrian-oriented city to a huge, modern metropolis with expanding physical boundaries. Unlike some major industrial cities in developed Western countries experiencing serious urban decay, Seoul has not undergone major urban deterioration, rather the city was challenged by an accelerated physical expansion and growth, sometimes orchestrated by the Seoul municipal government. Thus it is important that we begin our story with a historical perspective of urban development, including a case study of a newly created, large district in the southwestern portion of Seoul. As the available space for development and growth continues to become extremely limited, intense development pressures for urban redevelopment, mostly in already heavily built city centers, have emerged.

Most urban development projects for large cities, including Seoul, adopted land readjustment (replotment) methods which dominated all aspects of urban development projects until the 1970s. Government policy-makers favored this method mainly for the purpose of maintaining efficiency (Daeham Gookto Gaehoyk Hakhoy, 1984). During the overall process of urban planning and development, it was possible for government agencies to create an economically feasible and efficient project which reduced their dependence on public funding for such projects. Moreover, a general contractor for any given project could easily sell a small parcel of the development site to generate sufficient funds dedicated to the project. Finally, once the city planning and development plans were approved, the protection of private land ownership was effectively maintained throughout the entire development process. The protection of private property significantly reduced the possible friction between government agencies and private individuals, creating an amicable working environment at even some of the potentially sensitive project sites.

The land readjustment method originated in 1902 in Germany. This method, also known as the Adickes Law in Germany, was first adopted in the City of Frankfurt to guide orderly city growth and development. The basic concept of the method was borrowed from an idea of parceling out rural farmland for a more efficient use of land. Immediately after its initial application in Germany, many more European countries followed suit, and Japan was reputed to be the first non-Western nation that imported and applied this method to both urban development and redevelopment projects since 1909 (Kim Euy Won, 1985).

This new method was officially adopted in Korea in 1934 during the Japanese colonial period. The colonial government had previously generated a growth plan for approximately seven small districts in Seoul based on this acquired method in 1928, but failed to implement it successfully. After its adoption as law in 1934, this new method was used in the city of Rajin, a port city in Hamkyongbuk-do Province in the extreme northern part of North Korea, to provide orderly development for city growth, though it was limited to only the creation of new city development sites and some new city streets. The total area covered under the new law was three million square meters (City of Seoul, 1961–1994). The first group of projects for the City of Seoul that was based on this method was actually carried out at a number of small districts north of the Han River in 1937. Even if the movement of population from rural areas to Seoul was strictly controlled, the large population exodus to Seoul remained, congregating at the edge of the city, just outside the four main gates. Perhaps this was the main reason why the Japanese colonial government attempted to use this method in preparing new city growth and development. Several city districts, totaling 52.3 km^2 in physical size, that represented about 38.5% of the entire city development area of

135.7 km^2 were designated. Until Korea was liberated from Japanese domination, a total area of 14.26 km^2 was completed using this newly acquired method. During the 1950s, Korea was recovering from its tragic civil war and thus most projects were limited to the reconstruction of city centers and the rehabilitation of damaged buildings. The projects were small in size (less than 330 000 m^2) and concentrated in the primary-core area of the city, within the four main gates. Consequently, only an area of 1.23 km^2 was completed during this tumultuous period (City of Seoul, 1961–1994).

Beginning in the early 1960s, most urban development projects relied heavily on this new method. As Korea underwent a drastic transformation from an agrarian economy to an export-oriented modern industrial power, the stream of migrants to Seoul added to the swelling of its population and gave rise to new problems related to urban development and growth. In 1962, the first City Planning Law was passed and it was followed by strengthening of the existing development method into the Land Readjustment Law in 1966. The creation of this new law was the government's first attempt to weigh and recognize the importance of this method for city development projects. Urban development projects boomed during this particular period and this newly created law was instrumental in completing approximately 42% of the total city projects encompassing 17 districts and 58.81 km^2. Most of the projects were located within a radius of 5 to 15 km from the primary core area of the city center, thereby expanding the edges of the city farther and farther away from the existing city boundaries.

Two major freeways connecting Seoul with the southern port city of Pusan and the western port city of Inchon were under construction during this period. New available sites were identified paralleling the two freeways, and more urban development projects were built at these sites. In fact, the massive development that was concentrated at the southern edges of the city limits ignited the beginning of a major population shift from north of the Han River to the south, where many more new sites with ample amounts of open space were continuously developed. While this intense urban growth took place, particularly in the areas south of the Han River, the Seoul municipal government failed to provide an effective overall city growth and development plan. Subsequently, uncontrolled urban sprawl continued to threaten any opportunity for orderly growth and became a major factor in contributing to the disjointed district by district growth and development process.

The population concentration in Seoul continued well into the 1970s and the Seoul municipal government was desperate to meet the demand for public infrastructure. New development projects expanded at all locations in the city, though the existing reality of rapid population growth and the lack of physical space forced an increase in urban density. Most low density urban developments, particularly single-story housing units that were prevalent during the 1950s and 1960s, gave way to much higher density development; it marked the beginning of a boom in high-rise apartment construction in most areas south of the Han River. A number of large apartment housing districts were completed and most areas within a radius of 15 km from the primary core area of the city center were almost completely filled during this period.

A turning point in the area of urban development came in the early 1980s. Although the land readjustment method was widely practised for more than 40 years of Seoul's modern development history, the inherent obstacles associated with it were largely responsible for its eventual demise. Because the majority of urban development projects were based on economic efficiency and more flexible methods of construction financing, profits from the projects, usually due to the drastic increase in land prices, were pocketed by a small group of individuals who included some general contractors. This practice was mainly responsible for escalated land speculation and became a focus of social issues which drove a wedge between the haves and have-nots. As new sites were continuously graded and developed for more growth, urban sprawl continued and most completed sites, in the form of high-rise apartment complexes and small convenience shops, became monotonous in style, against the grain of the varied social mosaic.

As the housing crisis became more acute, the national government in 1980 announced a plan for constructing five million housing units to mitigate the crisis. To attain this ambitious goal and simultaneously reduce the accumulated negative impact of the land readjustment method, the Residential Land Development Law was enacted in 1980. Under this law, government-initiated urban land development became a dominant force in urban development and made the land readjustment method obsolete. To ensure the availability of future development sites, the national government identified and designated huge areas of undeveloped land as future housing development sites. Following in the footsteps of the central government, the Seoul municipal government also designated large segments of undeveloped land for future housing sites.

As population growth and the shortage of affordable housing persisted, the municipal government was forced to relinquish some of the already preserved land for housing projects, all in the areas south of the Han River. Thus four housing districts totaling about 14.27 km^2 were soon developed based on the previously used land readjustment method. Although additional monotonous high-rise apartment complexes were

Table 4.6   Land readjustment projects completed for Seoul

	Area (m^2)		
	Residential	Commercial	School
Before 1945 (10 projects)	6 311 378	23 912	99 780
1950s (nine projects)	840 363	2314	24 843
1960s (17 projects)	40 706 827	324 278	1 360 644
1970s (11 projects)	25 840 049	95 169	930 158
1980s (four projects)	6 130 453	4527	824 412
Korea Housing Corporation, Land Owners Union (seven projects)	6 584 740	50 592	124 980
Total (58 projects)	86 413 810	500 792	3 364 817

Source: Seoul Metropolis, 1984a.

created, these latest districts were allowed to exercise a higher use of public space and the development of a pleasing residential environment. The preservation of land for public use in these districts was kept between 50 and 70%, compared with that of 30–40% in the 1970s. As the primary benefit of public space went to all residents in the district, most land-owners resisted this generous offering of more public space, but to no avail. This unusual reverting to the already ceased land adjustment method came about not because government policy-makers lacked the initiative for government-sponsored projects under the new law, but because they did not have the means to purchase the necessary development sites. During the early 1980s, the priorities of the central government emphasized the preparations for hosting the upcoming 1988 Summer Olympics; a drain of financial resources to such a massive event was indeed inevitable.

As Table 4.6 illustrates, the contribution of the land adjustment method to the overall development of Seoul was clearly significant, however imperfectly the method might have been applied over the years. It peaked during the 1960s and 1970s, when more than 67×10^6 m^2 of residential areas and more than 2.6×10^6 m^2 of school and commercial areas were completed. More often than not, however, strong-willed politicians who were largely responsible for carrying out urban development projects often dictated the use of the method until public outcry against the lack of affordable housing as well as social injustice intensified. In the following section, we turn our attention to government-initiated urban land development methods and see how they in turn affected the existing urban mosaic.

Government-initiated urban land development methods

With more urban development projects under government control, a number of large housing projects, often much like new town developments, were undertaken during the 1980s. In general, there were three distinct types of government-initiated urban land development methods. Government agencies or quasi-government agencies would purchase the required land and prepare sites for development. Private individuals were then asked to participate in the leasing and construction of housing under a contractual agreement between government agencies and the individuals involved. This particular method was first used in a new town development for the city of Canberra in Australia. A second method involved government agencies not only purchasing the required land, but completing the entire project for citizens. The government then either leased or sold the completed units to prospective residents. This practice was widely used for new town development in England. Under the third method, government agencies prepared sites for development and subsequently sold available lots to individual buyers for housing construction (Daehan Gookto Gaehoyk Hakhoy, 1984).

Although most urban development projects in Seoul used a combination of all three methods, recent government-initiated projects adopted the second method, particularly in the 1980s (Hwang, 1983). The primary benefits of this particular method were indeed very attractive to government policy-makers. Chief among them was that, as the government was responsible for site selection and development, profits from selling commercial sites to individuals who wish to start businesses were preserved and used for providing affordable housing sites to low income families. In short, affordable housing could be subsidised mainly from the profits. As one of the major drawbacks from the previously used land readjustment method was a huge sum from private gains from similar projects that was never applied to benefit the public, the use of windfall profits for low and moderate-income families was enthusiastically received by the general public. In addition, as the Residential Land Development Promotion Law of 1980 allowed a generous use of public space and the preservation of a pleasing residential environment, it became possible for government agencies to develop an overall plan for creating such surroundings.

On the other hand, most government-initiated projects required a sound fiscal foundation on the part of the relevant government agencies. As many government agencies, particularly those outside the central government, lacked strong financial resources, the ability to purchase the required sites immediately became problematic, which was often detrimental to the proposed projects. Also, the strong friction between agencies and private land-owners continued to be a major issue during the purchasing stage (Lee, 1987). An escalation of land prices surrounding certain project areas remained as critical as ever; there appeared to be no practical mechanism to alleviate this unpleasant reality under the existing market economy. Nevertheless, the Seoul municipal government engaged in such developments, beginning with the Mokdong district project in the early 1980s and expanding to other districts such as Sanggae, Munjong, and Joongaee with the help of both the Korea Housing Corporation and Korea Land Development Corporation. Table 4.7 and Figure 4.3 illustrate some of the major projects initiated by the government during this period.

Among them, the largest project was the Mokdong district project, with an area larger than 4.3×10^6 m^2, an enormous physical size for any type of apartment complex previously developed in Seoul. The darkest area in the far southwestern corner south of the Han River in Figure 4.3 is the Mokdong district. Though slightly smaller, another large development was the Sanggae district project, some distance north of the Han River (Figure 4.3). One of the difficulties that most residents are facing with this particular district since the completion of the project is the lack of major and arterial roads leading to the project site. Many residents, however, rely heavily on the available subway lines for their commuting needs.

When many of these projects were accelerated, the City of Seoul in 1989 created a quasi-government agency, the Urban Development Corporation (UDC), for more efficient processing of the proposed projects. The main purpose of the UDC was to oversee and implement new urban land development as well as urban redevelopment projects. However, in recent years the UDC has mainly participated in the construction of leased housing for low income households throughout the city. Given the lack of other viable options at the present time, it is expected that projects sponsored by the UDC and other government-initiated urban land development will continue for some time to come.

A development project for the Mokdong District

As previously mentioned, a turning point in Korea's development programs and policies came with the implementation of the government-initiated urban land development method in 1980.

The development of the Mokdong district, about 10 km from the primary core area of the central city, was the first project that relied completely on this new method. The Seoul municipal government purchased a giant parcel of open land, approximately 430 ha, located in

Table 4.7 Government-initiated urban land development projects

Project name	Project area	Area (000 m²)	Planned population		Developer	Project period
			No. of households	Population		
Mokdong	Kangso-ku Mokdong, Shinjongdong	4345	20 000	120 000	Seoul Metropolis	December 1983–December 1986
Sanggae	Tobong-ku Sanggae, Changdong, Wolgaedong	3307	30 500	122 000	Korea Housing Corporation	March 1986–June 1988
Chunggae	Tobong-ku Chunggae, Hagaedong	1484	16 250	65 000	Korea Land Development Corporation	1986–December 1988
Munjong	Kangdong-ku Munjong, Karakdong	429	3900	15 600	Korea Housing Corporation	1986–April 1988
Chunggae 2	Tobong-ku Chunggae, Hagaedong	1403	1100	44 000	Korea Housing Corporation	–

Source: Seoul Metropolis, 1987–1993.

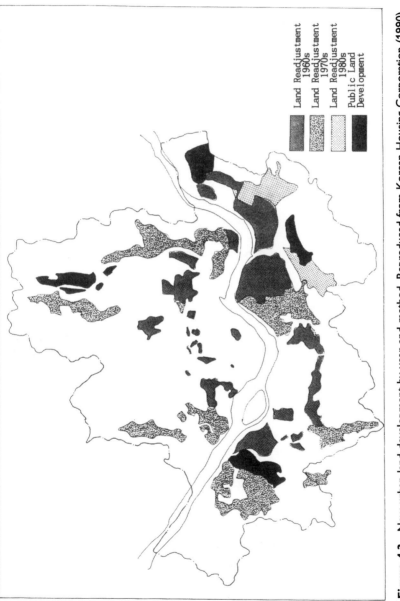

Figure 4.3 New urban land development by year and method. Reproduced from Korean Housing Corporation (1990) by permission of Seoul Metropolitan Government

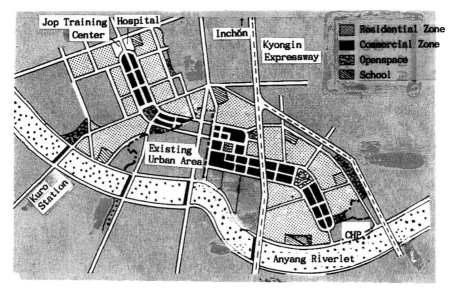

Figure 4.4 Mokdong district development plan. Reproduced from Seoul Metropolis (1983)

the southwestern section of the city and began massive site preparations for the development in 1983. Originally, this area was a string of rice fields characterized as a wetland that was often covered with water during the heavy rainy season. As this project was considered a show-case for the city, unusual steps were taken compared with any other previous urban development project in Korea. An open design competition for the complete project site was held, an unprecedented event for a project of this size in Korea, and the Office of the Mokdong District Development (OMDD) was created to supervise all phases of the project. It was believed that the creation of the office would enhance project efficiency and contribute to the overall improvement of the project. The conceptual design for the Mokdong district development is presented in Figure 4.4.

A project team that combined an award-winning consultant from the competition and planners from the city was created to carry out and oversee the entire project. The main reason for the development of the Mokdong district was to serve the ever-increasing population in the southwestern portion of the capital. Designating this development area would identify it as a main central district of the southwestern section. Accordingly, it was planned for a total population of 120 000 with 25 000 housing units configured as a mixed development with some commercial activities. It was also expected that, with this newly created

Table 4.8   Mokdong development scheme

Area	434.5 ha
Planned population	120 000
Total cost	1110 billion won
Development period	1983–1988
Land use (%)	Residential, 18.3
	Commercial, 10.1
	Open space, 7.4
	Street, 15.6
	School, 4.9
	Others, 13.7
Housing construction	26 629 dweling units (DU)
	Ownership 18 512 DU
	Rental 8117 DU
Major facilities	24 parks, two hospitals, 17 schools, integrated conduit and incinerator-thermal power plant

residential environment, the development could alleviate the existing housing shortage for residents not only at this section, but also in all areas of Seoul. The OMDD purchased the entire project area and then sold commercial lots to those individuals who were interested in business ventures at the site. As the development was mainly preserved for residential use, the allowed business activities were limited to serve the daily functions of residents: small grocery stores, neighborhood pubs and restaurants, photo shops, and other convenience-type outlets for after-school activities for children or routine neighborhood activities (An, 1983).

As shown in Figure 4.4, the overall pattern of the development was shaped to provide linear street patterns approaching the center of the district. Streets and transportation routes were developed based on a circular pathway encircling the district center of the project area, but each sub-district maintained its own streets and pathways primarily geared for bicycle and pedestrian use (An, 1983). The residential density was maintained at medium to high density, but a mix of high and medium density apartment complexes was strongly encouraged. Most of all, the overall concept emphasized that each sub-district should be developed as a semi-self-contained community where most daily routine functions could be fulfilled by the existing commercial and business areas. The entire Mokdong district was therefore seen as a secondary core area of the city. Small buses which served all neighborhood areas in the project district were put into operation and public transportation stops for buses and subways were also conveniently located. Table 4.8 shows the overall concept of the development.

At present, the development of Mokdong district is complete and the entire district is an additional dimension to the ever-expanding urban landscape of the capital city. Although a critical assessment of the project may take some time before an informed judgment can be made about the overall effectiveness of the project, many of the original goals appear to have been achieved. Generous open spaces for public use, designated as neighborhood parks, pedestrian paths, and malls and schools, are provided. Also, most profits from the project have been reinvested into providing affordable housing for low and moderate income families. The overall residential environment is far more pleasing than many other apartment complexes already developed and scattered around the city.

However, there have also been some serious problems associated with the project, some expected and others not expected. During the initial stage of acquiring land, tension between the government agency and land-owners ran very high. To make matters worse, there was no provision for tenants who considered themselves an integral part of the neighborhood. Their economic well-being depended on the jobs and informal social network that existed in the area. As most tenants were forcibly relocated without just compensation, this situation created much social tension during the entire development process.

Furthermore, like previous new urban land projects, the escalation in land prices and speculation surrounding the project site were never effectively controlled. An inequality resulting from the project between those who were fortunate enough to occupy units in the project area and others who were left out of the project boundary, yet resided in old, dilapidated houses adjacent to the project area, remained an important social issue to be resolved. As the original plan did not anticipate a sudden increase in traffic flow in and out of the project area, traffic congestion has worsened ever since the completion of the project. As most families in the area now own at least one or more private automobiles, traffic problems surrounding the site are likely to continue.

Small-scale residential and industrial site development

Although the extensive wave of large-scale urban development projects initiated either by the government or by major private development companies has been in full force over the last 40 years, the Seoul municipal government has sponsored other small-scale, yet rather distinct development activities since the early 1960s. The following is one example. Once a site between 10 000 and 50 000 m² in total size was located for small-scale residential development, it was developed either by individual owners of each lot or by the city with public funds. Most sites, small in their development scale, were located near the city limit and consisted of mainly single-family dwelling units. Until 1989, the total development area encompassed only about 8.66×10^6 m^2, but its contribution to the overall growth of the city should not be under-estimated (City of Seoul, 1989).

Before Seoul reached saturation point in terms of growth and environmental limitations, industrial site development within the city limits was strongly encouraged, particularly during the early 1960s. When Korea was forging ahead with her export-oriented economic development, the central government led efforts for the development of industrial factories concentrated at several locations in Seoul. If the size of a proposed industrial site exceeded 30 000 m^2, it was prepared for industrial factories. In 1964, the central government introduced a special tax incentive for factories locating at these sites as well as providing public land for development. Between 1965 and 1976 there were four large industrial districts, totaling about 2.05×10^6 m^2, completed in the western section of the city (City of Seoul, 1961–1994). By the late 1970s this industrial site policy came to a sudden end, however. The explosive concentration of population, policies of decentralization of the popu-lation and the relocation of industrial factories were heavily promoted during the 1970s, thus making this type of small-scale industrial site development within the city limit too difficult to carry out.

Companies in these industrial districts that have survived or resisted the relocation policy in the mid-1970s are still actively engaged in export-related economic activities. In fact, many small companies in high-tech manufacturing appear to spring up daily, perhaps availing themselves of the many research and development ties that were offered by the existing large firms in the districts.

Urban redevelopment

Urban redevelopment is generally a function of how intensely cities have gone through the cycle of growth and development. The age and economic base of a city contributes to its growth cycle. Factors including population changes and politics also affect urban growth.

Older cities are often challenged by a need to provide a meaningful and functional urban environment when finally faced with limited land for further growth and expansion. Many industrial cities in the Western world have had to deal with growing physical needs by relying on urban redevelopment (i.e. urban renewal) projects since the early and mid-20th century. However, the general experience in many US cities during the 1950s and 1960s with urban renewal projects was not very positive. Many residents in the affected areas were forced to relocate, neighborhoods had to be destroyed to make room for housing developments for middle and upper-middle income families, and existing long-term social networks were completely ruptured (Gans, 1962; Fried, 1963; Laska and Spain, 1980). Most urban renewal projects simply failed to consider and accommodate the existing social fabric of the affected community.

History of Seoul's urban redevelopment

With the explosive growth in both population and physical space, Seoul had to turn its attention to urban redevelopment in the early 1960s. Although the continuing urban sprawl pushed the city periphery further and further away from the city center and a mix of residential and commercial development had sprung up in greater intensity at many of the outlying areas, most of the vital economic and political activities still occurred in districts around the primary core area of the city. Thus it became inevitable that more redevelopment efforts had to be concentrated within the primary core area even though the price of land had substantially increased. In an attempt to provide an orderly redevelopment process, the City Planning Law, which included a provision for urban renewal, was first introduced in 1965 and allowed the City of Seoul to begin redevelopment projects oriented towards urban slum clearance almost immediately (City of Seoul, 1961–1994).

The first redevelopment project for the City of Seoul was a mixed use development of the Sewoonsangga project that cut across a significant number of major city blocks, north and south in direction, in the primary core area of the city. The main purpose of this project was to create a mixed use living environment with four major, medium- to high-rise, buildings that included both residential and commercial uses. The lower floors were reserved for business activities, while the upper floors were exclusively planned for housing. The second floor of each building was connected to pedestrian bridges that ensured a continuous traffic flow of the major east–west streets below (City of Seoul, 1961–1994). Although this project was hailed as one of the most exciting urban renewal projects in Korea's modern history, it quickly became a dinosaur as the living environment in and around the project area steadily deteriorated. Even though this downturn in the living environment might have been the natural progression in the urban life cycle, the straight-line design without any sense of coherent identity connecting all four major buildings did not produce a pleasing environment that facilitated a lively neighborhood interaction among residents. Moreover, the lack of facilities for daily neighborhood living also contributed to the eventual demise of the project. Currently, the entire project area has been converted for either commercial use or small-scale manufacturing factories.

In the meantime, the expansion of sub-standard houses built without proper permits accelerated after the war. As previously mentioned, most of these homes were located on various hilltops or alongside streams and lacked the necessary public infrastructure such as roads, sanitation and drinking water facilities. In 1968 the Seoul municipal government designated the majority of these areas, encompassing approximately 1.4 million pyong, as urban slum clearance districts and tried to curtail the future growth of such illegal housing construction. However, very few slum clearance projects took place during the late 1960s and they were limited to steering residents towards building safer houses by disciplining them with the applicable building codes, and prohibiting residents from constructing homes on government-owned land. This ineffective method of urban redevelopment was severely handicapped in 1971 when the revised City Planning Law was passed and negated the legal recognition of the designated urban slum clearance districts.

In 1976 the Urban Redevelopment Law was instituted, following the 1973 Housing Improvement Promotion Law. Subsequently, urban redevelopment projects were divided into two separate components: redevelopment projects for the core areas of the city center and urban slum clearance projects in sub-standard housing districts. Most projects during the 1970s were small in scale and few in number, due in part to the lack of financial support from the government, limited participation from land owners, and insufficient private funds. However, urban redevelopment projects took a radical turn in the 1980s when Seoul was designated to host both the 1986 Asian Games and the 1988 Summer Olympics.

During this period a number of the powerful major corporations (*Jaebols*) developed a keen interest in locating their corporate headquarters in various districts in the primary core area of the city. With active encouragement from the central government, these major corporations participated not only in the creation of their own headquarters, but also in the development of office buildings by actively clearing designated urban slum districts at different locations. Because of the corporate desire to manifest their own individual identity, particularly at corporate headquarters, a somewhat disjointed and uncoordinated spatial structure emerged at key locations in the primary core areas. As was indicated earlier, these buildings seem to float on an urban plane without any sign of belonging to the rest of the surrounding urban structure. Owing to a heavy concentration of office buildings in limited, designated areas of the primary core, urban problems such as traffic congestion and the physical separation between their place of residence and employment became a daily challenge for most residents in Seoul.

While the intense development for commercial use in the center of Seoul continued, slum clearance projects at many locations of the city were also instituted. Most projects were carried out without any consideration for the unique character of the affected community. The sole purpose appeared to be the beautification of the city for the Olympics. Existing communities were replaced by high-rise apartment complexes for middle and upper-middle income families. Even though most projects emphasized improving the physical environment of the affected community, the residents were neither contacted about nor involved in the improvements. This had the effect of neglecting the existing social intercourse among all the residents, including tenants. Without any just compensation for the affected tenants, clashes between tenants and the city government during the redevelopment process quickly emerged as a critical social issue in the latter part of the 1980s.

Most urban redevelopment projects took place in a very short period of time and brought profound changes in the existing urban spatial structure of the city. Because urban redevelopment will continue to intensify, not only in Seoul but also in most major cities in Korea, it is important to fully understand the redevelopment process and how it has affected the city. The negative implications of the projects may then be redirected towards positive changes for future projects.

Urban core area redevelopment projects

As the capital city, Seoul has a 600 year history, but the most concentrated development efforts actually began in the 1960s. Because of ineffective overall urban growth strategies and the random placement of some developments, scarce public open space, limited street development and non-conforming land uses became commonplace (Yeo, 1982). Faced with a higher rate of urban expansion than other modern cities in the developed world, Seoul's municipal government had to restructure the existing urban configuration of the capital city, thus the birth of urban redevelopment in the urban core areas.

The main purposes of the projects included the following objectives. Firstly, the primary functions of the city were to be restored in the primary core area. Secondly, not only the improvement of urban infrastructure facilities, but also the supply of such facilities were to be enhanced for future urban spatial structure. Thirdly, the city center development plan required uniform standards as part of the overall city-wide planning effort. Finally, the provision of livable urban spaces to create a pleasing environment away from a hectic urban life for citizens was encouraged (City of Seoul, 1961–1994).

It was expected that once urban redevelopment projects were completed, a harmonious urban spatial structure combining the traditional and more modern cityscapes would be established. When new development districts were located adjacent to the old, unique city districts, the preservation of the city districts was strongly promoted. Therefore, new development areas could employ modern land use patterns that did not necessarily upset the existing balance between the two. Although the newly developed sites were supposed to provide a livable urban environment, they also had to generate a geographical area large enough for sufficient economic activities. With this general goal in mind, an article of the Urban Redevelopment Law states the following provision for the potential designation of a site.

If the area (1) is an essentially low density development district, (2) is overcrowded in population and business activities that may require a higher density use, (3) is covered with buildings that are too old or substandard to be used efficiently, (4) is lacking rational land use and public benefits, (5) is contributing to the decline of the overall physical environment due to the deficiencies of public facilities, (6) if two-thirds of the buildings do not have fire prevention measures, (7) is comprised of buildings where half do not meet height requirements, and (8) if two-thirds of the buildings do not reach height requirements and are also susceptible to fire hazards, then the city government may designate the area as a potential redevelopment district. In addition, the delineation of the district is based on street patterns and blocks encircled by roads (Ministry of Construction, 1987).

Figure 4.5 illustrates urban core sites and their designation phases. Though not specified in the figure, 34 districts and 421 areas have been designated as potential urban redevelopment sites since 1973. Of the 7.95 km^2 that comprises the primary core area of the city, about 1.93 km^2 have been designated as project areas and districts. Almost 80% of the potential project districts are located within the four main gates of the city. Important features characterizing these areas include the relative permanence of the residents (over commuters), perhaps indicating neighborhood stability, and the age of the buildings, with most lacking fire prevention measures. Although the areas are mainly occupied by low-rise buildings, the concentration of such buildings is nevertheless very dense, requiring much needed open space for daily leisure activities (City of Seoul, 1989). With the aging of the capital city, most districts

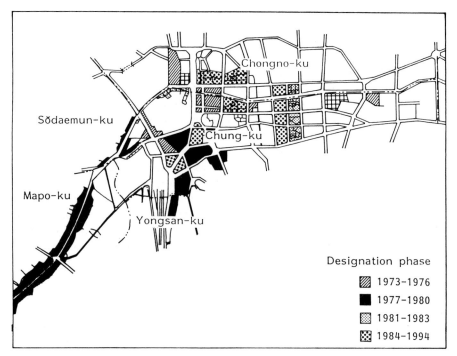

Figure 4.5   Urban core redevelopment sites. Reproduced with permission from Seoul Metropolitan Government (1991)

with commercial activities in the primary core area have characteristics similar to those of potential development sites. Therefore, for public safety reasons, they may have to be designated as potential redevelopment sites in the near future.

The completed redevelopment projects range from Daewoo's headquarters building near the Seoul rail station to corporate buildings around the city hall; this stretch of city blocks in the primary core area has always been considered the heart of Seoul. Although approximately 121 redevelopment areas have been either completed or are still in progress, they represent less than 33% of the total potential sites. One of the main reasons for this slower rate of completion is the method of land acquisition used during the redevelopment process. As government agencies or general contractors involved in the projects purchased the affected land outright from existing property owners and prepared the sites for development, the financial costs were burdensome when the affected areas were either very large or land prices were prohibitively high. In some districts, other options were extremely limited because highly irregular and non-conforming land uses along with rapidly deteriorating buildings made a sensible overall development plan difficult to delineate. During the process of land acquisition, the lack of financial resources automatically limited the number of owners who could participate in the projects, which heightened the tension between those who could afford to participate and others who could not, and so were left out of the project. In addition, some land-owners with very limited financial means demanded more than their fair share of the offer they received, arguing that they did not receive equitable treatment throughout the entire redevelopment process. Some projects were stalled, as increasing friction between agencies and land-owners became so severe that any settlement was difficult to reach.

Many of the central redevelopment projects created a new urban environment, clusters of high-rise office towers alongside commercial and service-related giant buildings in the primary core area of the city. Reliable accounts have revealed that the physical results fell short of meeting most of the original goals, one of which was to form a pleasing urban environment that was an essential component of the entire city (City of Seoul, 1989). When most redevelopment projects were carried out by major corporations, most residents in the affected areas, who tended to be low income households, were forced to relocate to outlying areas of the city where the daily employment opportunities were limited. The displacement threatened their daily survival. Therefore, most financial benefits from the project, however unfairly they might have been perceived, were largely realized by private developers. In addition, as most projects emphasized office and commercial functions, existing residential uses were replaced by multi-functional office and service-oriented structures. In recent years, many districts within the primary core area have been populated by day-time workers who commuted home in the evenings. Most buildings provided few activities for nightlife and became deserted at night.

As previously noted, most redevelopment projects were located within the four main gates. The development of secondary core areas, as a result, was largely overlooked. As more and more business and commercial activities were concentrated in the primary core area, other government policies that encouraged the decentralization of population and economic activities in Seoul quickly evaporated. As most projects failed to acknowledge the negative impacts of traffic congestion and air pollution from substantially increased automobile movement surrounding the area, not only were there significant traffic problems, but the responsibility for the provision of adequate secondary roads linking most of the project areas was left also to the municipal government.

Upon recognizing the inherent problems associated with most redevelopment projects, policy-makers and the general public called for reforms (City of Seoul, 1989). Rather than abandon the redevelopment efforts, they proposed that all urban core redevelopment projects should be incorporated into overall city-wide planning activities, particularly those issues dealing with consistent land uses, the formation of secondary core areas and the development of sensible core redevelopment plans. Although some designated areas would yield tremendous benefits to the public, or have a large number of landowners with insufficient financial means, public agencies such as the Korea Housing Corporation, the Korea Land Corporation or the municipal government should actively participate in the areas to ensure a smooth transition to the new environment and to recover development windfalls from the private developers. The transfer of land use from commercial to residential should be carefully monitored so that future redevelopment areas could maintain a mix of residential and business activities. To alleviate the increasing tension between residents and the city, active public participation, especially by residents who would be directly affected, should be encouraged.

Urban slum clearance projects

As previously discussed, the development of urban slums intensified from 1945. Most settlers came from rural areas for better employment opportunities, particularly during the 1960s when Korea pushed export-oriented policies for national economic development. A large proportion of homes were devastated during the civil war and many residents, who lacked the financial means to rebuild, had to rely on unsafe and inexpensive temporary living quarters at various city locations. Newcomers tended to locate themselves close to their place of employment, which was typically near the city center in the 1960s (Kim, Joochul, 1989; City of Seoul, 1961–1994).

Although the rapid rate of urban settlement prevailed between 1945 and the late 1960s, government policies dealing with such development were few and sporadic. During most of the 1950s, the municipal government ignored the formation of urban slums and often participated in the forced relocation of some residents. In 1959, however, a relocation policy was introduced to settle some residents away from the city center and along major streets. The City of Seoul provided a small parcel of land, usually 23.1–39.6 m² (7–12 pyong) for each household, mostly located in outlying areas of the city, and left the designated area residents there to begin their new life. As this new policy only concentrated on providing physical space for new housing and completely neglected the social fabric of the affected and future communities, most relocated residents suffered a drastically lowered quality of life: loss of employment opportunities, a disruption of schooling for their children, discontinuation of their social network, and, most of all, the end of familiar surroundings for all family members. Amid all the turmoil associated with the forced relocation, the municipal government continued this rigid policy until the mid-1960s. Exemplifying the policy aftermath is the city of Sungnam, located adjacent to the southeastern edge of Seoul. A major recipient of this policy, the city grew to be a major satellite city with over 500 000 people, yet reflected an unpleasant city environment filled with social problems and inadequate public facilities.

In the early 1970s, based on the 1973 Housing Improvement Promotion Law, the municipal government began limited housing rehabilitation projects at a number of selected slum areas. The residents in some districts were allowed to apply for legal ownership of the government land that they occupied, even though they did not have proper housing permits, and were subsequently encouraged to improve their current housing by meeting the existing building codes. Though helpful to a few selected residents in terms of enabling legal home ownership, the law could not alleviate the overall physical deterioration of an entire district. Many of the slum districts lacked adequate public infrastructure, including primary and secondary roads, water supply, and proper sanitation facilities, and consequently posed serious public health hazards. Though in addition to ongoing renewal efforts such as forced relocation and the development of small-scale low income public housing, this law did not contribute positively to the overall growth of Seoul (Kim Yong Ho, 1985).

A large majority of urban renewal projects actually took place during the 1980s, after the Urban Redevelopment Law was passed in 1976. There were two factors responsible for this renewed interest and increased activities: the preparation for the 1986 Asian Games and the 1988 Summer Olympics and the entrance by some powerful corporations into the urban renewal picture. Once the city of Seoul was awarded the Olympics, it was extremely important for the central government to showcase the city. As an important part of the efficient preparation for the Olympics, the city had to be beautified; to the government, it was unacceptable that any physical signs of unattractiveness were shown to foreign visitors. The capital city and the best face of the country had to be on display. Although a few more urban slum clearance projects other than those that had already been in progress came from the designated districts within the primary core area of the city, many more project areas were identified and cleared for site preparation near places where the Olympic venues were scheduled.

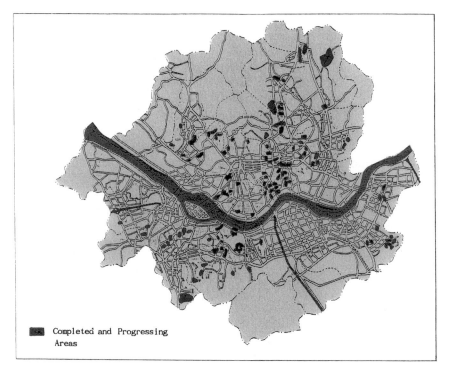

Completed and Progressing
Areas

Figure 4.6 Urban slum clearance and improvement areas. Reproduced from Seoul Metropolis (1991)

Figure 4.6 shows the physical locations of the slum districts that have been either completed or are still in the process of being finished. As discussed earlier, most project areas are heavily concentrated in the older city districts north of the Han River, though some scattered areas south of the Han River are also represented.

Originally, all the projects were initiated by the municipal government and participating residents were required to build their own houses once the city put in the necessary public infrastructure. Using this method, the city was responsible for the provision of public facilities, while private home-owners bore the burden of completing construction within a specified time period (Kim Yong Ho, 1985). Although the former method was used until the early 1980s, a new method which emphasized a private–public partnership for urban slum clearance projects was introduced. Involving active participation by most *Jaebols*, the new method was hailed as an innovative tool for urban redevelopment during the 1980s. Even though this method, in theory, seemed to be very attractive to all parties involved, it became a nightmare when applied to

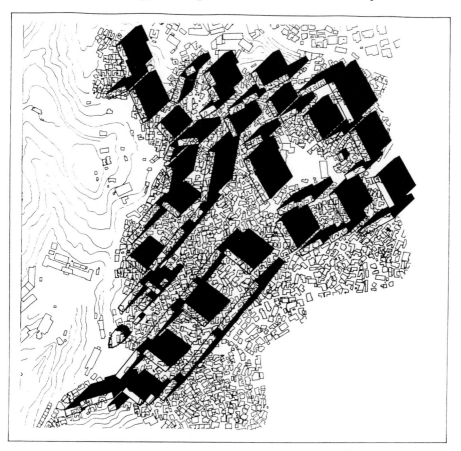

Figure 4.7 Private–public partnership renewal project at Kumho district. Reproduced from Seoul Metropolis (1991)

real situations involving most project areas. The profit motive of the powerful major corporations (*Jaebols*), coupled with the lack of political foresight and wisdom by the municipal government, simply did not mix well with the low socio-economic status of the affected residents. The private–public partnership was based on the concept that once a renewal site was located and a major construction company agreed to participate in the project, then a non-profit corporation largely representing residents from the selected site would be created to work with both residents and the construction company. A typical site under the partnership is shown in Figure 4.7.

As seen, a large proportion of the residential areas, though mostly older and dilapidated housing stocks, at Kumho district is affected by this newly initiated project scheme. At any project site such as this, the primary responsibility of the non-profit corporation was to obtain the required two-thirds vote for project approval from its members who were, in turn, supposed to be resident in the area. Based on this initial approval, each member was then provided with the right to own an apartment unit once constructed: a payment of one to two million won was required from each resident who wished to acquire the finished apartment. As it was initially agreed that the construction company was allowed to build more units than was required to house all available members of the area, any excess units beyond the total required were allocated to any buyers in the market. This arrangement was mainly justified based on the understanding that on covering the total costs, reasonable profits for the *Jaebols* involved in the projects should be realized. Consequently, the municipal government did not have to drain its already tight financial resources for such renewal projects (Kim, 1990; 1991).

However, the private–public partnership in reality was significantly less effective than originally anticipated. There were many reasons for this, but one of the main reasons was that the agreement between the corporation and the area residents was an illusion for most households. Most corporations were set up either by the municipal government or by a selected group of outsiders who vested major financial interests in the projects, without soliciting the participation of the area residents. After the construction was complete, the right to own an apartment unit became an unattainable dream for most residents as the corporations raised the initial moving cost of one to two million won to 10 to 12 million won for each household. Most corporations insisted that unforeseen inflationary pressures during the construction phase caused this unfortunate adjustment in moving costs, and that they could not provide any financial help if residents could not make this payment. As most residents in the affected areas tended to be low income families, the increased moving cost was beyond their reach. Although most residents became bitter about the agreement that the corporations touted throughout the approval process, they quickly realized that their political power base was very weak in bringing any court challenge addressing this predicament.

From the inception this program did not take into consideration the relocation of tenants who had resided there as long as most homeowners and who were very similar to owners in all aspects of their socio-economic characteristics. Once the demolition of buildings began, many tenants demanded just compensation for their plight. They argued that after many years of community and family ties, a sensible program should be created to reduce their financial difficulties during the relocation process. Although the arduous financial circumstances of the tenants were well known in the project areas, most corporations refused to respond to their requests by citing that, given the free market system and the pre-arrangement for the projects, it was not their social responsibility to provide any financial compensation. As tension increased between the corporations and tenants and demonstrations by the tenants became more violent, the entire private–public partnership program came under public scrutiny. Although the public were sympathetic to the plight of the tenants and the deceptive initial moving cost used by the corporations became widely publicized, most projects, with the blessing of the municipal government, moved according to plan. Only some projects were delayed. In the meantime, many residents had to give up their lifelong dream of owning an apartment unit by selling their rights to buyers from outside the project areas.

Perhaps the original intention of the partnership – creating a physically improved environment for all residents – was indeed noble, but it was estimated that less than 10% of the original residents were able to purchase an apartment unit that they could identify as their dream home. Consequently, it appeared that many of these renewal projects did not benefit the original residents who did not have adequate financial resources. What did result was a vicious cycle of forced relocation for the majority of residents in the project areas, whose existing community unity and social network were systematically destroyed (Kim, 1990; 1991). Even amid the continuing social tension surrounding all the clearance projects, the municipal government hastened its quest to complete more projects. By 1992, the total geographical area representing slum clearance projects was about 10×10^6 m^2 covering 208 districts in the entire city. Of the total, approximately 128 districts totaling about 5.4×10^6 m^2 have been completed or are still under construction. About 61 districts, comprising a total of 2.2×10^6 m^2, have been redeveloped based on the private–public partnership method, while in the remaining districts, which encompassed approximately 3.2×10^6 m^2, the old method was primarily used, requiring home-owners to build their own houses after the city put in the necessary public infrastructure within the project sites (City of Seoul, 1992).

Once the urban slum clearance projects were in full swing, the consequences emerged, some foreseen and others not. They contributed to the already long list of critical social problems. Most of the main objectives of the clearance projects – improvement of the physical environment, efficient use of land, and increase in the standard of living for low income families in the project areas – have hardly been met in the project areas. In fact, most residents, their home ownership notwithstanding, experienced another painful forced relocation, which added to their life-long struggle to find a permanent home to provide a strong social network and familiar physical surroundings. Many of the residents, after having been subjected to many unexpected forced relocations during their lifetime, wondered when and how they would be relocated again from their current temporary residence. Moreover, as most apartments built in the project areas were spacious, with approximately 100 m² of living space, most residents could not afford to become participating members of this newly created residential environment. Even for the fortunate few who could actually move into a new environment, any drastic increases in house payments, including monthly maintenance costs or the inability to assimilate into the newly created middle-class lifestyle, forced them to sell their homes, which ended their residential dream. It appeared that an increase in the housing stock contributed by the project areas became a significant factor in decreasing the housing shortage for middle and upper-middle income families. In reality, the projects actually reduced the number of available housing units for low income households (Kim Hyung Gook, 1989).

Both urban core redevelopment and slum clearance projects in Seoul seem to indicate that most projects were not based on a clear understanding of the potential needs of all affected residents and likely future changes, particularly in community dynamics. Perhaps the social inequalities and inequitable treatment that resulted from most of the projects were by-products that could have been avoided had the process shaping most urban redevelopment projects been well thought out and planned. However, the officials responsible for the projects appeared to lack both political sensitivity and a sense of fairness when carrying out their mission. The widening gap between the interests of the affected residents and those of the private developers rendered the municipal government unable to perform its critical role of safeguarding the long-term interests and welfare of the general public (Kim, 1991). It is only hoped that the lessons learned from these projects are used for the creation of more humane, productive policies and programs, not only for future urban redevelopment efforts, but also for the overall housing strategies in Korea.

Current housing supply system and future housing policies

The overall housing situation in Seoul is indeed very serious. Although city officials, with the help of the central government, have introduced various programs to provide more affordable housing to all segments of the population, it seems that they have not succeeded in meeting their goals. Housing shortages still persist, while urban redevelopment attempts appear to have polarized the worsening rift between the haves and have-nots.

As previously discussed, the three major providers of housing in Seoul have been the City of Seoul, the Korea Housing Corporation and private housing companies. In 1989 the City of Seoul created the Urban Development Corporation to supply adequate public housing for low income families. It has participated in limited urban redevelopment projects that supplied small-sized, single-family dwelling units. In the meantime, the Korea Housing Corporation replaced their goal of providing housing for middle and upper-middle income families after the mid-1970s and have since concentrated on supplying a sufficient number of housing units for middle-income families, usually with less than 86 m^2 (26 pyong) of living space. Although these two government-supported organizations have consolidated their resources in meeting the housing demand of low and middle income families, most private housing companies, often a subsidiary of the *Jaebols*, have continued to provide large apartment units to middle and upper-middle income families.

As a system of mortgage finance has not been introduced in Korea, housing financing programs are limited to two mechanisms. Originally, the Korea Housing Bank provided most of the necessary housing financing to home buyers, but in 1987 the central government passed a law that permitted other commercial banks to participate in the provision of housing finance. To improve the transition to a wider participation from various banking institutions, the central government adopted a government-guaranteed insurance system that protected the amount of housing loans (Park, Moon Bae, 1989). The second mechanism of housing financing has been the use of public funds. This has been widely used since the establishment of the National Housing Fund in 1981. The overall housing supply and available housing programs for Seoul are described in Figure 4.8.

Since 1987, there have been more open debates on the general housing crisis in Seoul. Some policy-makers argued that a correlation existed between the lack of housing and social instability and urged that some solutions to the increasing isolation felt by low and moderate income families should be found. Paralleling the central government's campaign for developing two million houses nationwide, the municipal government launched a plan to create 400 000 more houses between 1988 and 1992. It was believed that this additional housing could increase the rate of housing supply to 64.2% in 1992, up about 6% from that of 1988 (Seoul Metropolis, 1992). In addition, the central government in 1989 pushed for a new town development located in a large open field in

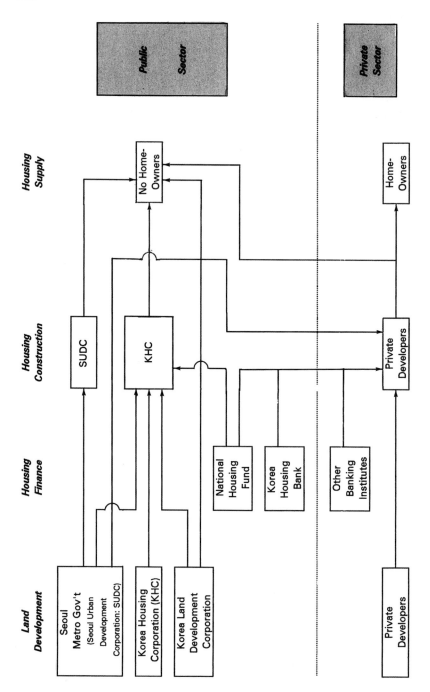

Figure 4.8 Overall housing supply system in Seoul

Kyonggi-do Province, some distance from the southwestern edge of the central city. The Pundang and Ilsan new town developments were supposed to create an additional 180 000 dwelling units to alleviate the ever-worsening housing shortage situation in Seoul – 105 000 units in Pundang and 75 000 units in Ilsan. Escalating housing costs and limited sites for new housing development in the capital city could be eased with additional housing at the new towns, argued the policy-makers. At present, the Pundang and Ilsan new towns have nearly been completed, including a subway line to the central city. The rate of housing supply for Seoul currently fluctuates around 60% as the expected goal of providing 400 000 additional units has never been met (Seoul Metropolis, 1992).

The main objectives of the Pundang and Ilsan new town developments were to develop additional housing units for middle and upper-middle income families living south of the Han River, to provide incentives for businesses to relocate in new areas and to promote the decentralization of population and commercial activities from Seoul. However, the development of two new towns does not appear to have achieved many of these original goals. In fact, the pressure for urban sprawl continues to intensify, adding more satellite cities and towns between the edges of the city and the new town sites. Since the completion of the project, home to work traffic has worsened and business and commercial activities have not made as smooth a transition as anticipated, resulting in the lack of necessary services to area residents. Furthermore, as the new town development was based on the anticipated housing demand from middle and upper-middle income families, it neglected the need from other income groups, particularly those with a low to moderate income. This practice, coupled with the disruption of daily lives and the existing social network of the original settlers, has again increased the feeling of isolation among these segments of the population. In general, this has been one consistent result of urban redevelopment projects in Seoul (Ha, 1989; Kim Hyung Gook, 1989).

Recent studies have shown that the provision of public housing in developing countries has not only reduced the possibility of urban riots, but also increased social stability for the nation (Castells et al., 1990). As Korea is continuing her economic growth as well as the development of democratic institutions, more demand will be placed on economic equity and social justice. Housing policies in the future must address the plight of low income families. Stable environments, decent housing and adequate physical amenities should be provided so that residents can become active, vital participants in social reconstruction and the equitable distribution of benefits should be ensured. It is expected that the housing shortage is not going to be substantially reduced in the near future. The supply of more affordable housing is a critical aspect of any housing policy, but it is equally important to recognize that a system of housing financing such as a mortgage program needs to be introduced to generate the needed financial help for future home buyers. A significant improvement in providing housing for all segments of the population would assure Korea's progress in becoming a more equitable and harmonious society in the future.

5

City planning, administration and finance

Throughout the previous chapters, it has been described how Seoul has evolved into a huge, metropolitan city that continues to undergo dramatic changes. With its enormous, and increasing, population the city has clearly become the most powerful center for economic and political activities. Its rich cultural heritage sets a future direction for the nation. On the other hand, due to a never-ending expansion, it battles with serious transportation and housing problems, exhibits a disharmonious urban landscape, and suffers from the emergence of residential segregation as well as the unequal distribution of economic wealth. This chapter concentrates on how the processes of local planning and city politics have contributed to the overall situation facing the city.

Imagine an extremely small, castled city, untouched by the outside world for over 500 years, which was forced to open reluctantly by an invading foreign country. Long based on a harmonious relationship with nature and deep-rooted Korean tradition, the city was suddenly shattered, not only by the introduction of modern ideas and technologies, but also by steadily increasing population growth and industrial development. The restructuring of the city was often directly managed and planned by the invading country. This actually transpired in Seoul between its first era as the capital city of the Yi Dynasty, in 1394, and the end of Japanese colonialism in 1945. Upon liberation, considering Seoul's limited resources at the time, the modern development visible in Seoul today has indeed been remarkable. Among the many incidences of dramatic growth are the expansion of the public infrastructure and constant applications of contemporary city planning methods. However, if the current cityscape is any indication, the planning process has had a minimum impact in providing effective growth guidelines and making significant, profound changes during Seoul's various stages of development.

City planning

The origin of city planning

When the Yi Dynasty decided to locate its capital city in Seoul in 1394, the city then known as Hanyang was a very small town, though it exhibited tremendous potential to become the capital city of the Kingdom. Its geographical composition was especially appealing to the regime. It was located in the middle of the nation, with the Han River flowing along the edge of the town to serve as a convenient, important transportation channel. Not only was it ideal as the nerve center for political and economic functions, but it was also seen as a possible military safe haven with its vast open fields and surrounding rolling hills and mountains.

The idea of city planning during the Yi Dynasty is believed to have originated from the ancient oriental spatial concept that was initially practised during the Warring Kingdom Period between 3 and 5 BC in China and known as *Chuli*. The *Chuli* put emphasis, not on the specific geographical location of the city, but rather on the harmonious spatial use of all elements within the city. It was expected that the physical shape of the city should be a perfect square, with major streets forming a right-angle where they crossed. The width of major streets was such that nine-horse carriages could run smoothly. The location of the palace was the most important consideration and this was placed in the center of the city (Choe, 1989). The first known cities based on this concept were the cities of Loyang and Changan (now Xian) in China. The city of Changan adopted a slightly modified version of the original *Chuli* concept, however. The palace was still located in the middle of the city, but at the farthest northern edge of the perfect square. Market areas were placed in front of the centrally located palace on either side and were identified as an eastern market and a western market. Japanese cities such as Nagoya and Kyoto were also believed to be heavily influenced by this modified Changan method. Closely following the Changan method, Seoul during the Yi Dynasty continued to emphasize the oriental spatial concept that was based on a close, harmonious relationship with nature (Choe, 1989). Many of the primary streets that were constructed during the Yi Dynasty are still in use in Seoul today as secondary roads.

Although some city planning efforts were underway during Japanese domination, most activities evolved around the physical infrastructure: new road construction, the improvement of old, narrow roads, and the redesign of city districts with street names and numbers. The first known modern planning effort for Seoul was probably introduced in 1930. As the Japanese colonial government attempted to dismantle the nature of the castle city, this modern plan called for expanded development beyond the walls and encompassed a total area of about 109×10^6 m^2, including the surrounding areas outside the four main gates. The plan, covering the period between 1929 and 1959, projected a total population of approximately 700 000 by 1959. (The total population in 1929 was approximately 415 000.) As it was not legally adopted by the colonial government, this plan was never implemented (Seoul Metropolis, 1977).

However, the Japanese colonial government continued its pursuit of developing workable city plans for the occupied land and in 1934 the Governor-General's Decree on Planned Urban Development was announced for general city development plans for the entire country. Following this decree, the colonial city government, which relied on the concept previously created yet subsequently shelved in 1930, created a comprehensive city plan for Seoul in 1935. The 1936 comprehensive city plan under the Japanese rule is considered to be the beginning of modern city planning efforts in Korea (Choe, 1989). Most experts in the field of planning in Korea feel that this particular aspect of the planning history was unpleasant and humiliating, as the original plan was a product of the colonial past and not derived from using the talent and ability of self-trained Koreans. The legacy of colonial attitudes and oppression persisted in Korea for many years after the end of occupation. Not only was there a limited opportunity to explore and pursue independent thinking among Koreans, but deviation from the colonial doctrines during the entire period of occupation was not allowed. Some believe that the slow development of democratic principles in Korea has been largely due to these remnants of the colonial past.

In any event, this plan expanded the total planning area to 135.3 km^2. Including the areas immediately surrounding the city boundary, the planning area was proposed to accommodate about 1.1 million people by 1965. The ambitious, detailed plan also called for five total incremental development stages, with each stage requiring a five-year period until the completion of the plan. Basic land uses were divided into four major categories: 68% of the total area for residential use, 4.4% for commercial use, 4.9% for industrial use, and 22.7% for undesignated use. For residential development, the plan recommended that each citizen occupy about 83.4 m^2 of land for living space. The construction of 720 roads and streets was outlined, extending to 310 km in total length, while 19 large, open plaza areas were also proposed. To provide leisure space, approximately 140 residential parks were recommended throughout the entire city (Seoul Metropolis, 1977). Although most of the elements in the plan were never fully implemented, this conceptual plan remained in effect and was used sparingly until the city of Seoul proposed its own modern plan in the mid-1960s.

From 1945, the following two decades were a volatile period during which Seoul faced sharp population surges, reconstruction from the tragic Korean civil war, and unlimited physical expansion. Although a newly revised modern plan for the city was urgently needed, the city officials failed to produce a meaningful plan. Instead, in an attempt to respond to post-war reconstruction efforts, a temporary city plan was introduced in 1951. Even though this plan was the first devised by Korean planning experts, their general lack of experience produced a plan that did not substantially deviate from the comprehensive colonial plan of 1936. It is doubtful, however, given the explosive growth the city was experiencing at the time, that whatever plan the city might have adopted could have provided any forceful guidelines for growth. Consequently, most city planning efforts continued to be based on the 1936 comprehensive plan, incorporating a few incremental modifications to some basic elements whenever necessary (Seoul Metropolis, 1977).

Development stages for modern city plans

As Seoul continued its unfettered growth, the pressure for a modern city plan which could address various critical issues associated with the city's physical expansion intensified. By 1963, for example, the total population of Seoul surpassed the three million mark, and its physical area was extended to approximately 713.2 km^2. With national economic development strategies shifting to an export-oriented industrial economy, the rate of urbanization for many large cities also increased drastically. Seoul, in particular, faced not only an explosive population growth, but the increasing settlement of various manufacturing firms that further encouraged in-migration from rural areas. In an effort to address the critical problems stemming from uncontrolled urban growth and to plan Seoul as a proud capital city that could provide enough livable urban space for about five million people for the next 20 years, the city of Seoul initiated a modern development plan in 1966. It was contracted out to the Korean Planners Association. The plan was to emphasize the handling of the city's present conditions as well as preparing for an internationally renowned modern city.

The 1966 comprehensive plan (also known as the 1966 master plan) was the first conceptual city planning document completed by experts who were native Koreans. Although the field of city planning was in its infancy during the early 1960s, this contractual arrangement was an important milestone in Korean city planning history in that a small number of trained planning experts, however limited they were in their knowledge of modern city planning concepts and methods, were able to put together a master plan that not only expanded the existing physical aspects, but also brought in the broader social and economic aspects of planning. On completion of this modern planning task, the city officials decided in August 1966 to showcase the 1966 master plan by constructing a large exhibition hall in front of the city hall plaza and inviting all Seoul residents to the display (Choe, 1989).

The original purpose of the 1966 master plan was to develop Seoul as a modern capital city with a carrying capacity of five million people by the year 1985 (Seoul Metropolis, 1977). Borrowing heavily from the master plan for London, UK, the 1966 master plan divided the city into four major districts and recommended reasonable future growth policies for each district. For the existing primary core area within the four main gates, the creation of a dense central business district (CBD) area with intense commercial and business activities was encouraged. High-rise residential apartment buildings and some industrial firms were located at the edge of the primary core area. To reduce the escalating movement of population towards the center of the city, it was suggested that secondary core areas should be developed in the other districts. The creation of greenbelt areas along the city boundary was heavily promoted, not only to discourage the unending urban sprawl, but also to encourage the small-scale subsistent production of vegetables, poultry, and other daily necessities for nearby residents. In the satellite cities and towns near Seoul, it was recommended that low-density, single-story residential houses were built. A number of small industrial and manufacturing firms with sufficient housing to prevent a further concentration of the population inside the city would also be strategically located.

The existing CBD in the primary core area was proposed to remain as the nerve center of the city. The intended new spatial arrangement of Seoul was based on six pie-shaped sectors, each containing the secondary core area and developing its own unique, area-specific commercial and industrial activities. The primary core area and all six other secondary core areas were planned to be connected by a major circular ring road. Although no detailed plans were developed, activities related to the executive branch of the government were housed at various districts in the primary core area.

On the island of Youido, the plan specifically recommended a new building for the legislative branch. In addition, more open space for leisure activities and the existing airport for small and light commuter airplanes were to be kept on the island. A district for the judiciary branch was proposed to be created in the southeastern district, south of the Han River, where a major Olympic scale stadium, along with major athletic fields, was also to be developed. In addition, the 1966 master plan included the elimination of existing street cars and endorsed the immediate construction of an extensive network of subways serving most areas of the city, initially totaling 68 km in length. For the anticipated future increase in automobiles, an estimated 630 000 cars by the year 1985, the 1966 master plan additionally called for the development of four major ring roads and 14 radial roads for a more efficient transportation network (Seoul Metropolis, 1977). The original concept of the 1966 master plan is shown in Figure 5.1.

Although the professional planners who worked on the 1966 master plan had good intentions to provide much-needed urban development guidelines, they failed to foresee the growth rates that were truly unprecedented for Seoul. The maximum population of five million people targeted for the year 1985 was quickly exceeded in less than five years from the inception of the plan, and most elements in the 1966 master plan, however conceptual, soon became obsolete by July 1970. During this short period of time, two additional bridges connecting the areas beside the Han River were constructed; the resulting three bridges were instrumental in providing smooth traffic flows between the two areas. Subsequently, the island of Youido, as well as many districts south of the Han River, became active ingredients in the development boom that hit Seoul during the early 1970s. Recognizing this unexpected surge in all aspects of urban expansion, the Seoul municipal government understood the need to update the plan, not only to correct the already dated elements, but also to provide some official guidelines for the course of future growth. Again, the Korean Planners Association was asked to revise the existing plan to incorporate the current and future challenges facing Seoul.

Unlike the 1966 master plan, however, this newly updated plan was used only as internal guidelines within the appropriate city departments. It is not known why city officials decided to keep quiet about this modified 1972 plan, though we could speculate that they probably felt that their professional competence would be questioned if they changed the much heralded 1966 master plan so quickly. However, the new plan itself was similar in scope to that of the 1966 plan. It contained most previously discussed elements, including the broader socio-economic aspects of city planning.

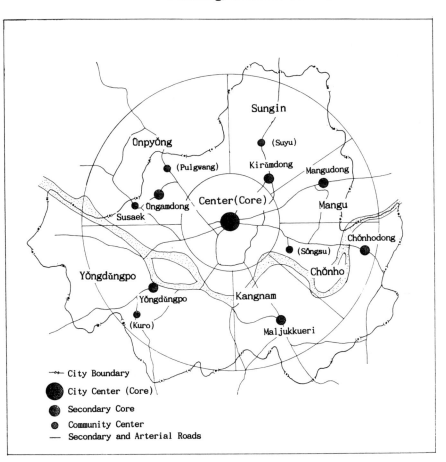

Figure 5.1   Basic concept of the 1966 master plan

The 1972 plan again emphasized a multi-nuclei concept by advocating one primary core area within the four main gates and seven other secondary core areas scattered evenly around the city. Given the fluid nature of city growth, this plan covered a period of ten years, which would facilitate modest medium-range goals and objectives. By 1985 it was anticipated that the total population of Seoul would reach around 7.5 million, and all elements in the plan, particularly the provisions promoting a pleasing urban environment, were modified to support population demands.

One of the main emphases in the 1972 plan, therefore, was to stress an effective and efficient transportation network system that recognized the important symbiotic relationship between people and goods. With the construction of more bridges connecting the areas beside the Han River, it was believed that a well-planned transportation system could accommodate smooth traffic flows for all residents. More infrastructure development projects were recommended to further improve the functions of the existing primary core area, while simultaneously developing seven other secondary core areas with their own unique characteristics. In addition, the 1972 plan continued to promote the increased designation of greenbelt areas to prevent uncontrolled urban sprawl (Seoul Metropolis, 1972).

The magnetic pull of urban growth intensified during the 1970s, however. By 1976, Seoul's total population easily surpassed the 7.5 million projected for the year 1985. By the mid-1970s, city officials faced another unpleasant reality, reassessing the existing plan. Although they were better prepared to deal with the painful experience of the many unexpected, unwelcome impacts of growth, the challenges were still an ordeal. In less than ten years after the inception of the 1966 master plan, events frequently forced city officials to either abandon or rethink their original plan. To their credit, city officials continued sincere efforts to modify and update both plans by extending another invitation to a private consulting firm in Seoul in 1978. More specific directions from city hall concerning the future growth of the city were given to the consultants this time around so that the consulting firm, aided by an advisory panel of experts appointed by city officials, could effectively carry out the new objectives.

One of the main objectives of the 1978 plan was to disperse the population concentration of the city of Seoul by the year 2001. Although the total population already exceeded 7.5 million by 1976, the new plan recommended stabilizing the population at about seven million people by 2001. The decentralization of government functions, wider designation and stricter control of the greenbelt areas, a ban on intensive growth for some areas north of the Han River for military reasons, a shift in commercial functions of the primary core area to other secondary core areas, and the eventual relocation of the capital city to a distant location in the center of the nation, were all aggressively pursued by this newly emerging plan to successfully control the growing population of Seoul (City of Seoul, 1990).

However, the 1978 plan was immediately disregarded by the central government when it introduced a new concept plan for the SMR. This marked the beginning of a vicious cycle that quashed frequent efforts to create Seoul's modern city plans until 1989 when a conceptual master plan was officially adopted. Although city officials announced another comprehensive plan that stressed long-term goals and objectives for the City of Seoul in the early months of 1980, the newly installed Fifth

Republic was none too eager to continue the previously pursued decentralization policy for Seoul. For example, after a revised city planning law was passed in 1981 to require a legal authorization from the government to develop any master plan, the 1980 long-range basic plan was quickly discarded and shelved, allegedly because the entire planning process did not follow the necessary legal steps. Government officials concentrated on preparing for the upcoming 1988 Summer Olympics and subsequently all planning policies shifted to the development of Seoul as an international city. Freeing up greenbelt areas for extensive residential development, accelerating urban renewal projects, developing new residential districts such as the Mokdong district, beautifying the Han River, and loosening population migration into the city all became an integral part of the Olympic fever that the government was actively staging.

Amid the uncertain policies affecting the development and implementation of basic local city plans, in 1981 city officials initiated a bold step in the preparation of another comprehensive plan for Seoul. The development plans at the district level. Because the city underwent changes so rapidly, a manageable master plan at the citywide level seemed impractical. City officials turned to experimenting with the new district level of city planning. Planning at this level was particularly appealing, as many small cities and towns with a population of 3000–50 000 were authorized to develop their own plans under Korea's centralized government system, yet each district in Seoul, exceeding a population of one million was not allowed to create its own plan because the same centralized political system did not recognize the political independence of each district. However, city officials encouraged all 17 city districts to conceptualize and create their own future vision with long-term perspectives as well as to solicit input from district residents. Although no administrative and legal system legitimized district planning activities, all 17 districts participated in the development of basic city plans between 1981 and 1983.

Even though city officials could not implement the district-level plans as official guidelines for the entire city, the exercise proved to be important and provided useful tools for planning in the near future. Firstly, as the decentralization of national government and local government autonomy became a reality in Korean politics, each district should be able to expand its vision based on the experiences gleaned in the early 1980s. Secondly, this grassroots level planning activity could be seen as a reversal from being a passive political observer under the centralized government function to being a dynamic participant in the newly created political arena where political diversity was more accepted. Thirdly, not only did it encourage active involvement from district residents throughout the long and difficult planning process, but it also succeeded in helping residents understand the arcane planning concepts by relating theory to day-to-day issues and problems. Finally, though the city officials were struggling with a feasible comprehensive plan that could be legally adopted, the 17 district-level plans, coupled with the existing 1980 basic plan, could serve as the building blocks for a new master plan when the time came.

Between 1980 and 1984 there were more drastic changes in the internal structure of Seoul. Four subway lines came into full operation, the population shifted, commercial and service activities in areas south of the Han River accelerated, and automobile ownership increased substantially. In 1984 city officials asked city planning experts at the Environmental Planning Institute of Seoul National University to revise the existing 1980 basic plan. City officials were eager to produce a plan that could be legally adopted based on the revised 1981 city planning law. A planning team from the institute concentrated on the development of the 1984 master plan, revising the 1980 basic plan, and also prepared for direct citizen participation through public hearings that were part of the legal requirements from the 1981 law. City officials, however, balked at the public hearings, fearing a unforeseen backlash from citizen groups. Even though the city officials hesitated to hold public hearings for almost two years, they nevertheless authorized two private development companies to go ahead with city projects based on the unofficial 1984 master plan; one company was to develop areas north of the Han River, while the other was designated areas south of the Han River. This clearly indicated how unprepared city officials had always been in the development of long-range, comprehensive local city plans; instead they consistently focused on incremental planning activities that tended to react to crisis, perceived or real.

Since the 1966 master plan was introduced, more than 20 years had passed without a revised plan that city officials could have used as a meaningful development guide. Both the 1986 Asian Games and the 1988 Summer Olympics came and went during this period, and the internal structure of the city was significantly transformed without an officially adopted plan. Additional attempts were made to revise not only the latest 1984 plan, but also to include all previous efforts before the city officials were ready to begin the process for their newest version of local city plans. The 1988 master plan, a product from the same planning team that had been involved since 1984, incorporated most of the critical lessons learned during the last two decades and was presented as the official plan for the city. Five public hearings were held before the 1988 master plan was approved by the Ministry of Construction and adopted by the City of Seoul in November 1989 (City of Seoul,

1990). (The concept of citizen participation was not a familiar term in Korea. By conducting five public hearings, not only were city officials able to solicit a wide range of concerns from the public directly, but they were also successful in introducing the concept of citizen participation throughout the planning process.) The 1988 plan was then the second master plan in Korea's modern planning history, but it was, more importantly, the first comprehensive plan that was legally adopted for Seoul.

Levels and the decision-making process of planning under the centralized government

In the previous section we discussed the origins of city planning, particularly the development process of the modern plans for the city of Seoul. Although city officials tried repeatedly to create rational city plans that could address many of the critical issues stemming from Seoul's rapid growth, they were unsuccessful in the preparation of final plans and often relied on incremental efforts in steering the process of urban expansion. The following section describes how different levels of city planning are interrelated with the decision-making process under the centralized government.

The process of city planning is generally under the overall guidelines of national and regional planning in Korea. Within the auspices of national and regional planning, activities and concerns relating to the nation, provinces, counties, and special districts with regional level implications are often planned and implemented, whereas local city planning, after receiving a strict guideline from the national level plans, deals specifically with citywide problems and has three different levels of local planning hierarchy. Figure 5.2 shows how each level of the hierarchy functions within the overall planning system.

An urban master plan (or comprehensive plan) is the most important concept plan which represents a future vision with a long-term outlook (20 years in general) and is uniquely suited to a particular city. As this planning activity emphasizes a broader framework during the development process of city plans, not only does it describe the spatial and physical aspects of the city, but also the critical interrelationship between these and other dimensions such as the social, economic, political, and cultural elements of planning. At the master plan level, the city mayor has public responsibility for implementing such a plan, including soliciting citizen participation through the legally bounded public hearings.

Once the master plan is completed, the next level of planning activity is the development of an official plan (urban development plan) that

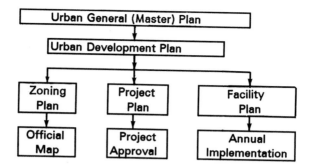

Figure 5.2 Urban planning system and hierarchy. Reproduced by permission from Korea Research Institute for Human Settlements (1984)

includes three specific areas of concern: zoning maps, development project, and facility plans. At this level most specific decisions concerning the overall planning concept would have already been made, and planning elements with medium-range goals and objectives (about 10 years) receive more detailed attention. The physical aspects of the plan are mainly emphasized during this stage of the plan-making, however. The third level in the planning process involves the notification of specific planning sites and a detailed yearly implementation plan. After the general concept and overall elements of the plan have been decided, the execution and implementation of the plan with short-range goals (one to five years) and simply described information on smaller scales are expected. A formal public hearing is not usually required for these two sub-levels of the planning process, however. The three different levels of the planning activities are further summarized in Table 5.1.

Although it is understood that planning issues and concerns at the city level are generally local matters, requiring particular attention from local residents, politicians, and planning experts, it is rare that local government is given complete freedom and flexibility to carve out its own unique planning objectives under a heavily centralized government system such as that in Korea. Most often, as the central government makes an attempt to define and control what kinds of planning issues are important in local areas, opportunities for the city government to engage in more diverse and innovative plan-making hardly exist. As a result, it is common to observe that the planning process requires an unnecessarily long period of time and that most local plans lack a strong local flavor and flexible outcomes. One of the main reasons for the rigidity is that plan-making in Korea is further divided into two separate and distinct components. The formulation of a city plan is under the

Table 5.1 Comparison of planning hierarchy

	Master plan	Development plan	Implementation plan
Planning goals	Policies and vision	Actual development and control	Project implementation
Main features	Comprehensive	Physical	Specific condition
Legal base	City planning law (CPL)	CPL	CPL and other by-laws
Planning period	20 years	10 years	1–5 years
Citizens' involvement	Public hearing	Notification	Notification and appeal
Concreteness	Conceptual	Statutory	Detailed plan and design
Map scale	1 : 25 000	1 : 5000	1 : 6000–1 : 1200

Source: Korea Research Institute for Human Settlements, 1984b.

authority of the city mayor, while the final approval of and ultimate decision of the local city plan is under the jurisdiction of the Ministry of Construction. In other words, although local government officials appear to be allowed to create their version of city plans, the final outcome, after being dictated and revised by the central authority, generally depends on the whims of the central government.

For example, Seoul's mayor may initiate the development of a master plan by working closely with various city departments to identify a wide variety of local issues such as urban redevelopment, the establishment of greenbelt areas, expansion of the public infrastructure, and others. Once a draft of the master plan is completed, public hearings are conducted to solicit direct citizen input. After incorporating citizens' suggestions and comments into the plan, a revised city plan is prepared and subsequently sent to both the Seoul City Planning Committee (SCPC) and the Standing Expert Group under the SCPC for advice and review. (Members of both groups are made up of planning groups appointed by the local mayor, and do not serve simultaneously as a member of the national advisory group. Their function is solely to advise the mayor during the development of a master plan.) On completing this review process, a final draft is prepared as a formal proposal for the master plan of Seoul and is forwarded to the Ministry of Construction for final approval. After receiving the proposal from the City of Seoul, the Ministry of Construction conducts its own review process by seeking comments from the Central City Planning Committee (CCPC), which is made up of city planning experts and is created for the sole purpose of advising the Minister of Construction during the approval process. Based on recommendations from the CCPC, the Minister then seeks further cooperative suggestions from other related central government offices before making a final decision on the plan. The master plan is officially adopted by the city of Seoul when the mayor makes a public announcement after receiving the final approved plan from the Ministry of Construction.

Although most plan-making activities must go through this tightly controlled and structured process, there is an exception. When the facility plan in the context of the general framework of the proposed master plan involves only a small area within a district with convenient daily functional needs, the city mayor is given full decision-making authority. Rarely, however, is the city mayor or the CCPC given enough flexibility to make an independent decision during the planning process.

In recent years, decentralization of some functions of the national government has been cautiously implemented. Local mayoral elections were completed in June 1995. Although it is anticipated that most local planning responsibilities will belong to the local government, it is not

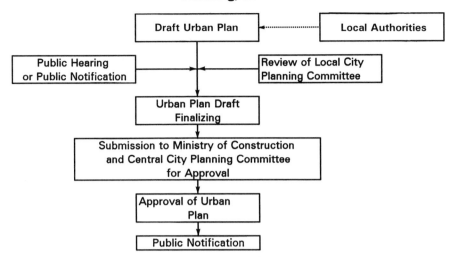

Figure 5.3 Urban planning process. Reproduced with permission from Korea Research Institute for Human Settlements (1984)

certain at the present time how much local autonomy will be realized even after the election. A flow chart describing the currently practised decision-making process is shown in Figure 5.3.

Historically, the main authority of the city planning process for the central government did not originate from the Ministry of Construction. In fact, it has evolved from involving various departments within central government. Beginning in 1946, a year after the liberation from Japanese domination, all city planning-related activities were under the control of the Division of City Planning in the Bureau of Civil Engineering of the Ministry of Commerce. When the national government for South Korea was officially established in 1948, most local planning matters were reorganized into the Division of City Planning under the supervision of the Bureau of Construction in the Ministry of Home Affairs. As Korea was rapidly rebuilding and modernizing after the civil war, the central government officials felt that it was necessary to combine all aspects of planning, such as national and regional planning, city planning, and local construction into one government department. In 1962, on the introduction of the new city planning law, all affairs concerning national and local planning were finally restructured and housed in the Ministry of Construction, where they remain today (Choe, 1989).

In the City of Seoul, the Japanese colonial government created the Division of City Planning in the early 1930s and the function of city planning stayed at that level until 1962 when the Bureau of City Planning was newly established. The Bureau of City Planning coordinates all aspects of city planning at 17 district offices and is responsible for the development and implementation of a citywide master plan. Within the Bureau, most professional tasks involving local city planning are systematically defined and organized by department lines. For example, the Division of City Planning is responsible for developing a master plan that includes the basic concept for general land use and zoning. The Division of Facility Planning oversees the overall facility plans during the implementation stage of planning. The general notification of planning sites is under the Division of Notification, while the Division of Redevelopment deals only with site planning and development. Most redevelopment projects are under the Bureau of Housing, while the Division of Redevelopment is responsible for urban redevelopment efforts in the central city. On the other hand, the Division of Housing Rehabilitation initiates and is responsible for urban renewal projects (City of Seoul, 1990). The Bureau of Housing was established from the reorganization of city offices. Divisions such as Construction and Mapping, Housing Management, and Housing Rehabilitation in the Bureau of Construction Management and the Division of Urban Redevelopment in the Bureau of City Planning were combined in 1990 to create a single entity, the Bureau of Housing. Inside the Bureau of City Planning, the Standing Expert Group under the SCPC advises the city mayor on various planning issues during the development process of a master plan and its members are from the professional city planning community.

As most planning activities are strictly controlled by the various planning-related offices at the main city hall, the structure of each district office is relatively inflexible. From time to time an implementation authority is given to a district office over simple facility planning tasks that address concrete concerns of district residents on a day-to-day basis. Although most city planning decisions generate serious impacts on private property, the process of city planning in Seoul has been insulated from the very citizens the plan is supposed to effectively serve. This exclusion of affected residents is not surprising, as the plan-making process, as previously discussed, has been a more or less heavily guarded privilege of the central government. Whenever either national or local political interests interfere with the terrain of planning issues, more often than not the integrity of the planning process has collapsed, thereby increasing the public's apathy towards general planning practices.

In terms of providing an open forum for the citizens, the Japanese colonial government did not allow any citizen participation during the planning process. The practice of excluding the citizen input continued during the 1950s and the 1960s, even after an enactment of the new city planning law in 1962. Although the city government created the City Planning Committee, comprised of the professional planning experts, this exercise was a far cry from genuine citizen participation as all members appointed by the city mayor were far removed from effectively representing the concerns of ordinary citizens.

A turning point in the area of citizen participation occurred in 1981 when the existing city planning law was revised. For the development of a master plan, this revised law required citizen participation through officially held public hearings. Even during the stages of facility planning or overall management planning, it was also required that the plans were displayed to the public. In theory, it was possible for members with opposing viewpoints to come forward and air their differences during public hearings. However, in reality, the level of citizen participation has consistently been low due in a large part to continuing apathy among the general public, the lack of public notices about the hearings, and the reluctance of the responsible city departments to solicit meaningful citizen input (Choe, 1989).

In recent years Korea has shown an increasing tendency towards more participatory democratic practices and the movement towards local government autonomy has gained momentum. District governments now have elected members of the local council who represent the district level. It is expected that after the mayoral elections in June 1995, the City of Seoul, with its own elected mayor, will become even more independent from the national government and most local city planning responsibilities will be transferred to the city council. Although it may be too soon to speculate how this will affect the level of citizen participation, especially for the general planning process, an increasing awareness of the various aspects of local planning issues has emerged. With more local control and self-reliance, the city government could invite more direct citizen participation, which would help to lower the level of political apathy. Furthermore, it seems that this new level of citizen participation could bring a significant improvement in the development of a future master plan, as the centralized planning previously practised and guided by professional planners, however profound their professional integrity, has failed to create a more livable, governable city.

There appear to be many factors that contributed to the unsuccessful attempts at developing workable master plans that could have been instrumental in creating a truly exciting capital city. Chief among them is the lack of a clear understanding of the political process involved in the plan-making process. Although numerous master plans developed during the last 30 years yielded beautiful, colorful pictures and designs, they were generally unsuccessful in presenting how political constraints and policy options, particularly relating to medium-range objectives, should be handled during the planning process. Furthermore, the guiding principles for most elements in the master plan were poorly applied, which failed to support the more efficient concepts of land use planning and zoning. The net effect was a disjointed plan for Seoul's urban development. Indeed, it is unfortunate that less care has consistently been given to an important symbiotic relationship between all planning elements and the potentially evolving spatial arrangement during the process of planning.

Development of city planning laws

Although city officials have struggled for and stumbled along the development of a meaningful master plan that could have given them a clear vision for an outstanding urban environment, the enactment of effective, enabling city planning laws does not appear to have occurred. Rather than making laws that emphasize rational reasoning and future visions, the majority of city planning laws responded to extremely explosive growth situations. Again, the laws were enacted to manage crisis conditions and addressed the symptoms of uncontrolled growth, not the causes.

Similar to different levels of the planning activities already discussed, however, most city planning laws are under the general direction of both the National Comprehensive Land Planning and the National Land Use and Management Laws. Therefore, though the laws preside over local land use planning and zoning, they have proved to be ineffective in addressing local needs. The central government held its complete authority over the development and enactment of most laws, including city planning laws, under the centralized political system. It was not uncommon to see that all cities implemented exactly the same land use regulations without any consideration for different population sizes or their own unique characteristics. Thus the city of Seoul, with more than ten million people covering a huge physical space, received the same consideration as a small, rural town of 50 000 population when it came to the practical application of land use regulations. Thus most cities and towns had to abide by national city planning laws with very little, if any, flexibility available for their own needs.

Table 5.2 illustrates how different development laws dictated various levels of the planning process as well as contributing to the overall system of national spatial development. The National Comprehensive Land Planning Law 1963 had set policy directions for areas ranging from provinces to the nation as a whole, while the National Land Use

Table 5.2 Planning systems in Korea

Scale	Laws	Plans
National and regional	National comprehensive land planning law	Nationl plan Special region plan Provincial plan
	National land use and management law	County plan National land use plan Detailed land use plan
Urban and site	City planning law	Zoning (urban land use plan)
	Land readjustment project law	Project plan Facility plan Land readjustment project plan
	Urban renewal law	Urban renewal project plan
Building and lot	Building law	Building permit Urban design control

Source: Korea Research Institute for Human Settlements, 1984b.

and Management Law 1972 encouraged the efficient management of land uses by dividing the nation's land into various areas of use. Once an urban area had been designated for development, the general city planning process was allowed to take place under the guidelines of the City Planning Law 1962. For specific sites and neighborhood areas, either the Land Readjustment Project Law or the Urban Renewal Law was used to facilitate the overall process. Following the steps summarized in Table 5.2, it is clear that all the planning and development activities adhered to strict guidelines provided by the national government, exemplifying a one-way, top-down channel of communication and authority.

Though enacted in 1934 under the decree of the Japanese colonial government, it was considered to be the first modern city planning law for planned urban development. Earlier crude planning guidelines for Seoul, such as the redrawing of city district lines in 1912 and the application of new building codes in 1913, appeared to have been treated as if they were local city planning laws. Based on these guidelines, for example, street expansion, secondary road construction, and the regulation of building construction actively occurred until the 1934 decree, which combined the development of general city planning and the regulation of building codes. For the general city planning component, the new regulation focused on three distinct planning aspects: site development and land management, street planning, and land use and zoning. Residential, commercial, and industrial use areas were identified, whereas three additional special districts were further classified under the law: scenic, fire prevention, and social action districts. Although the 1934 decree evolved under three major revisions to reflect the changing nature of urbanization between 1934 and 1945, significant regulation concerning fallout shelters was introduced in 1940. Although this regulation reflected the defensive stance of the Japanese government, it was initially developed to provide safe shelters from potential air-raids during the Second World War. Concentrating on the construction of secure shelters, fire prevention facilities, and essential road systems connecting most shelters, the 1940 regulation quickly fueled other aspects of city planning and development between 1940 and 1945. In fact, it wielded more legal power than any other local city planning laws during the same period (Choe, 1989).

Although the city of Seoul relied on the 1934 decree for most of the reconstruction period from 1945, the first modern city planning law for Korea was developed in 1962 to provide a much needed legal framework for urban growth and expansion. More importantly, not only was this law created by the country's own city planning experts, but it broke the colonial stronghold over city planning and development. The 1962 City Planning Law dealt mainly with city planning and development. New building codes were separately enacted to concentrate on building construction. To facilitate more active involvement from the professional city planning community, the Central City Planning Committee was created. At the same time, more detailed information on land use and zoning was allowed to be used. This first modern city planning law was revised twice between 1962 and 1967, and a section covering land readjustment projects was eliminated from the existing law and adopted as an independent law in 1965. The main reason for the separate creation of the land readjustment method was to provide a legal mechanism to effectively manage explosive urban growth, particularly in the City of Seoul during the early 1960s. It was felt that the existing law was ineffective for Seoul in managing not only high volumes of population growth, but also the laying of new city streets and physical infrastructure resulting from uncontrolled physical annexation.

While Seoul continued its explosive growth course, urban problems increased geometrically and were not amenable to immediate solutions. In 1971 another revision of the existing city planning law brought a wide range of changes. More stringent restrictions on general land use practices were enforced, while the greenbelt area was established to prevent uncontrolled future development. The restriction of land uses was enhanced by the enactment of the National Land Use and Management Law of 1972. Thus it became possible that national land uses regardless of city boundaries could be controlled by this particular law. In addition, the development and implementation process for a master plan was clearly rewritten for the general public for better comprehension, and the revised law of 1971 emphasized the protection of private property during the planning process. The urban redevelopment process was legalized and most redevelopment projects were selected from rapidly deteriorating urban districts with maximum protection for property owners provided (Lee, 1982). With intensified urban development during the 1970s, the 1971 city planning law had to be revised again in 1972 and 1975. The 1976 revised law, in particular, responded directly to the accelerated rate of urban redevelopment projects in Seoul, which led to the enactment of a new urban redevelopment law. Any relevant mention of urban redevelopment was removed from existing city planning laws, and all redevelopment projects fell under the jurisdiction of the newly created urban redevelopment law.

As most planning and development laws introduced during the last three decades aided the growth of urban cities, particularly the City of Seoul, the national housing situation steadily declined. In an attempt to increase the availability of housing for middle income families, the Housing Construction Promotion Law was created in 1977. This law provided an opportunity to create large-scale housing development sites in urban cities, and subsequently fueled the sudden growth of large-scale high-rise apartments, often densely situated, in Seoul. As the housing crisis continued to emerge as the most serious problem facing the country, the Residential Land Development Promotion Law was introduced in 1980. Under this law government-initiated urban development projects were allowed and became a dominant force in the City of Seoul. Most large, vacant sites were identified and developed as high-rise residential complexes, providing much needed relief for middle and upper-middle income households. Although these government-initiated projects were considered the most efficient during the development process, they could not easily escape the rising tension between government officials and affected property owners concerning just compensation and possible recoupment from development benefits.

Faced with continuing urban expansion, the existing city planning law had to be revised again in 1981. Owing to constantly improving economic conditions, coupled with the changing social fabric in Korea, the demands of the general public became diverse. Politicians and policy-makers reacted to the shifting public mood. The 1981 revised law was significant in that it provided for citizen participation during the general plan-making process. Not only did the law make it a legal requirement to adopt an official master plan for cities, but it also required a series of public hearings to solicit input from citizens. Furthermore, a yearly development and implementation plan was encouraged so that the public could be more informed about future projects and possible impacts. For example, all cities, including the city of Seoul, had to develop a long-term master plan, preferably with a 20 year horizon, that could guide them with a well thought out, clear vision. A yearly implementation plan had to be prepared and notified to the public well in advance so that the protection of private property from anticipated projects could be enhanced. In an attempt to further reduce the friction between the parties involved in the development of a project, an official mechanism for citizen participation was not only encouraged, but also became an essential element in the legal requirements. For private projects that affected public welfare, it was required that city officials notified the residents of the affected area to obtain their direct input. In addition, to ensure fairness and solicit professional advice during the planning process, the Standing Expert Group representing the professional planning community was established and supervised under the Local City Planning Committee (Lee, 1982).

However well intended, the revised 1981 law was directed towards direct citizen participation, but it fell short in practice. Perhaps it was partly due to the lack of familiarity with the concept of citizen participation in Korea, but the central control of the planning process was also largely responsible for the low level of citizen input. The more city planning laws were developed to respond to impending crises, the less future vision they provided. This led to decreasing common goals and mutual mistrust. As a result, the protection of private property was not widely realized and could not be enforced. Instead a small group of the privileged few who either obtained pertinent information on future projects or who could participate in the speculation game of urban development reaped substantial financial benefits from the projects. As the balance between private and public benefits from the projects became a political issue, which alienated more residents from the planning process, the wipeout of the windfall method was introduced to deal specifically with the issue of redistribution. Although this new method was able to slow down unwanted land speculation, thereby curtailing windfall benefits to some private individuals, it did not reduce the continuing tension among the affected residents concerning just compensation.

As Korea becomes more sophisticated in its social and political spheres, it is inevitable that the absolute control currently practised by the central government will be widely questioned. Since the beginning of the movement towards the decentralization of various political functions, including local city planning activities, many of the existing city planning laws have had to be revised to reflect the changing relationship between central and local government. It may not be too long before the general public begins to question official accountability, demand more equitable compensation from planning projects, particularly urban redevelopment projects, and to take direct control of the planning process.

City administration and finance

While the city of Seoul expanded its physical boundaries outwards, struggled to control urban growth with the development of effective master plans, and continued introducing and revising city planning and development laws within the general framework of the national planning system, Seoul's public administration structure also experienced tremendous increases over the years. Increases in population size and demand for public services made it necessary for city officials to respond by reorganizing the administrative structures. The reorganization included redefining the responsibilities and functions of key city offices, reassessing the financial capabilities for public infrastructure projects, and introducing a more efficient budgetary process to maintain a fiscally strong position. In this section we will examine both evolutionary changes that took place in the city administrative structure, including the physical expansion, and the increasing importance of fiscal responsibility, particularly with the introduction of political decentralization and local control.

Historical growth of city administrative areas

The continuing growth in the city's administrative area has paralleled the historical trend in population growth. As more people migrated into the capital city, it became necessary to expand its spatial configuration to accommodate such an influx of people. Seoul under the Yi Dynasty was extremely small in physical size, about 15.5 km^2 in total area, and did not expand for 500 years under the Kingdom. During this long historical period, the administrative area of Seoul (then called Hanyang or Hansung) reached far beyond the city boundary. Areas surrounded by walls within the four main gates were considered the important city center with five administrative districts, while areas extending to approximately 4 km from the city boundary were under the administrative control of Seoul. The total area under the two-layered administrative areas stretched to approximately 245 km². The areas outside the four main gates were treated as if they were rural towns, divided and assigned into areas, which was the separate distinction given to rural administrative areas. Toward the end of the Yi Dynasty these rural administrative areas were changed to wards, which were administered under the five districts (Seoul Metropolis, 1977; Kim An Jae, 1984).

During Japanese domination, Seoul underwent profound changes. The Japanese colonial government downgraded the status of Seoul from the capital city of Korea to an administrative center for Japan's colonial occupied land. After changing its name to Kyongsung, all administrative functions came under the control of the Kyonggi-do Province. The existing five districts remained, while the areas beyond the city center were rearranged into eight rural wards in 1910. As the Japanese colonial government experimented with more changes in terms of administrative areas and functions, the existing system of districts and myuns was completely eliminated and replaced with a new structure in 1914. A total area of 35.2 km² constituted the new administrative area for Seoul and consisted of one main district in the heart of the city, four satellite districts, and 186 field offices (*dongs*). Most areas that were designated as *dongs* in Seoul were later changed to *Jeong*, following the customary practice in Japan. By the year 1944, the administrative area for Seoul had expanded to 130 km² and the entire city was rearranged into eight districts by eliminating the existing multi-layered system (Kim An Jae, 1984).

Immediately after its liberation in 1945, the City of Seoul changed its name from the colonial Kyongsung and reclaimed its capital city status by establishing an independent administrative authority. The city government also removed previously assigned administrative responsibilities and functions away from Kyonggi-do Province and created three new levels of identification for the city (*dong, ka,* and *ro*); the colonial identification, *Jeong*, was completely dropped. By 1949 the city administrative area was expanded to 268.4 km² with nine districts. With its increasing physical size and population, satellite administrative offices within each district were also created to better serve the general public. As the City of Seoul aggressively pursued an annexation policy during the post civil war periods, the total administrative area grew substantially from 268.4 km² in 1949 to 613 km² in 1963 and 627.1 km² in 1973. This total administrative area represents Seoul's current size. At present, the City of Seoul has 25 districts (*ku*) and 475 field offices (*dongs*) covering the entire administrative area (City of Seoul, 1961–1994; Seoul Development Institute, 1994b). Figure 5.4 shows the expansion of Seoul's administrative area over time.

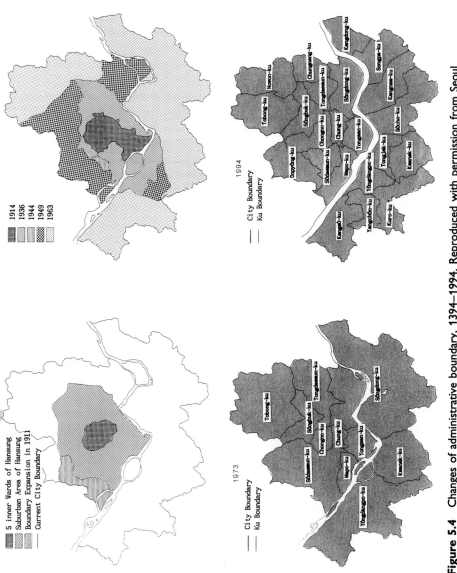

Figure 5.4 Changes of administrative boundary, 1394–1994. Reproduced with permission from Seoul Development Institute (1994)

Administrative structures and functions

On reclaiming its capital city status in 1945, the City of Seoul began maintaining its independent authority in terms of administrative functions, though the central government had the ultimate power under the constitution. The mayor was directly elected by popular ballot in Seoul and the city offices were divided into seven distinct bureaus: internal affairs, finance, industrial development, construction, water, social welfare, and police. After the military coup in 1961, the military government did not want to continue the power accorded to local governments, especially the capital city. It was believed that their grip on political power could best be exercised by consolidating all political practices under the authority of the central government. Consequently, Seoul became another layer in the administrative structure of the central government, directly controlled by the Prime Minister, from 1962.

Under the political and administrative control of the central government, the mayor was appointed by and served at the pleasure of the president. The city's budget was completely dictated by the central government and local concerns were not adequately addressed. Chief among the victories people earned through hard-fought democracy movements since 1961 was the reintroduction of a decentralized political system. In April 1988 the Local Autonomy Law was revised and, one month later, opened the door for the decentralization of various administrative functions from the central government. Thus Seoul again started to enjoy its independent authority and emerged with a three-tiered administrative structure: central office, district offices (*ku*) and field offices (*dong*). Although the City of Seoul already had a similar experience in terms of self-government between 1945 and 1961, its independent authority had been absent too long. Perhaps unknowingly the city became solely dependent on the central authority for direction. Therefore, this change, however pleasing to many concerned politicians and residents, brought a profound change in how the city's administrative structure needed to be organized to meet the daily functions. For example, all district offices became semi-autonomous entities. Not only were district offices given authority to plan for local concerns, but they were also empowered to implement programs, specifically those providing essential services to district residents.

Accordingly, both functional and budgetary concerns had to be redistributed, and new official responsibilities had to be created for the three different levels of offices. The central office would perform a liaison function for issues stemming from the central government and all other governmental offices, address overall concerns that had citywide implications and affected more than two districts, coordinate citywide general planning and development, and adopt uniform policies applicable to all districts. With their newly created self-governing power, district offices were given the following independent authorities: legislation, budget, personnel, tax assessment and collection, and the development and implementation of district-wide specific policies, particularly those affecting the general welfare of residents. It was clearly understood that all matters at the district level were supposed to be implemented by the district offices without direct interference from the central office. As expected, the field offices were the initial and routine contact point for residents. Their responsibilities included effectively implementing policies and recommendations, collecting fees and taxes, providing residents with efficient paper work, collecting pertinent information for future research, and soliciting direct citizen input regarding all aspects of city operations (Kim, Dong Goo, 1988; City of Seoul, 1989).

Because of political bickering, the mayoral elections for large cities including the City of Seoul were not scheduled until June 1995. However, Seoul's city council, including the district-level councils for Seoul, have been in operation since 1990 when district representatives were elected by popular vote. All reviews and approvals of the budget and audits of the city operation were placed under council control, no longer under the jurisdiction of the office of the Prime Minister. Although this decentralization movement has renewed the political process, it has also created a significant problem in government finance, albeit an expected outcome under any decentralized form of government. The uncertain fiscal position of the districts has contributed to a tremendous strain in the central budget as the shortfall of each district has had to be covered by the central office. For example, only about 53.5% of the budget for all districts in 1989 was generated by their own revenue programs, while the rest had to be absorbed by the central office (City of Seoul, 1989). As more revenue sources from central government will be transferred to the local level in the coming years, the financial situation is expected to improve, but the uneven fiscal distribution among different districts will continue to require direct intervention from central office.

Figures 5.5 and 5.6 illustrate the current organizational structures of the central and district offices. As Seoul grew larger and larger, its city administration developed into a huge bureaucracy. At present, the one central office and 25 district offices support 50 000 employees (excluding the police force), or one city employee per 269 citizens. The 50 000 employees can be classified as follows: 29 000 regular employees (57.9%); 11 600 special hires (23.1%); 3800 fire fighters (7.6%); and 2600 engineers (5.1%). Of the total, about 15.2% work in the central office, while 68.5% serve residents at or below district level offices and 15.7% are employed by such special offices as the Subway and Transit

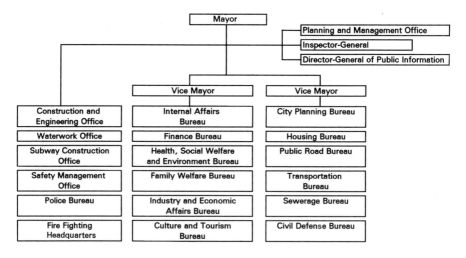

Figure 5.5 Seoul metropolitan government organization

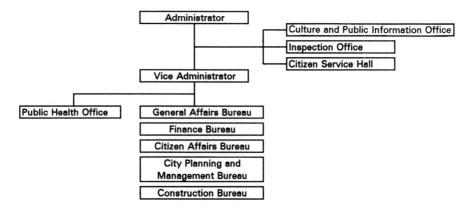

Figure 5.6 *Ku* (district) office organization

Corporation, the City Hospital Corporation and the Urban Development Corporation (City of Seoul, 1993).

This mammoth organization is unwieldy. The chain of communication and flow of information are often very difficult to maintain, not only within the central office alone, but between the central office and district offices. When the structure of the central office grew from seven bureaus into its present size, the main intention was to create several divisions or departments according to the general purpose they have, the types of clients they serve, and the special processes and tasks they involve. For example, the Bureau of Health, Social Welfare and Environment, the Bureau of Public Roads, the Bureau of Sewerage, and the Bureau of Transportation were developed for service purposes, whereas Bureaus such as Finance, City Planning, and Internal Affairs were formed to process certain programs and for decision-making. Currently there are 15 bureaus, four headquarters, and two independent offices of audits and public information located in the offices of the mayor. For each district office there are currently one office, five bureaus, and 23 departments, and it is expected that more changes will ensue following the additional assessment of existing functions.

In addition to this massive organizational structure, there are five government corporations established and operated by the city: the Corporations for Subway and Transit, Farm Product and Fish Wholesale and Management, Urban Development, Facility Management, and City Hospital. The main purpose of forming these corporations was to provide essential services to residents more efficiently and to bring more business-oriented practices and incentives to them. A separate account-ing system for each corporation was created from the general budget process and the operating expenses were expected to be fully supported by user fees. Furthermore, any profits generated by the services pro-vided were required to go back to the overall operation, though in reality none of these offices has generated enough profits to be self-sufficient. The Subway and Transit Corporation, which was created to operate the system with a higher level of efficiency, grew to almost 10 000 employees. As most initial construction and subsequent capital improvement costs were prohibitively high, the heavily subsidised user fees and interest payments for the international loans made to the projects outstripped reasonable revenues, thereby plunging them into an approximately 2000% debt ratio. Other special offices were generally small in scale and their main purposes often included social welfare functions. For example, the City Hospital, with a facility of about 400 beds and a 500 member staff, was founded in 1982 and served low income families. It continues to be one of the few municipal hospitals that caters exclusively for the lower end of the socio-economic spectrum (Yoo, 1985; Lee Sang Hee, 1985; City of Seoul, 1993).

Metropolitan association of governments

As the influence of Seoul spilled over to the SMR and beyond, not only did many municipalities and some provincial governments begin to question the validity of growth-related projects affecting their own residents, but they also demanded a cooperative approach to many of the critical problems resulting from the extension of urban growth. They argued that such area-wide problems as air pollution, water and sewerage, and transportation, with their negative externalities, deserved more active coordination among government entities.

Although there was no legal basis for the formation of the metropolitan council of governments in Korea during the early 1960s, the City of Seoul and the Kyonggi-do Province initiated their own by creating the Advisory Association of Metropolitan Administration in 1967. While this cooperative effort was being established between the two local governments, the central government recommended a coalition of cooperative governments in 1973. The legal procedures and management guidelines for the metropolitan association of governments were finally enacted in 1975. During the 1970s and 1980s, when the explosive growth of Seoul spilled into the surrounding cities and towns, a new form of metropolitan association of governments was created. It encompassed other local governments: the current membership of the organization includes Seoul, the City of Inchon, Kyonggi-do Province, Kangwon-do Province, and Chungchong buk-do Province. As the frequency of regular meetings for the association is not legally required, any one of the chief officers in the association is permitted to convene a meeting with a specific agenda.

In general, the agenda items for meetings relate to: area-wide planning and development, public facility and management, residential and industrial development, the prevention of environmental pollution, cost-sharing, infrastructure development and maintenance, realignment of the transportation system, including bus and subway routes, and regional development and administration. As shown in Table 5.3, meetings were infrequent over the years and most proposals for considerations came from Seoul and Kyonggi-do Province. Of the proposals initiated by each entity since 1968, about 76% were approved for the City of Seoul, while substantially less, 55%, were approved for Kyonggi-do province. Most items requested by Kyonggi-do province that received unfavorable treatment from the association were due to a lack of financial resources and generally included programs such as subway and bus line extension, water and sewage treatment facilities, and the location of mortuary facilities.

Although there are many factors other than budgetary considerations that contributed to the ineffectiveness of the Metropolitan Association of Governments, one single important element has been the impact of the heavily centralized political system on local governments. More often than not, proposals from the association have required authorization from central government and the association was prohibited from actively engaging in the decision-making process of issues under the control of the national government. Therefore, the association became a

Table 5.3 Summary of meetings of the Metropolitan Association of Governments

	Rejections			Agreed proposals*		
		Kyonggi-do			Kyonggi-do	
Date	Total	Province	Seoul	Total	Province	Seoul
October 1968	23	20	3	21 (91)	18 (90)	3 (100)
April 1969	11	9	2	8 (73)	6 (67)	2 (100)
July 1970	20	9	11	18 (90)	7 (78)	11 (100)
March 1971	17	11	6	14 (82)	8 (73)	6 (100)
September 1971	7	6	1	6 (86)	5 (83)	1 (100)
December 1975	10	1	4	8 (80)	4 (67)	4 (100)
May 1976	14	4	4	10 (71)	7 (70)	3 (75)
May 1982	26	4	13	12 (46)	5 (39)	7 (54)
July 1985	21	13	7	8 (38)	5 (36)	3 (43)
December 1985	14	7	5	5 (36)	3 (33)	2 (40)
June 1989	15	5	2	7 (47)	6 (46)	1 (50)
Total	178	120	58	117 (68)	18 (55)	43 (76)

* Values given are number (%).

Source: Korea Regional Administration Institute, 1990.

recommending body to the national government without any legal authority for implementation. To make the situation even worse, the association convened meetings on an *ad hoc* basis and had neither enough staff support nor legal power to follow up or implement their own recommendations. As with any other organization there was a continuing power struggle among the chief officers of the association. The mayor from the City of Seoul, for example, felt that he should be given more power than any other member given the size and political position he holds in the association. As expected, the operation of the association has not really been harmonious. Finally, when a proposal concerning spatial development came to the association, it often conflicted with the spatial development plan at the national or SMR level, thus making it harder for the association to consider any other alternatives (Choe Sang Chuel, 1989).

With local governments becoming more independent under the newly constituted decentralized political system, territorial and compensation battles among the local governments are expected to become fiercer. Under the current fiscal condition of each local government, each will negotiate and fight rigorously using their own fiscal and political strengths to reach a preferred position during association sessions. However, given that the transfer of political and financial arrangements from central government has not fully materialized, it is unclear at this time how cooperative local governments in general will become, as the future expectations or aspirations for each government entity will differ. It is also uncertain whether the Metropolitan Association of Governments can emerge as a strong regional government with clear vision and leadership.

Finance

Local public finance is generally shaped by the vitality of the local economy as well as by the ability of local government to generate enough revenues to provide sufficient services to its local residents. The cycle of population growth is also closely linked to the fiscal condition of the local government. With more people, it is expected that revenue sources would expand, thereby providing enough services even if there was a sudden increase in demand from the general public. A higher level of efficient public services can be achieved when the local government enjoys a strong fiscal position and a wide range of flexibility in generating the required revenues, while simultaneously maintaining its independence from the national government. In a heavily centralized political system such as Korea, however, the national government wields the most powerful, national budgetary authority and thwarts the ability of most local governments to become financially self-sufficient. The intricate relationship between local and national governments in terms of identifying and sharing revenue sources has not been fully developed, and consequently local government, more often than not, looks to the national government for a large majority of the local budget needed to provide adequate services for residents.

Although it enjoys its special capital city status, Seoul has maintained a stronger fiscal self-sufficiency than other local and provincial governments, but has yet to achieve either political or fiscal independence from the central government. When the population surges were slowed and the available resources of funds increasingly limited in the early 1980s, the Seoul municipal government initiated a drastic change in the local budgetary system in 1981. While this new financial system placed heavier emphasis on a financial plan with medium-range goals, its main purpose was to create an efficient local budget system based on well defined and targeted service objectives. As shown in Figure 5.7, all financial plans, management, and evaluations were based on long- and medium-range goals, whereas any immediate, short-term financial concerns and programs were expected to follow the already established long-term framework by employing both a critical review process for public investment decisions and a zero-based budgeting technique.

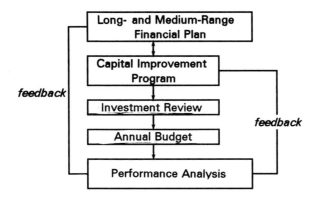

Figure 5.7 Schematic flow of financial management, Seoul Metropolitan Government. Reproduced with permission from Seoul Metropolitan Government

Under the process of zero-based budgeting, a higher rate of efficiency for new programs and services was considered one of the most important criteria in the selection stage. Following the technical budget review process, it was further expected that some programs, after final evaluation and feedback, would go back to the initial stage for further study, thus implementing the budgetary process in an efficient and effective manner (Park Huang Suek, 1983; City of Seoul, 1989).

Historically, the overall budget for the City of Seoul has undergone a continuous increase, paralleling the trend in population growth. For example, the share of the city budget measured by total revenue sources was 5.3, 7.4, and 8.65% of the Gross Regional Development Product for 1970, 1980, and 1987, respectively. Accordingly, the total tax contribution for each taxpayer also increased over the years: 3000 won in 1970 to 359 000 won in 1980, and 990 000 won per capita in 1988 (City of Seoul, 1989).

Table 5.4 shows the overall trend in the budget between 1960 and 1992. The results show a tremendous increase in the amount of total budget from 17.6 billion won in 1960 to 8.7 trillion won in 1992, a geometric growth. They also seem to indicate that there has been a steadily decreasing trend in general purpose accounts, indicating an emerging pattern of dominance for special purpose accounts in Seoul's budgetary system. This trend is consistent for both revenues and expenditures for the same period. The general purpose accounts are closely related to the fluctuation in population and are usually reliant on local taxes. On the revenue side, for example, more than 71% of the total revenue of 17.6 billion won in 1960 reflected general purpose accounts. The share was drastically reduced to a mere 58% of the total revenue in

Table 5.4 Summary of city budget between 1960 and 1992. Values given are in million won (%)

Year	Revenues			Expenditures		
	Total	General accounts	Special accounts	Total	General accounts	Special accounts
1960	17 587 (100)	12 557 (71.4)	5030 (18.6)	15 005 (100)	10 386 (69.2)	4619 (30.8)
1970	44 257 (100)	25 329 (57.2)	18 928 (42.8)	44 038 (100)	24 828 (56.4)	19 210 (43.6)
1980	722 175 (100)	429 794 (57.5)	292 381 (40.5)	672 890 (100)	407 483 (60.6)	265 407 (39.4)
1988	2 806 763 (100)	1 266 054 (45.1)	1 540 709 (54.9)	2 011 597 (100)	12 746 (50.3)	998 851 (49.7)
1992	8 727 270 (100)	5 097 799 (58.4)	3 629 471 (41.6)	7 339 362 (100)	4 258 837 (58)	3 080 525 (42)

Sources: City of Seoul, 1961–1994; Seoul Metropolis, 1960; Ministry of Home Affairs, 1971–1981.

1992. On the expenditure side, the magnitude of decrease is less during the same period. The general purpose accounts were nevertheless reduced from 69% of the total expenditure in 1960 to 58% in 1992.

As mentioned earlier, the fiscal status of Seoul has fared much better than other municipal and provincial governments due to the uninterrupted influx of population and the continuing expansion of economic activities. In terms of self-sufficiency measured by the revenue-generating capacity over the years, Seoul's status has improved constantly. The main sources of general purpose accounts have always been local taxes, a reliance which has shifted dramatically from 67.5% in 1970 to 80.4% in 1988. Moreover, by 1988 the City of Seoul was able to generate almost 98% of its general purpose accounts from local taxes and other revenue sources. The proportion of other revenue sources for Seoul has not been insignificant, but has declined to a point where they are almost negligible with respect to the size of the total revenue. For example, other revenue sources including user charges represented 23% in 1970 and declined to 17% in 1988, while the combination of grants-in-aid and subsidies from the national government decreased from about 10% of the total general purpose accounts in 1970 to a mere 2% in 1988 (City of Seoul, 1990).

With the implementation of a decentralized political system since the late 1980s, the increasing level of national tax revenue sources has been transferred to local government, thus adding yet another layer of local taxation. Programs supported by general purpose accounts are typically in the areas of general administration, social welfare, industrial development, regional development, education and culture, and civil defense. Specific expenditures for these programs have not significantly fluctuated over the years. The distribution of these programs for Seoul in 1984 and 1993 as shown in Figure 5.8 exemplifies the continuing increase in spending for infrastructure development (public utilities and local development) and social welfare, whereas spending for other areas has decreased. General administration and other spending categories appear to have been stable, however (City of Seoul, 1961–1994; 1993).

The increasing dominance of the special purpose accounts in the overall budget became prevalent after the implementation of the revised budgetary system in 1981. Paralleling efficient business operations in the private sector, most special purpose accounts are based on the "pay as you go" approach. User charges are common in the financing mechanism and special fees that are supposed to reflect the actual market prices are charged for services such as water, sewerage, public housing, urban development, site and services, housing rehabilitation, subway operations, parking, toll roads, health insurance, the city hospital, special building permits, and others. As shown in Table 5.4, there has been a

Figure 5.8 Comparison of general account expenditures between 1984 and 1993

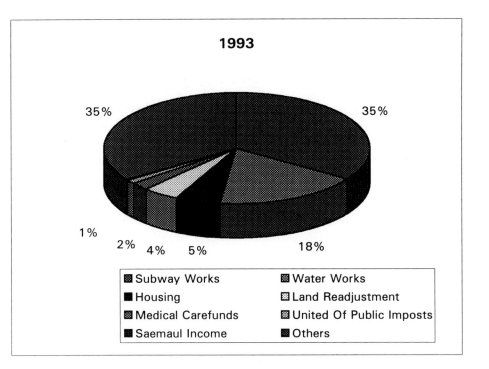

Figure 5.9   Comparison of special purpose accounts in 1984 and 1993

steady increase in the special purpose accounts in the city budget, and this is expected to continue. Of the special purpose accounts shown in Figure 5.9; services related to the physical infrastructure represented more than half the services provided (City of Seoul, 1961–1994; 1993). However, some service categories have not achieved a higher degree of financial self-sufficiency under the special purpose funds as originally anticipated. Subway operations, for example, have never been able to attain financial self-reliance. Not only were the fees charged to residents substantially subsidised, but the capital costs of subway construction for extended services became prohibitively high over the years. Most revenues from user fees have therefore been used for paying off the principal balances and interests on foreign loans and municipal debts incurred during the capital construction phases.

One of the most difficult situations facing the capital city is the heavy dependence on intergovernmental transfers from the national government for local budget shortfalls. Even with a budget capacity increased by local tax revenues, the proportion of local taxes to overall taxes is relatively small. This inhibits the Seoul municipal government from exercising its independent budgetary control through public services. Of all the local taxes, the national government directly controls both income tax and sales tax, whereas the less flexible revenue sources such as benefit taxes are given to local government. This strict constraint exerted by the national government is another reason why Seoul has not yet reached financial independence. Even with its own city council and mayor, this trend is expected to continue under the current political system.

As discussed in previous chapters, Seoul's growth has been fueled without any practical management strategies. Many critical urban issues such as transportation, the environment, housing (including public housing for lower income families), water, and open space will undoubtedly require increasing financial support. Without meaningful financial independence from the national government it would be extremely difficult for the Seoul municipal government to focus attention on many of these problems. Efficient financial operations, coupled with the "pay as you go" approach for many services is going to receive close public scrutiny. Unless the national government relinquishes more of its existing budgetary controls, sufficient provision of public services would be difficult to obtain. With the completion of mayoral election, however, the political landscape in Seoul could change. Instead of a mayoral figurehead without political power, a newly elected mayor supported by a new, wide political base under a local autonomous system could work with the existing city council to govern the city they represent.

We now turn our attention to how urban forms have evolved in Seoul.

6

Urban form

Thus far, we have discussed various factors that influenced the development of Seoul, particularly since the beginning of the Yi Dynasty. We have related Seoul's explosive population growth not only to its constantly expanding physical size, but also to the shortage of affordable housing for many families. The nation's economic growth was instrumental in generating more diverse economic activities associated with a growing industrial base. At the same time, it fueled a strong population movement towards Seoul, due in large part to the rapidly expanding employment opportunities in labor-intensive manufacturing and service industries.

Although capital accumulation for one segment of the population did not transfer into a more equitable income distribution for all, the economic expansion during the last three decades did bring an overall improvement in the standard of living for most households. The result is that residents in Seoul have enjoyed a wide variety of economic resources and cultural offerings. They have also become active participants in changing the urban landscape, developing the urban infrastructure, shaping the urban spatial forms, and setting and shifting local priorities. Therefore, the current physical environment of the capital city is a product of the interrelationship of all the factors discussed previously. Urban form is not shaped overnight by one dominant force of society, but is gradually created by various influencing factors at work. It is a series of statements made in a certain historical period during the process of general growth and development.

At first sight the present urban form in Seoul is indeed impressive. Its many imposing features include the presence of apartment communities in varying sizes on the wide city terrain, the emergence of high-rise apartment blocks depicting modern and post-modern architecture, and a cityscape developed at extremely high density. The rapid rate of change of urban construction is evident everywhere, as many roads are torn open for subway construction, new buildings seem to appear overnight, and a traditional low-density commercial district seemingly disappears only to be replaced by completely new, intensive uses within a few months. However, an overall "legibility" of the city environment appears to be lacking. According to Lynch (1975), a legible city possesses a particular visual quality that includes districts or landmarks that could be easily grouped and identified. The legible city thus represents a poetic and symbolic urban environment that should speak of individuals and the complex nature of society. Its emphasis is on a harmonious co-existence between the historical tradition and the natural setting.

Although Seoul does have numerous landmarks, districts, and focal points, a definite linkage among these elements does not seem to exist. The current urban environment seems unable to provide a meaningful, powerful interpretation of its experience. Perhaps the unknown territory of urban design or architectural guidelines, coupled with the lack of consistent building regulations during the city's earlier periods of modern development, added to the present condition. When many urban development projects occur without proper regard for historical preservation, the city's historical heritage neither effectively connects to its modern spatial structure, nor is easily identified in the current urban landscape. Existing visually pleasing districts are often well hidden, and modern landmarks have been created with a lack of appreciation for the important historical meaning within the overall urban spatial continuum. Only in recent years has the preservation of historical buildings and districts received much-deserved recognition with some innovative building designs that incorporate traditional architecture.

The resulting cityscape appears disjointed in terms of urban form. Although the capital city environment currently appears to be diverse, it seems to lack a coherent visual image or meaning to residents or visitors to Seoul. In this chapter, we will examine how Seoul's urban form has evolved over time. Our discussion begins with high-rise apartment towers, one urban spatial feature that dominates the cityscape.

Apartment towers as emerging city districts

Most urban development before the 1960s consisted of single family dwelling units, either detached or attached. The units were targeted to house Seoul's rapidly swelling population. As mentioned in Chapter 4, apartment living was a foreign concept to most Koreans. The traditional

Plate 6.1 Traditional hanok architecture

Korean house (*hanok*) was single story, with an inner court yard covered by a clay (tiled) roof. An urban neighborhood often consisted of 10 to 20 clustered *hanoks*, depending on the physical layout of city streets at a given location, and was small in physical scale (Plate 6.1).

Most social interaction took place within this well-defined physical neighborhood boundary and in the courtyard of the *hanok*. Following the Confucian tradition in honoring the harmonious family and social order, elders in the neighborhood were generally accepted as leaders, and the neighborhood unit behaved as if it were a large extended family. Special occasions such as weddings and births were happily celebrated in the neighborhood. Neighbors knew each other, greeting one another by name. When there was sadness in a family, it was shared by all in the neighborhood. The neighborhood environment created a social network that provided vital community information and support for the residents' daily lives.

Many of these characteristics typify other urban neighborhood residents, not only in developed countries, but also in developing nations before urbanization. Before any city is totally transformed by urbanization, it is believed that life was simpler and serene while the urban

Plate 6.2 Typical view of large apartment complexes

spatial arrangement was less complex. In Seoul, the concerted efforts of the government in orchestrating the development of large-scale apartment complexes during the last 30 years seem to have contributed to the degeneration of the long-standing neighborhood social mosaic. In addition, sequential influences stemming from an accelerated rate of urbanization also added to this steady decline. Although many of the apartment complexes with large, tall towers touted the concept of a self-contained community and attempted to introduce a human scale in their design, their enormous physical size alone was not conducive to such ideals (Plate 6.2). Consequently, many of the traditional neighborhood characteristics that had been cherished over the years have either disappeared altogether or are only sporadically practised.

Earlier developments: mostly public housing

In 1962 the Korea Housing Corporation (KHC) initiated the first ever large-scale apartment project in Seoul. Completed in 1964, this particular project, known as the Mapo apartment project, was small compared with the giant projects of today, but was nevertheless a significant beginning for Seoul. It represented a clear departure from the single-family housing developments that were then common, and further contributed to residential development at much higher densities. The modern amenities associated with apartment living were introduced to the general public. The Mapo project, an apartment community comprised of 10 separate towers, was carefully designed to house 642 low and low-middle income families; each unit in the tower contained about 26–60 m^2 in living floor space (Sohn, 1983). Each apartment building was designed to be six stories high, a modest height for today's apartments, and the concept of a self-contained community was used to provide a feeling of neighborhood among the residents. The Mapo project was also unique in that it was used as a test case in assessing the effectiveness of the building technology available for medium- to high-rise apartments in Korea.

During the mid- and late 1960s, the KHC, following the successful completion of the Mapo project, was actively involved in developing more public housing projects for low and low-middle income families. The KHC located the projects in the southwestern section of the city where vast open land could be converted into residential areas, approximately 1×10^6 m^2 in total size. Most houses were single story with 40–56 m^2 of living floor space and the residential sites included an elementary school, neighborhood parks, local markets, and public facilities, which all provided a convenient location for the resident families. Given the giant project size, it was not clear how many of the residential sites effectively created viable neighborhoods. Soon after the completion of the project, not only did it become a catalyst in encouraging the orderly expansion of city growth in the section, but also grew to become a secondary core of Seoul.

A critical turning point in high-rise apartment development came in 1968 when the KHC participated in another large apartment development project. Located in a district close to the primary core of the city, this particular project site was originally occupied by squatter settlers and located in a mostly flood-prone area. After being targeted as an urban renewal project, the entire area was cleared for the development of 34 large apartment towers, planned for about 1310 families. The living floor space of each unit varied from 40 to 83 m^2, at the time the most spacious living area thus far. Unlike other projects previously completed by the KHC, all the apartments were for middle income families. To ensure a community where simple daily functions could be met, a variety of open spaces and public facilities was provided. These functions included an elementary school, middle schools, a market, a post office, banks, and neighborhood playgrounds (Sohn, 1983).

Having learned from the experiences of the Mapo project, officials wanted to adopt a different layout that would be simple, yet create a more diverse environment. To ensure maximum public open space between the high-rise towers, a straight line, parallel layout with a southerly orientation was used throughout the entire project, resulting in an environment resembling military barracks. Before the city officials became aware of this faulty design, the parallel layout had quickly spread and was widely adopted for more apartment projects in Seoul. Not only was this considered an efficient use of buildable land, but it also maximized profits for developers. This unfortunate trend was largely responsible for the creation of a series of monotonous complexes, which led to a dehumanized urban environment in many sections of the capital city (Plate 6.3).

Although many of these large apartment projects were successful in setting the trend for more high-rise apartment developments, most middle and upper-middle income families did not enthusiastically embrace them due in a large part to a prevailing perception that most projects were targeted for low and low-middle income families and the building safety record was yet to be proved. To make matters even worse, one of the apartment projects for low income families collapsed in 1970, as already discussed in Chapter 4. Undeterred by this tragic accident, city officials continued to pursue their commitment to additional apartment construction, while campaigning for better building safety and an improvement in construction technology. Middle and upper-middle income families continued to be skeptical of such apartments well into the mid-1970s. In the meantime, the city's decision to develop more apartments for middle and upper-middle income families in Youido facilitated the active involvement of a number of major private construction companies.

Intense development and active participation by private developers

In the early 1970s most apartment complex developments, though varied in size, were mainly developed in the area north of the Han River.

Development in the area south of the Han River became significant in 1972, when the KHC was authorized to construct a huge apartment complex known as the Banpo apartment project. Though this particular

Plate 6.3   One of the earlier apartment complexes based on parallel layout method

site, more than a 500 000 m² in total area, was located south of the Han
River, it was only a few kilometers from the project just completed for
government workers. The living floor space of a unit ranged from 73 to
210 m², thus providing a wider selection of choices for potential
residents. It was by far the most spacious living space available at the
time. The entire project was completed in 1974, accommodating almost
3800 families. Again, the project included schools, centrally located
markets, and other convenient public facilities to create a self-contained
community for residents. With the maximum height of each building at
five stories, the public open space between the buildings was maintained
at one and a half times the vertical height. The generous open space,
combined with an open living area in each unit oriented to the south,
provided much needed sunlight for each apartment unit. This concept of
providing maximum public open space became an important element
for future high-rise apartment towers. However, the "military barracks"
physical design continued to add to the existing hard cityscape, which
hindered the development of neighborhoods fit to live in (Choo, 1986).

The development of large apartment complexes by the KHC and other small-scale housing developments by a few private developers increased, particularly in the Banpo district. These developments fueled the escalation of speculative housing and land prices. A few powerful corporations began to participate in the construction market boom in the mid-1970s. Profits to be made seemed to justify their involvement in the domestic market, although most of their construction activities took place in Middle Eastern countries such as Saudi Arabia and Iraq.

Between 1975 and 1983 the Hyundai Construction Company, a subsidiary of the parent company, Hyundai Corporation, developed large-scale luxury apartments for upper-middle and upper-income families. The project site was located along the south bank of the Han River, only a few kilometers from the primary city center to the north. It was completed in stages, 74 separate towers with the parallel layout method, and housed about 5661 families. Compared with most other apartments, each apartment was very spacious, with a living floor space of more than 165 m^2. All the units were quickly purchased by upper-income households; the ownership of an apartment unit in this project area was considered important as a status symbol and as an indication of wealth.

Over the years the city blocks adjacent to the Hyundai apartment project site in the Apkujong-dong district were developed to highlight a variety of Western cultures: fashionable stores with European and American designed clothes, trendy Western restaurants that included American fast-food chains, and other luxury goods shops. In general, most stores and establishments catered specifically for teenagers and college-aged young people, not only from the surrounding Hyundai apartments, but also from other districts in Seoul.

During most of the 1970s, the area south of the Han River attracted most of the high-rise apartment construction. Almost 10×10^6 m^2 of the flood-prone area that was routinely inundated during the monsoon season were graded and developed for low and low-middle income families. Some families who were displaced by urban renewal projects from the primary core area were relocated here. The entire project area, known as the Jamsil district apartments, was eventually developed to house more than 20 000 families. The living floor area per unit ranged from 43 to 70 m^2. A total of 483 apartment towers was built with heights varying from five to 15 stories. To avoid another military barracks environment, four high-rise towers were clustered together around a central common public open space (Sohn, 1983).

Although the original intention of this newly adopted design was to provide diverse and more manageable physical surroundings where residents would feel comfortable as part of a neighborhood, the drastic design change created major confusion in spatial orientation for both

Apartment complex along the Han River

Plate 6.4   Aerial view of the Jamsil apartment complex: the parallel layout and imposing physical dimension are well shown here

residents and visitors. The anticipated social network among residents in the project area failed to materialize, perhaps due to the higher rate of residential density and the enormous physical size of the project (Plate 6.4).

The 1980s was marked by escalating land speculation. New and revised laws dealing with housing and urban redevelopment were introduced to curtail some of the speculation. Urban renewal projects were vigorously carried out and were scattered throughout the city. Continuing protests by the affected residents at many of the urban renewal sites increased, particularly tenants with limited financial resources. Consequently, housing developments by private companies decreased substantially, while government-initiated urban development projects for most high-rise apartment construction increased during the 1980s. Approximately 11 large projects housing about 166 000 families, encompassing more than 23.7×10^6 m^2 in total area were constructed (City of Seoul, 1961–1994). Owing to their immense physical scale, many sites developed with high-rise apartment projects emerged like new towns.

One project in particular was the Olympic Village, built for the athletes participating in the 1988 summer games. A large open space, approximately 660 000 m^2 across from Olympic Park in the Jamsil district was developed for the village. The village itself contained over

Plate 6.5 Partial view of the Olympic Village

122 apartment towers and 5540 units. In an attempt to correct the past mistakes in using the military barracks design, these towers were laid out in the shape of an oriental fan, with heights ranging from six to 24 stories. The living floor space varied between 83 and 211 m². Additional attempts were made to reintroduce the traditional courtyard concept of the *hanok* by clustering a small number of apartment towers together with a common open space in the middle. Thus more attractive open fields with trees and green areas amid the high-rise apartment towers were created. A road system that separated pedestrians from automobile traffic was also introduced: ring roads encircling the towers were created for automobile use, while pedestrian walkways were developed along the public open space that connected each tower with neighborhood parks and other public facilities. Only service vehicles for the public facilities were allowed to enter the service roads within the site.

Schools for K-12, a satellite district city office, a post office, a police station, local markets, a hospital, neighborhood parks with various sports facilities, and other convenient shops were provided to create a self-contained community for approximately 30 000 people (Plate 6.5). After the Olympic games, all the units were sold to mostly upper-middle income families. Many design features used for the village set a new trend for other high-rise apartment development, but, more importantly, the village emerged as a distinctly different apartment community in Seoul.

As self-contained communities became prevalent, they attracted additional business development, thereby becoming important sub-centers or apartment districts within the existing urban facade. Although the patterns of the overt residential segregation did not exist during most of Seoul's growth periods, the presence of various sub-centers and particular apartment districts in the Apkujong-dong district became increasingly associated with and represented by a certain class of residents.

Public concerns for apartment living

At present, the appearance of huge apartment towers as a dominant cityscape challenges Seoul's future urban fabric. As long as amenities such as a central heating system and Western-style bathrooms are accepted as norms in modern living, the apartment towers will remain as an important residential choice for most residents in Seoul.

The impact of apartment living on residents' social and psychological well-being, particularly that of children growing up in a highly urbanized, concrete physical environment, has recently been questioned. The lack of natural open space may not be conducive to the well-balanced growth of children during their early years. As Mumford (1968) had stated, an ideal city environment should present a varying combination of many associated activities and intensities progressing through the life cycles of residents.

Concerns have been raised about whether the current residential lifestyle in many of the high-rise apartment communities is indeed healthy for young children, as it is so radically different from the traditional Korean *hanok* and its surrounding neighborhood environment. Gathering places for children have been greatly reduced and delegated to cement-covered parking areas between apartment towers. Perhaps the recent phenomenon of out-migration from Seoul to nearby cities and towns in the Kyonggi-do Province may be explained by this. Many have expressed their desire for change, others wished to own homes with small yards, and still others longed to retreat to a more natural environment.

Although the concept of a neighborhood in an urban environment may differ from the traditional use of the term, the enormous physical size of most development sites has become an obstacle to creating and enhancing neighborhoods that preserve the social network of residents. Narrow hallways and steps surrounding the apartment units, brief rides in the elevators, and short distances to parked automobiles may not be conducive in making personal contacts or meeting mutual acquaintances among residents. In addition, the physical design of the existing apartment towers encourages residents to become alienated from events occurring outside each unit once they step into their own physical space. Familiar surroundings where many of the residents do not have to arm themselves against urban crimes require gathering places where individual contacts with meaningful conversations are frequently made and special occasions can be mutually celebrated. It is in this manner that a community's social fabric is woven.

The rationale for the routine construction of massive high-rise apartment complexes was solely based on the fact that Seoul has very limited buildable land for an ever-increasing population. City officials have already begun the construction of five more new towns at even higher residential densities than before. It appears that mass-produced housing such as high-rise apartment towers has become embedded in the urban spatial structure. It will probably remain so through the 1990s and beyond.

Urban design and cityscape

The spatial development of Seoul during the early period of its 600 years of growth relied on the concept of geomancy. Although the physical layout of buildings respected the harmonious relationship with local currents of the cosmic breath, indigenous local building materials were mainly used for construction. The concept of modern urban design was neither known nor needed for a tranquil spatial arrangement that endured until Korea was invaded by the Japanese.

Early modern architecture

With Japanese domination came the development of modern public infrastructure and urbanization in Korea. At various locations in the primary core of the city, the colonial government erected a number of key public buildings to symbolize their colonization, thereby introducing modern architectural design to Seoul's urban facade. Many buildings from the colonial period were subsequently destroyed to make way for urban redevelopment projects. While others were replaced by modern office buildings, the Seoul rail station (Plate 6.6), Bank of Korea (Plate 6.7), and the city hall (Plate 6.8) have become permanent fixtures and important focal points in Seoul's landscape.

Plate 6.6   Seoul Rail Station

Plate 6.7   Bank of Korea

Plate 6.8 City hall

In yet another attempt to obliterate Korean culture and national heritage, the Japanese constructed a central government office building (Choongang Chung) in front of the royal palace, which was a symbol of the Yi Dynasty. Of modern design, the massive government office building was constructed in such a way that the view of the royal palace from the center of the city was completely blocked. It was believed that by eliminating the view from the general public, the presence of the royal palace and its traditional importance to the Korean people would gradually diminish. After the liberation in 1945, the celebration for the newly constituted government took place in front of Choongang Chung (Plate 6.9). Although this building has served as the national museum in recent years, it became controversial for many Koreans. Some argued that it should be permanently removed from its present location to eliminate the shame of Korea's colonial past and that the original physical layout of the royal palace should be reinstated. Others wanted to save the building for its historical value, whatever connotations it bore. Most recently, however, the government of President Kim Yong Sam decided to dismantle the building and the project began in late 1995. Recently, the Seoul municipal government also decided to build a new city hall on the present site, further eradicating the colonial imprint from Seoul.

Adding to this national humiliation, the colonial government had opened up many royal palaces to the public and converted a summer

Plate 6.9   Central government building – Choongang Chung

garden (Ch'anggyungwon) into a zoo. Again, the summer garden has been restored to its original form in recent years by relocating the zoo to a new, modern facility. During the colonial period, many other modern buildings were constructed at some royal palaces that were clearly out of scale and design with the original palace architecture (Plate 6.10). Again, the main intention of the Japanese was to discredit the final years of the Kingdom and dispel the traditional Korean culture. As the general public increases its critical awareness of Korea's colonial past, the fate of other buildings is an issue that will be debated for some time to come.

International modernism and urban design controls

Evidence of Seoul's explosive growth during the last 50 years has been discussed in previous chapters. Seoul experienced extremely rapid urban construction that broke away from the traditional concept of geomancy and embraced modern designs and international influences. However, urban design guidelines that could integrate and balance both traditional Korean and modern architectural designs were lacking. Not only were most buildings constructed by private owners without review by design specialists, but responsible government offices that were

Plate 6.10 Present view of Toksugung, one of the remaining palaces: the modern architecture in the middle was built by the Japanese

supposed to oversee the development process did not provide any leadership in design controls.

Most office buildings, regardless of their physical size, were designed along the prevailing trend at the time. Thus, until the mid-1980s, buildings representative of modern architecture remained a dominant force in shaping and rearranging the urban fabric of Seoul. As many powerful major corporations carved out certain districts within the primary core of the city for their own corporate headquarters, commercial skyscrapers that were large-scale, physically imposing, internationally fashionable, and ultra-modern in architecture rapidly mushroomed. Many of these corporations used the buildings as signature statements that were their own permanent seal in Seoul's cityscape.

Similar to points identified by Harvey (1990) through a survey of international spatial designs, the resulting theme of these buildings was closely tied to the preservation of monotonous modern characteristics that typify production based on linear progression and positivistic and technocentric rationality (Plates 6.11 and 6.12).

Over the years there were efforts to preserve some historical districts and their architecture, but the concept of urban design during the urban development process was not formally introduced until 1980. The legal language describing urban design controls was included in the revised Building Law 1980 to promote a more pleasing urban environment. Other urban development and zoning laws were frequently used to encourage the orderly development of construction projects by limiting heights and lot sizes as well as requiring adequate open space. The main emphasis of the newly adopted urban design controls was to improve the existing physical environment by legally designating an urban design district. Most urban design districts were located either inside the primary core or along the major arterial roads throughout the city (City of Seoul, 1961–1994).

Once an urban design district is identified and design controls are incorporated into an overall urban design plan, the mayor of Seoul is required to display the plan for 30 days for public review. After revising the plan according to citizen's comments, the mayor then sends the plan to the Ministry of Construction for review. The Minister of Construction, on receiving recommendations from the Central City Planning Committee, approves the plan with or without modifications and remands it to the city for implementation. The mayor then notifies the plan to the general public and the project is subsequently implemented. Although this planning process has sometimes resulted in lengthy delays because central government approval was mandatory, city officials welcomed the new urban design control measures as guidelines for enhancing project environments. The adoption of these measures arrived at an opportune time, as city officials had concentrated mainly on the preparation of the 1986 Asian Games and the 1988 Summer Olympics as well as city beautification projects.

Since 1983 there have been 16 urban design districts designated, covering approximately 20×10^6 m^2 in total area. Many of these projects were expected to contribute to the creation of a more diverse and physically pleasing urban environment with the help of urban designers. In addition, city officials welcomed the concept of design controls, tools that could be used to curtail the ever-increasing urban sprawl and the production of unattractive buildings scattered around Seoul. With more projects coming to an end, it appears that the urban design controls under the revised Building Law have met with little success. Although

Plate 6.11   A series of modern buildings

Plate 6.12   DLI63 building, the tallest building in Korea today

city officials had hoped to implement the urban design controls, they soon discovered that most plans incorporating design controls remained conceptual. Not only did city officials lack the legal authority to implement the necessary design controls, but they also learned that many of the design recommendations did not fully address the needs of the district or residents, thus isolating the affected public from the plan. The residents in most urban design districts complained loudly that the design controls were used only to restrict their building construction and that unrealistic design plans did not incorporate their immediate concerns and needs.

Furthermore, most urban design specialists, though initially supportive of urban design controls, expressed frustration with the current rigid design process and the ineffective implementation of urban design controls. It has been argued that closer linkages between the urban design controls and urban redevelopment projects, combined with special land use districts that allow variances, are needed to substantially affect Seoul's future landscape.

Back to traditional roots and the emergence of post-modernism

Although most projects during the period when the city was preparing for the Olympics did not positively contribute to an overall improvement of the existing urban mosaic, two important factors emerged that could alter Seoul's cityscape: rediscovering traditional Korean architecture and the shift from modern to post-modern architecture.

An important component of the overall Olympic facilities, Olympic Park, about 3.5 km southwest of the main Olympic complex, was created in the Jamsil district. Olympic Park comprised more than 1.67×10^6 m^2 of total land area and housed sports facilities such as cycling, fencing, gymnastics, weight lifting, swimming, and tennis. However, the main purpose of the park was ultimately to create a natural environment that could be permanently enjoyed by Seoul's residents after the Olympics.

During its early construction phase it was discovered that a section of the proposed park was home to the archeological site of the Mongchon mud walls during the Baekche Kingdom of the Three Kingdom Period. Preservation of this important historical tradition replaced the common practice of bulldozing that leveled many urban project sites. Thus a major design theme for the park included not only the creation of the sports facilities that could later be used by residents, but also the integration of Korean traditional designs into modern architecture. A sports-related high school and college, youth center, and an outdoor theater were constructed, whereas a historical park was developed around the recreated Mongchon mud walls. The harmonious co-existence between historical elements and modern sports facilities in the park was promoted throughout the entire design process. On entering, visitors find themselves in an interior reminiscent of traditional Korean culture by its spatial arrangement, but they also experience international sports culture at the sports park.

Although areas immediately adjacent to the park were densely developed, the presence of schools, open plazas, Olympic memorials, and wide open spaces for the park entrances served as a sufficient buffer zone to protect the park's natural environment. At present, the park has become a favorite spot for families and young couples, providing residents a space in an urban setting to escape from their daily hectic activities (Plates 6.13 and 6.14).

Plate 6.13 Olympic Park: the open area to the far left is the preserved Mongchon mud walls

Most houses in the primary core area of Seoul were traditional Korean *hanoks*. With Seoul's growth accelerating at higher rates and over more space, signs of tradition and historical heritage in many districts in the city core began to fade.

As there were no laws for the preservation of historic buildings to curtail unnecessary urban projects until 1983, many *hanoks* were replaced by modern office buildings. A large proportion of the remaining *hanoks* were converted to commercial use. A number of districts in the primary core area, including a very high density of *hanoks*, was designated as a special historic preservation area in 1983, and relevant building codes and zoning laws have been enforced to prevent the alteration and destruction of Seoul's historical environment (Plates 6.15 and 6.16).

However, these actions appear to have come too late. Distressed residents experiencing unwanted changes in their districts moved to apartment communities in the area south of the Han River in pursuit of more convenient modern amenities. After many high schools with a long tradition in the districts had also been encouraged to relocate to various areas south of the Han River, modern office buildings were erected on the relocated high school sites without any consideration of

Plate 6.14 Olympic memorials

the impact on the existing historical urban fabric. It seemed that more and more urban development projects for office and commercial uses in the districts destroyed whatever delicate historical value the traditional *hanoks* had in the districts. Of the total buildings located in the preservation area in 1985, about 55% or 1518 buildings were *hanoks*. Only about 23 *hanoks* were built before 1910. The remaining majority were constructed between 1910 and 1950; the devastating fallout of urban development ignored the historical importance of the *hanoks* in these districts (City of Seoul, 1961–1994).

Spurred by an increased awareness of the preservation of Korean culture and historical tradition, the special preservation area had two main purposes. Firstly, the existing narrow alleys and streets and arrangement of the *hanoks*, which emphasized pedestrian use and smaller

Plate 6.15 *Hanoks* with modern buildings

physical areas to foster a more intimate neighborhood environment, were to be maintained and recreated whenever possible. The maximum heights for new buildings would be strictly enforced and the architecture for new buildings should blend in with traditional Korean architecture. Automobile traffic on streets in the area was restricted, while open spaces with trees would be designated for neighborhood gatherings. Secondly, most *hanoks* would be classified by the years built and categorized by

Plate 6.16 One of the main gates, Namdaemoon, is completely isolated by streets and modern office buildings

historical periods. At the same time, newly identified historical buildings or sites would be permanently preserved.

Even with these noble objectives, the current outlook for the preservation area is bleak. Required to distinguish historical homes or sites, various agencies at different government levels typically exerted their control over the decisions of others, eliminating any possible coordination among themselves. In addition, as only the oldest historical buildings or sites with some connection to the Yi Dynasty were perceived to be of any value, most residents living in old *hanoks* or in the *hanok* districts were not routinely considered for historical designation, thus receiving no special program funds or benefits under the historical preservation acts. With very limited public funds available for such programs, most residents were advised to rehabilitate the residences with their own financial resources. As fewer and fewer residents were able to improve their own homes, the physical environment in the area continued its downward slide. In addition, more commercial and office development has encroached over the years. Unless the central government makes a substantial financial commitment to preserve Korean *hanok* districts, it is likely that most *hanoks* or traditional Korean architecture will completely disappear from Seoul, only to be found in historical museums.

Post-modernism

While the movement towards defining Korean culture and tradition continued, particularly in the areas of popular culture and food, another distinct spatial development emerged in Seoul's landscape: post-modern buildings.

In terms of spatial concept, post-modern architecture is a radical departure from modern architecture. In general, post-modernists view space according to aesthetic aims and principles and treat it as something independent and autonomous. As a result, post-modern architecture is a self-conscious and ironic use of historical styles and imagery (Knox, 1987; Harvey, 1990). Harvey (1990) further argues that it also emphasizes individualism, financial power, and eclecticism.

Perhaps some design specialists became tired of producing and seeing the massive, modernistic architectural form predominate Seoul's development periods since the 1960s. The trend towards the post-modernistic spatial arrangement seems to have come after the 1988 Olympics. The majority of post-modern buildings were constructed in the area south of the Han River. The area commanded most of the accumulation of capital through its real estate boom cycles, and the area's rapid expansion as a newly developing section of Seoul since the late 1970s provided more vacant tracts for large urban development projects. Even though major construction projects had slowed after the Olympics, new projects adopted the post-modern facade and a few major hotels incorporated the physical flavor with the traditional Korean architecture, thereby helping to break up the existing dominant, monotonous spatial arrangement (Plate 6.17).

Although the particular trend of the imageable building in an urban space will undoubtedly continue, it is not clear at the present time how it will alter the current cityscape in Seoul. It is not certain what interest major private corporations have in adapting their next urban spatial project to the post-modernistic approach. Moreover, existing private

Plate 6.17 Main building of the Korean Foreign Trade Association, one of the newest post-modern buildings in Seoul

developers, particularly those in apartment development, may be reluctant to participate in changing their present design methods which have consistently generated uniform modernistic buildings at minimum construction costs.

Artistic expression of streetscape

Although post-modern architecture remains a newly added element in the overall urban structure, efforts towards a softer and more pleasing urban environment are underway.

With decades of Korea's continuous economic growth, more diverse economic activities began to spread in Seoul. As most shops came to rely

Plate 6.18   Street signs without any design coordination

on advertising signs to attract customers, street signs which were not controlled by sign ordinances became major contributors to creating a more chaotic physical environment (Plate 6.18). This situation worsened when increasingly dense commercial developments were allowed in all parts of the city and these new establishments all required some form of name recognition for their products and services. In recent years, however, many commercial buildings have begun to display an array of well-coordinated signs in front of their buildings, thereby creating more effective advertisements as well as a more pleasing visual environment for pedestrians (Plate 6.19).

The exhibition of art works in and around office buildings has become common practice, while permanent sculptures and murals have been added to many of the courtyards and available open spaces at major corporation and public office buildings (Plates 6.20 and 6.21). Not only

Plate 6.19 Coordinated sign boards

have many of these newly created artistic displays improved the quality of the streetscape, but they have also provided residents with softer, more soothing user-friendly places in Seoul's modern spatial surroundings.

Other urban cultures: churches and underground shops

There are two other significant urban cultures that deserve some attention: the omnipresence of churches and underground shopping districts that cannot be seen at ground level in Seoul.

In addition to the Confucian tradition, Korean society has historically been influenced by Buddhism. However, because of the tradition of self-meditation, most Buddhist temples were located in remote mountains some distance away from civilization. The introduction of Christianity to Korea is relatively new, though its influence on modern Korean society has steadily increased. When Christian missionaries arrived in Korea during the late nineteenth century, the Kingdom did not understand this newly invading Western religion and banned it completely. The executions of Christian missionaries on arrival continued. During the Japanese colonial period, however, the spread of Christianity was tacitly approved. Not only did the practice of Christian religion become immediately widespread in Korea, but ironically some members of the newly formed religious organization participated actively in the independence movement against Japanese rule.

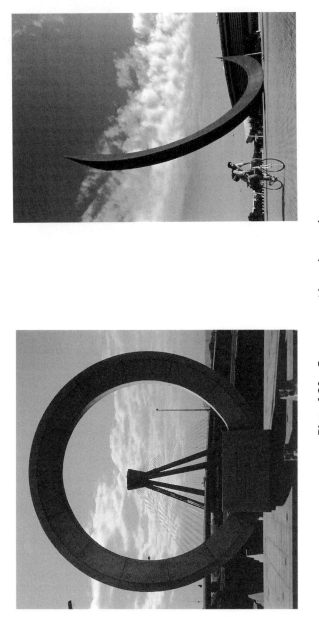

Plate 6.20 Open space with modern sculpture

Plate 6.21 Modern sculpture and indoor garden

At present, the appearance of churches can be noted everywhere in Seoul's cityscape. There are many small churches scattered around the city serving particular neighborhoods. Many are also located in apartment communities. A significant number of large churches, some even post-modern architectural in design, are physically imposing and have quickly become dominant focal points in Seoul's urban landscape. One of the most prominent churches is Myungdong Cathedral, located in the heart of the primary core area (Plate 6.22). Myungdong Cathedral, one of the oldest churches built in Seoul, is unique not only because it incorporated Gothic architecture into its original design, but also because it provided a safe haven for pro-democracy activists as well as urban dwellers who protested against many of the urban renewal projects during the tumultuous periods of the 1970s and 1980s. As a sanctuary, the cathedral became a forceful, symbolic focal point for democratic movements.

Borrowing the concept of underground shops from Tokyo, city officials actively promoted the development of underground shopping districts at many of the highly populated areas of the city. It was believed that the limited space available for commercial development made this method a more efficient use of land, particularly as the cost of rent continued to climb and became prohibitively high. Therefore, most

Plate 6.22 Myungdong Cathedral, one of the oldest cathedrals in Korea

Plate 6.23   A view of an underground shopping district

underground shopping districts are connected to major subway stations, hotels, and department stores where traffic is heavily concentrated. At some locations, the total underground shopping area encompasses more than 2 km². Almost all major consumer items such as clothing, jewelry, electronics, books, and food can be found in underground shops (Plate 6.23).

Inadequate air ventilation, coupled with airborne dust and cigarette smoke, degrades the air quality in all underground shopping districts. In fact, the air pollution measured at many underground districts, such as one close to the City Hall or the shops connecting to a major subway station in the area south of the Han River, is consistently two to three times higher than the permitted air pollution standard (City of Seoul, 1990).

During the day, most shopkeepers never see the sun and become completely isolated from the activities outside. With the ever-increasing urban density in Seoul, the expansion of underground shopping districts is expected to continue and will remain an important urban culture, however serious the health hazards it might pose to workers, regular customers, and occasional visitors.

Open space

Most modern cities struggle with providing a variety of open space for their inhabitants. Owing to uncontrolled urbanization, open space is rapidly dwindling. As life in today's cities becomes more complicated, urban residents increasingly retreat to the natural environment not only for their leisure, but also as a temporary retreat from the fast pace of urban life. Although the types of natural surroundings and their subsequent development priorities may vary from city to city, the availability of river levees, ocean fronts, hills, large urban parks, and other natural settings has become an integral part of the urban environment that substantially enhances the quality of life.

Traditional to modern concept

The concept of open space in the Korean tradition also originates from the practice of geomancy. As spatial development was supposed to create a harmonious relationship with nature, open space in old, traditional Korean settlements meant a naturally inviting place for gathering or recreation.

More often than not, these open areas were places naturally formed over time. Though lacking modern public facilities, a small shaded area under an old oak tree in front of the village entrance, the space around a public well for drinking water, and an open plaza in the village all served the purpose of providing much needed public open space (Kwon Sang Jun, 1983). Even today people can be observed gathering for conversation at any of the hills in Seoul where underground natural spring water is readily available. Nearby residents not only enjoy a better quality of drinking water, but also participate in daily exercises and neighborly interaction (Plate 6.24).

The modern concept of open space in Seoul was first introduced during the 1930s. Open space was classified into five major uses: parks for children, neighborhood parks, city parks, parks with sports facilities, and parks with untouched natural surroundings. Approximately 10% of the city's total land was designated as open space (Lee, 1983). Although increasing development pressures continued to eliminate the available open space around the city, no serious attempt was made to curtail such projects by revising existing city ordinances relating to open space until the mid-1960s.

The main purpose of the Park Law was to regulate and oversee the development of natural areas for future use. First enacted in 1967, the law stipulated and implemented environmental policies concerning natural

Plate 6.24 A newly designed gathering place for the elderly: a traditional gathering place would have been similar to this, with natural shade and trees

areas that have yet to be reached by urban growth. The existing open space was reorganized into three major categories: national parks, provincial parks, and city parks. Most existing natural preservation areas were incorporated into national or provincial parks, whereas city parks were further divided into children's parks, neighborhood parks, cemeteries, and natural parks. As expected, both neighborhood and children's parks were easy to access and designed to be used daily, whereas the others were meant for weekend use and on special occasions. The total area preserved for parks in 1990 was about 153.4 km² representing approximately 25.3% of the city's administrative area, but only about 57% of this total provided park facilities for residents (City of Seoul, 1990).

The designation of the greenbelt by the revised City Planning Law of 1971 was another attempt to protect the natural environment in and around Seoul, but, as we have shown earlier, it did not encourage orderly development. Instead, the city expanded in an uncontrolled leapfrog development pattern. The public facilities needed for leisure activities within the designated greenbelt areas were never developed, thus severely limiting their use as a public open space for residents. Some city officials have argued that some public facilities should be provided until future decisions are made about growth in the existing greenbelt areas (City of Seoul, 1990).

In an attempt to address the rapidly expanding physical growth and its continuing negative effects on the environment, the Park Law was revised in 1980, not only to minimize the speed of environmental degradation, but also to address the ever-diminishing quality of life in Seoul. Two separate laws were enacted: the Natural Park Law and the Urban Park Law. Buffer zones and natural beauty zones were additionally designated to protect the city's natural environment from unforeseen future development. Paralleling the environmental regulation movement, street beautification projects, including the planting of trees, were also carried out from 1977, but they could not keep up with the rapid pace of growth (Yang Byung Yee, 1985; City of Seoul, 1990). The resulting landscape in Seoul is uneven in terms of its physical characteristics: some newly developed areas, particularly the neighborhoods of upper-middle income families, are provided with trees and other environmentally pleasing amenities, whereas many other areas seem to lack trees or green spaces, thus projecting a physically bare image. This unevenness may contribute to creating an overall cityscape that is unattractive.

Uneven distribution of open space

Originally, the natural setting of Seoul was beautiful. Surrounding the capital, some distance away, were majestic mountains. Dissecting the city from east to west was the magnificent Han River. Small hills dotted the landscape at intermittent locations within the city boundary.

Seoul's current urban form is very different from the cityscape that could have been had better coordination of and commitment to environmental conservation existed (Plate 6.25). The total area of open space is still substantial: approximately 50.8% or 359.6 km^2 of Seoul's administrative area (Plate 6.26).

Only about 1.3% of the open space is agricultural land; the remaining, 98.7% is covered by natural green areas. Because of Seoul's greenbelt control, urban development is prohibited in about 167 km^2 of the natural green areas encircling the city boundary (City of Seoul, 1990). Although most open spaces appear to be scattered around the city, the largest single open space lies in the area north of the Han River and is a national park that includes Pukhan Mountain, one of the most popular places for hiking and weekend outings for residents.

One of the most critical issues concerning open space in Seoul is the uneven distribution of parks and other recreational facilities in the city. At issue is the difficulty of residents in accessing some of the facilities. Most districts (wards) located in the area north of the Han River lack

Plate 6.25 City scene with open space

city parks serving children and the local neighborhoods, mainly because urban development has always been so densely concentrated. Taking a child to a nearby park becomes a serious effort. Therefore, parking lots at many of the apartment tower communities commonly serve as children's play areas. Owing to the ever-increasing demand of automobile parking, however, the safety of children has become a major issue, thus taking away even this marginal open space from their use.

The availability of park facilities is another major concern facing the city. Except for the national parks inside the city, most city parks have inadequate public facilities. Some city parks are nothing more than open fields, an extremely uninviting environment for active public use. Perhaps the most difficult challenge facing Seoul is the ownership of parks. Although almost 60% of the parks belong to the government, about 52% of the neighborhood parks are under private ownership. The amount of leverage, financial or legal, that the city government has in terms of their future land use, even though current zoning classifies them as open space, is an important question to be addressed in the near future.

Importance of the Han River

Historically, the Han River, with a total length of 469 km, was vital to the development of Seoul. Not only did it supply drinking water, but it also served as an essential water transportation route until Seoul fully developed other modes of transportation.

Plate 6.26 Aerial view of Namsan Mountain in Seoul: a drive for the restoration of the mountain to its natural state is being carried out by the Seoul municipal government

It was also a continuing cause for anxiety and pain to some residents, as it often flooded during Korea's famous summer monsoon season. Over the years, more dams upstream were constructed to prevent flooding. Meanwhile, urban development polluted the river to a point where swimming, fishing, and other recreational activities were prohibited. Although its potential benefit as a major recreational site for all residents in Seoul has always existed, the Han River Development Plan did not fully materialize until Seoul prepared for the 1988 Olympics. To impress the world community, both city and central government officials realized that the Han River had to be cleaned and beautified; thus the Comprehensive Han River Development Project began in 1981.

Although one of the main objectives of the comprehensive project was the successful presentation of the refined Han River to the world during the 1986 Asian Games and the 1988 Summer Olympics, the cultivation of natural resources was also an important part of the project. Environmental clean-up efforts were actively carried out in order to regenerate a rich habitat for the fish and birds that originally lived in and around the river. To allow recreational river cruisers to serve the public safely in the river, the maximum depth and width of the river were carefully redesigned and facilities to monitor and control the velocity of the river were constructed. The banks at either side of the river were raised and reinforced to prevent future flooding during the rainy season.

Approximately 6.9 km^2 of the levee land along the river were graded and developed for recreational uses. There are now nine city parks with sports facilities such as soccer and softball fields, and tennis and basketball courts. About 3.8 km^2 of additional land were preserved as a natural wildlife area; fishing is now allowed and outdoor classes exploring the natural habitat around the river are routinely held there. More access roads and pedestrian pathways have been created for a more convenient approach to many of these newly developed sites. With the development of two permanent water treatment facilities the water has become clearer. Although the comprehensive project took four years to finish, restoration and improvement of the Han River have not been fully completed. More political and financial commitment from city officials may be required to provide more diverse and complete public recreational facilities along the entire river. Only then will the Han River become an important site of natural beauty for all the residents of Seoul (Plate 6.27).

Although the main Olympic stadium and other major fields were constructed in the Jamsil district, urban expressways along both sides of the Han River were also developed. The main purpose of the expressways, which were later named the 88 urban expressway to the south and the Kangbuk expressway to the north, were to create a scenic route along the river. They also provided an efficient east–west traffic flow for residents in the area south of the river, particularly from Kimpo International Airport in the extreme southwestern corner of the city to the Olympic sites. At key locations five bridges and 11 interchanges were built as smooth linkages between both sides of the Han River. Many sections of the 88 expressway have now been expanded to eight lanes to ease bottle-necks, but the traffic jams and ever-increasing volume of traffic persist all day long.

As mentioned earlier in this chapter, the legible web of an urban landscape, however complex its presentation may be, can create a

Plate 6.27   Development of the Han River facilities

positive image to most residents in the city. Even though intertwining urban roads, complicated mass transit systems, disjointed physical spaces presented by uninviting buildings and incomprehensible spatial designs, and the intense movement of people could provide an imposing environment for urban dwellers, the presence of familiar surroundings often provides a sense of belonging and relief to residents of a hectic and unprotected urban environment. How many sections of Seoul qualify for this definition of a comfortable neighborhood environment?

Parks and recreational facilities are integral parts of urban life because most people pursue leisure activities in places away from where they conduct their work, home, or school routines. Family members require their own outings from time to time, while single people need gathering places for their own social functions. It has become a common practice that many of the newly developed apartment communities provide a small open space where residents can participate in activities such as jogging, badminton, and floor exercises. However, the lack of recreational facilities may explain why so many of the residents of Seoul seem to spend most of their leisure time in front of their television sets at home (City of Seoul, 1990).

The movement to rediscover a national heritage has significantly contributed to the resurgence of traditional Korean architecture. However, modern architecture remains the dominant cityscape of Seoul, far removed from the city's historical form. Therefore, the great challenges facing the capital city may include the creation of an urban environment that successfully integrates international modern forms with traditional Korean culture. Quality of life depends on an exciting, vibrant, yet orderly urban environment.

7

Conclusions: what challenges lie ahead?

A daily radio program from the Transportation Broadcasting Services in Seoul delivers frequent traffic updates during the morning and evening rush hours, alerting drivers about specific locations to avoid. The 20 minute drive between offices in the primary core of the city and apartment complexes in districts south of the Han River typically stretches into a two hour trip during the rush hours because of heavy traffic delays. Beginning in January 1995, city officials, hoping to alleviate the ever-increasing traffic congestion, instituted a pilot program that required residents in Seoul to leave their cars at home once every ten days and commute by public transportation. Violators were fined a substantial amount of money during the program period, which was scheduled to end in May 1995. However, due to its initial success, and continuing traffic problems, it has become a permanent fixture in Seoul's transportation policy.

In recent years, public awareness of the environment has significantly increased. Subsequently, electronic display panels at various sites in the city have been installed, illuminating daily air pollution levels. Citizen groups have been organized to educate residents about the possible health problems from drinking water, automobile emissions, hazardous chemicals, and the deteriorating environmental quality in the city.

On national holidays and Sundays it has become a common practice that many residents hike along the numerous scenic trails traversing the nearby mountains and national parks. The large numbers of people participating in such leisure activities not only generates congested traffic conditions, but also creates a continuous human wave that prevents them from enjoying weekend outings. It is a reminder of how crowded and suffocating the capital city has actually become. Politicians and civic leaders alike express deep concern and debate whether Seoul, with its over-burdened infrastructure and carrying capacity, has reached a point where it is ungovernable and rapidly becoming uninhabitable.

As discussed in previous chapters, the economic and social trans-formation of the capital city from a tranquil, small town to the present day metropolis has occurred quickly, often guided by national government policies. It has resulted, at times, in abrupt and pervasive social relations. The continuing physical expansion of Seoul, along with the growing number of satellite cities in the SMR, has fueled public infrastructure development that includes subway extensions and new urban expressways. Today Seoul is indeed vibrant and lively, with more than 11 million people active in diverse and highly specialized urban functions. Its population has also become more involved in constantly changing and reshaping its urban structures.

As discussed in Chapter 1, the overall growth patterns of Seoul do not seem to fit one particular theoretical presentation about the formation of a city. Perhaps the formation of a city is generally constrained by the particular space, culture, and time, and additional theories should consider such profound limitations when describing a city's structure. Seoul's existing urban structure and functions will certainly continue changing in the future, requiring new approaches in managing all aspects of urban growth and development.

Although there are now numerous difficult, challenging issues facing Seoul, one of the most critical problems is restructuring the intricate political relationship between the central government and Seoul's municipal government following the mayoral election in June 1995. After the revision of the Local Autonomy Law 1988, a decentralized political system was instituted and Seoul was given independent authority to have its own city council. The vertical relationship that has existed between the central government and the Seoul municipal government has changed. Rather than remain a passive local govern-ment subservient to the national government, Seoul should emerge after the election as a powerful, independent political unit that asserts itself in any future political and economic issues. As long as the political move-ment towards local autonomy is fully implemented, Seoul, with its broad financial resources and large population base, should become a most powerful local government that not only steers and sets its own future, but also strongly influences the nation as a whole. Even though the national government may not relinquish its political grip on all local governments, it is still expected that a popularly elected mayor will try to serve his or her own political constituents and pursue a local political agenda, however unpopular that agenda might seem to the rest of the country. Therefore, national politicians and the popularly elected mayor and city council members may have to enter new and unfamiliar political territory that requires genuine coordination and negotiation.

The newly acquired local autonomy will probably force the City of Seoul to redefine its own administrative structure, particularly with the existing 25 district offices. No longer will they remain satellite offices, managing and fulfilling orders and guidelines given by City Hall. In June 1995, the heads of all 25 city districts were elected by popular ballots and each council member is obligated to represent his or her own council district throughout a four year political term. As each district develops its own physical growth and economic development strategies, it could add even more tension about the overall city budget and management unless the mayor and city council develop clear official guidelines that ensure an equitable distribution of citywide financial resources. This is particularly important because wide disparities exist among the districts, not only in their financial capabilities, but also in political power. Given a renewed interest in citizen participation and the steady growth of citizen organizations concerned about environmental and other political issues, it is also anticipated that district residents will become fairly vocal about issues that they perceive will affect their quality of life. The concerns include locally unwanted land uses, roadway expansion that threatens to disrupt residents and neighborhoods, and the location of factories that pollute their own districts. It is currently not clear, however, how well Seoul's city council will work together to pursue common goals pertaining to citywide concerns. Will council members become parochial in their political outlook?

The decentralized political system, fully implemented after the June 1995 election, will also affect the SMR. As described in Chapter 5, an intergovernmental advisory organization, the Seoul Metropolitan Association of Governments (SMAG), has been established to handle issues affecting member cities and nearby provinces. Without any legal authority to implement policies and plans, the SMAG has been relatively ineffective, shadowed by Seoul's dominance over the region. However, newly elected governors from Kyonggi-do Province and other provinces, the mayor from a nearby large city such as Inchon, and other elected city officials adjacent to the capital city will undoubtedly demand their fair share in future political debates that affect their communities. As regional migration has slowed substantially in recent years, more people are now born and raised in one place. Many young people in Seoul, for example, have never left the city and are less sensitive to non-urban cultures and lifestyles. The demands of this new segment of the population will clearly differ from those who originally migrated from rural areas and still have a strong attachment to their place of origin. Friction over the different needs and expectations among the municipal and provincial governments in the SMR and in the surrounding region may intensify. Perhaps the time has come to encourage more intergovernmental cooperation for the various aspects of growth and public management by making the existing SMAG a more responsible and responsive regional government.

The unexpected failure of the Sungsoo Bridge in October 1994 amplified just how fragile the existing public infrastructure can be when its construction phases are not carefully monitored during periods of unprecedented growth. The lesson learned from the collapse of the bridge countered the prevailing view that completing public work projects quickly was a success and signified progress. Public safety and welfare should no longer be overlooked and considered secondary to speedy construction. After the accident, all 13 remaining bridges connecting both sides of the Han River were closely scrutinized. The necessary repairs are underway. As a result, the traffic jams that choked the capital city worsen. Possible solutions to the existing transportation problems do not appear to be within reach at the present time.

The improved standard of living is associated with private automobile ownership. More cars will occupy the existing roads, further stalling traffic in the city. When addressing the increasing dominance of automobiles in cities, Mumford (1961) argued that although ample space for automobile use should be provided, cars need not be allowed in every part of a city so that all other activities are disrupted. Along with the extremely high urban density in Seoul, automobiles are everywhere. In many alleyways once reserved for pedestrian use, cars are parked in a way that leaves little room for pedestrian traffic. Cars are commonly parked along one side of many secondary roads, making them into one-way streets that block smooth traffic flows and add to the tension of urban living for many residents.

To alleviate the existing traffic congestion, more expressways are being built, while existing arterial and secondary roads have been widened to accommodate even more cars. New subway lines have been added to provide adequate public transportation services to newly developing sections of the city, whereas innovative mass transportation programs such as flexible hours, exclusive bus lanes, and preferential treatment of high occupancy vehicles have been introduced. Still, however, the traffic crawls practically all day and continues into the evening hours. Idling automobiles emit an increasing rate of carbon monoxide, thus adding to the ever-increasing health hazard for all residents. It seems that the extremely limited open space and present street layouts of the capital city cannot possibly cope with the rapidly increasing demands brought by automobiles.

Any solution to the current transportation problem, which have been repeatedly cited as the most serious threat to Seoul's urban environment, may need to begin with a serious re-examination of the prevailing value system within the existing political, cultural, and economic system. The growth of automobile ownership and usage has been closely identified with the increased demand for privacy, comfort, flexibility, and an efficient mode of transportation at an individual level. Perhaps we need to introduce the concept of a social contract within the framework of a civil society where some individual gains are sacrificed to benefit common needs and goals. However, we must ensure that it does not discourage newcomers who aspire to enjoy their improved standard of living by acquiring goods that were otherwise simply not available to them. As long as all members of society feel that they are entitled to the benefits that automobiles bring to their private transportation needs, the current dilemma will probably reach crisis levels with no feasible solution in sight.

Korea has a strong automobile industry that exports its products world-wide. Although the individual desire to enjoy a privately owned automobile increases with their improved economic circumstances for many residents in the country, the automobile industry may need to put less emphasis on the domestic market. It perhaps needs to recognize that the physical size of the country is too small to provide private automobiles to all deserving individuals. The costs of progress appear dire when the city's roadway capacity cannot handle the rapidly increasing traffic volumes. Average speeds of 5 to 8 km/h on many existing roads and emissions from the idling cars that threaten environmental quality are among the sobering consequences of ill-managed growth.

The existing urban density of Seoul is expected to increase with continuing urban renewal projects in the city. High-rise apartment towers based on assembly-line like mass production will continue to be constructed to alleviate housing shortages for all segments of the population. A mixture of modern and post-modern commercial buildings will slowly add to the existing cityscape. When strolling along the streets of Seoul, particularly in the island of Youido, one is left with the impression that it is like any other modern Western city. Buildings, street designs, business activities and other city functions closely resemble cities such as New York, Tokyo, and London. A uniquely Korean tradition in architectural and cultural presentation is lacking. The absence of traditional Korean influences, along with a substantial increase in urban density and crowding, reduces the overall legibility of the city environment: the city looks too disjointed, chaotic, and unattractive. The development of special functional districts within the city might enhance its image and ambiance. At present, a number of special districts such as theaters, antiques, general consumer goods, and electronic products have been created in various sections of the city, but others, such as foreign embassies, historic sites, and the arts, are not available. The creation of such special districts cannot be brought about by zoning or other enforcement mechanisms alone, but rather through a historical process of urban growth and development.

Seoul has been the engine of the nation's economic development, spreading innovation, invention, and culture to other parts of the country. Negative externalities following its intense growth in population and physical size have continued to degrade the quality of life in the capital city. In recent years, some residents have decided to move out of the city in pursuit of a better living environment. However, it is likely that the capital city will remain the powerful center for economic, political, social, and cultural activities, and that the population will continue to grow. Furthermore, residents will continue to develop a strong, distinct cultural pride and heritage that could eventually be claimed as their own.

When faced with the coming information age, particularly with the constant advancement in telecommunications and computers, policy options for the deconcentration of the capital city, not only in terms of population, but also in government functions could make sense. Personal computers allow communication to take place without physical contact. Provided that social, psychological, and institutional obstacles are easily removed, the successful dispersal of government offices and the population from the capital city would result in an enhancement of the quality of life for all segments of the population.

Additional consideration should be given to an effective private–public partnership in the management of local government. To be more responsive to the needs of residents, the massive bureaucracy that has been a dominant form in the Seoul municipal government needs to be restructured. Some middle layers of the vertical organizational structure that have often hindered efficient decision-making could be eliminated, while various functions of the city services could be delegated to the private or quasi-public sector.

It would be an ideal situation if we all could anticipate future changes for Seoul and plan actions to meet such challenges accordingly. On the basis of what we have charted throughout 600 years of growth and development, one aspect appears to be certain for the future: the city will remain symbolic as an important capital city for generations to come. Provided that the currently evolving urban system in northeast Asia and the Pacific Rim countries continues, Seoul is expected to play an increasingly important part in this emerging new international order. In an inverted S-shaped corridor from Beijing to Pyongyang, North Korea to Seoul to Tokyo, the present total urban population is about 97 million residing in 109 cities. With the opening of China and Russia, this particular region is rapidly becoming a borderless urban corridor. The part that Seoul should play within this emerging international arena is an important question facing the capital city.

Seoul should also prepare for an eventual reunification, when the national border between the two Koreas will carry little significance. How Seoul will be reshaped and molded to emerge as a city in the next century will largely depend on its residents' imagination, relentless determination, flexibility, and, most of all, their ability to embrace an uncertain future.

References:
English language publications

Bello, W. and Rosenfeld, S. 1990. *Dragons in Distress: Asia's Miracle Economies in Crisis*. San Francisco: A Food First Book Press.

Berry, B.J.L. 1981. *Comparative Urbanization: Divergent Paths in the Twentieth Century*. New York: St. Martin's.

Blumenfeld, H. 1949. A theory of city form, past and present. *Journal of Architectural Historians*, 8(3–4), 7–16.

Blumenfeld, H. 1967. *The Modern Metropolis: its Origins Growth, Characteristics, and Planning, Selected Essays*. Cambridge: MIT Press.

Bourne, L.S. (ed.) 1982. *Internal Structure of the City: Readings on Urban Form, Growth, and Policy*. New York: Oxford University Press.

Castells, M. 1977. *The Urban Question: a Marxist Approach*. London: Edward Arnold and Cambridge: MIT Press.

Castells, M. 1983. *The City and the Grassroots*. Berkeley: University of California Press.

Castells, M. *et al.* 1990. *The Shek Kip Mei Syndrome: Economic Development and Public Housing in Hong Kong and Singapore*. London: Pion.

Chapin, Jr, S.F. 1974. *Human Activity Patterns in the City*. New York: Wiley International.

Cooke, P. 1983. *Theories of Planning and Spatial Development*. London: Hutchinson.

Davis, K. 1965. The urbanization of human population. *Scientific American*, 213(3), 41–53.

Doebele, W. 1982. *Land Readjustment*. Lexington: Lexington Press.

Dogan, M. and Kasarda, J.D. (eds) 1988. *The Metropolis Era: a World of Giant Cities*. Vols. 1 & 2. Newbury Park: Sage.

Edel, M. and Sclar, E. 1974. Taxes, spending, and property values: supply adjustment in a Tiebout Oates model. *Journal of Political Economy*, 82(2), 941–54.

Foley, D.L. 1964. An approach to metropolitan spatial structure. In: *Explorations into Urban Structure*. Webber, M.M. *et al.* (eds). Philadelphia: University of Pennsylvania Press.

Fried, M. 1963. Grieving for a lost home. In: *The Urban Condition*. Duhl, L.J. (ed.). New York: Basic Books.

Gans, H.J. 1962. *The Urban Villagers*. New York: Free Press.

Geddes, P. 1949. *Cities in Evolution*. London: Williams & Norgate.

Gordon, D.M. 1978. Capitalist development and the history of American cities. In: *Marxism and the Metropolis: New Perspectives in Urban Political Economy*. Tabb, W.K. and Sawers, L. (eds), pp. 25–63. New York: Oxford University Press.

Hall, P.G. 1984. *The World Cities*. London: Weidenfeld & Nicolson.

Harvey, D. 1973. *Social Justice and the City*. Baltimore: Johns Hopkins University Press.

Harvey D. 1985. *The Urbanization of Capital*. Baltimore: Johns Hopkins University Press.

Harvey, D. 1990. *The Condition of Post Modernity*. Oxford: Basil Blackwell.

Holand, S. 1976. *Capital Versus the Region*. London: Macmillan.

Kim, Joochul 1990. Housing development and reforms in China. In: *Housing Policy in Developing Countries*. Shidlo, Gil (ed.), pp. 104–120. New York: Routledge.

Kim, Joochul 1991. Urban redevelopment of greenbelt-area villages: a case study of Seoul, Korea. *Bulletin of Concerned Asian Scholars*, **23**(2), 20–29.

Kim, Kwang Suk and Roemer, M. 1981. *Growth and Structural Transformation*. Cambridge: Harvard University Press.

Knox, P. 1987. The social production of built environment: architects, architecture and the post-modern city. *Progress in Human Geography*, **11**, 354–377.

Laska, S.B. and Spain, D. (eds) 1980. *Back to the City: Issues in Neighborhood Renovation*. New York: Pergamon Press.

Lim, Hyun Chin 1985. *Dependent Development in Korea, 1963–1979*. Seoul: Seoul National University Press.

Lynch, K. 1975. *The Image of the City*. Cambridge: MIT Press.

Lynch, K. and Rodwin, L. 1958. A theory of urban form. *Journal of the American Institute of Planners*, **24**, 201–214.

Macdonald, D.S. 1990. *The Koreans: Contemporary Politics and Society*. Boulder: Westview Press.

Mumford, L. 1961. *The City in History: its Origins, its Transformations, and its Prospects*. New York: HBJ Books.

Mumford, L. 1968. *The Urban Prospect*. New York: HBJ Books.

Norwood, H.C. 1975. Informal industry in developing countries. *Town Planning Review*.

Oates, W.E. 1969. The effects of property taxes and local public spending on property values: an empirical study of tax capitalization and the Tiebout hypothesis. *Journal of Political Economy*, Nov/Dec, 957–971.

Pae, Mooki 1985. Industrial development and structural changes in labor market: the case of Korea. *Institute of Developing Economies*, **26**(2), 67.

Park, R.E. *et al.* 1925. *The City*. Chicago: University of Chicago Press.

Portes, A., Castells, M. and Benton, L.A. (eds) 1989. *The Informal Economy: Studies in Advanced and Less Developed Countries*. Baltimore: Johns Hopkins University Press.

Raban, J. 1974. *Soft City*. London: Fontana.

Saunders, P. 1983. *Urban Politics: a Sociological Interpretation*. London: Hutchinson.

Smith, M.P. 1979. *The City and Social Theory*. New York: St. Martin's.

Tabb, W.K. and Sawers, L. (eds) 1978. *Marxism and the Metropolis: New Perspectives in Urban Political Economy*. New York: Oxford University Press.

Tankel, S.B. 1963. The importance of open space in the urban patterns. In: *Cities and Space*. Baltimore: Johns Hopkins Press.

Tiebout, C.M. 1956. A pure theory of local expenditures. *Journal of Political Economy*, Oct, 416–424.

Ward, P.M. 1990. *Mexico City: the Production and Reproduction of an Urban Environment*. London: Belhaven Press.

Webber, M.M. 1964. The urban place and the non-place urban realm. In: *Exploration into Urban Structure*. Webber, M.M. *et al.* (eds). Philadelphia: University of Pennsylvania Press.

References:
Korean language publications

An, Sang Young 1983. Mokdong Jikoo Kongyoung Kaebaleuy Banghyangkwa Naeyong (The development concept for Mokdong District Development). In: *Dosi Moonjae (Urban Affairs)*. Seoul: Daehan Jibang Haengjueng Kongjaehoy.

Bank of Korea 1983. *GNP of Korea*. Seoul: Bank of Korea.

Bureau of National Rail Service 1988. *Rail Statistical Yearbook*. Seoul: Office of National Rail Service.

Cha, Byoung Gwon 1986. Dosioa Saneob (City and industry). In: *Dosi Moonjae (Urban Affairs)*. Seoul: City of Seoul.

Choe, Sang Chuel 1989. Hankook Dosi Kaehoik Yuksajeok Jeonmangkwa Kwajae (Problems and historical perspectives for city planning in Korea). In: *Jibang Jachywa Dosi Kaehoikae kwanhan Kookjae Haksool Seminar Nonmoonjip (Proceedings of International Conference on Local Autonomous Government and City Planning)*. Seoul: City of Seoul.

Choe, Sang Chuel and Song, Byung Nak 1984. An evaluation of industrial policies for urban decentralization in Seoul Region. In: *Hwankyung NonChong (Environmental Review)*. Seoul: City of Seoul.

Choo, Jong Won 1986. HanGook Dangi Kaehoikmit Dosiseolkaeeuy Banseaky (A half-century of city planning and site development for Korea). In: *Dosi Moonjae (Urban Affairs)*. Seoul: City of Seoul.

Choongang Daily 1990. August 24.

City of Seoul 1961–1994. *Seoul Statistical Year Book*. Seoul: City of Seoul.

City of Seoul 1984. *Seoul Municipal Handbook*. Seoul: City of Seoul.

City of Seoul 1987. *Si Jung (City Administration)*. Seoul: City of Seoul.

City of Seoul 1988. *Seoul Metropolitan Administration*. Seoul: City of Seoul.

Daehan Gookto Gaehoyk Hakhoy (Korea Planners Association) 1984. *Kookto Kaehoyk (National Development Plan)*. Seoul: City of Seoul.

Economic Planning Board 1960–1990. *Report of Population & House Census*. Seoul: National Government Printing.

Economic Planning Board 1962–1994. *Korea Statistical Yearbook*. Seoul: National Government Printing.

Economic Planning Board 1970–1991. *Population Housing Census*. Seoul: National Government Printing.

Economic Planning Board 1978–1986. *Major Economic Index*. Seoul: National Government Printing.

Economic Planning Board 1983–1993. *Joo Yo Kyung Jae Ji Pyo (Economic Indicators)*. Seoul: National Government Printing.

Ha, Seong Kyu 1989. Jootaek Moonjaewa Sindosi Kaebal (Housing problems and new town development). In: *Jootaek keumyung. (Housing Finance)*. Seoul: City of Seoul.

Hankook Daily 1993. August 6; August 8; June 3.

Hwang, Myung Chan 1983. Kong Young Kaebaleuy Euymiwa Pilyosueng (Government initiated urban development). In: *Dosi Moonjae (Urban Problems)*. Seoul: Daehan Jibang Kongjaehoy.

Kang, Dae Gi 1987. *Hyundae Dosiron (Modern Urban Theory)*. Seoul: Mineumsa.

Kang, Hong Bin 1986. Yuksa hwankyungeuy yoojiwa Bojeon (Historical preservation). In: *Dosi Moonjae (Urban Problems)*. Seoul: City of Seoul.

Kim, An Jae 1984. *Hwankyungkwa Kookto (Environment and the Nation)*. Seoul: Pakyoungsa.

Kim, Dong Goo 1988. Jachigooeuy Samoo (Problems of local autonomous government). In: *Dosi Moonjae (Urban Affairs)*. Seoul: City of Seoul.

Kim, Euy Won 1985. Woorinara Togi Koohiok Juengri Sauepeuy Doypkwa Juenkae (Implementation of land development method in Korea). In: *Tojy Juengchaekron (Theory of Land Policy)*. Seoul: Kyung Young Moonhwawon.

Kim, Hyung Gook 1989. *Boolyangchonkwa Jaekaebal (Urban Slums and Renewal)*. Seoul: Nanam.

Kim, In 1984. *Dosi Jirihak (Urban Geography)*. Seoul: Beobmoonsa.

Kim, Won 1983. *Dosi Haengjungron (City Administration Theory)*. Seoul: Pakyoungsa.

Kim, Yong Ho 1985. *Seoulsi Boolyang Jootaekjigoo Jaekaebal Kibuebae Kwanhan Yungoo (Analysis of Urban Renewal Project in Seoul)*. Seoul: City of Seoul.

Korea Housing Bank 1985–1993. *A Survey of Housing Price by Cities*. Seoul: Korea Housing Bank.

Korea Housing Bank 1989–1991. *Housing Economic Data Book*. Seoul: Korea Housing Bank.

Korea Housing Corporation 1979. *Daehan Jootaek Kongsa 20nyunsa (20 Years of History of Korea Housing Corporation)*. Seoul: City of Seoul.

Korea Housing Corporation 1989. *Jootaek Handbook (Housing Handbook)*. Seoul: City of Seoul.

Korea Housing Corporation 1990. *Seoul*. Seoul: City of Seoul.

Korea Regional Administration Institute 1990. *Study of Administrative Systems for SMR*. Seoul: City of Seoul.

Korea Research Institute for Human Settlement (KRIHS) 1984a. *Soodogwon Gipjoon Gineung Boonsan Bangan Yungoo (Depopulation of the Seoul Metropolitan Region)*. Seoul: KRIHS.

Korea Research Institute for Human Settlement (KRIHS) 1984b. *Dosi Kaehiok Pyunram (Introduction to City Planning)*. Seoul: KRIHS.

Korea Research Institute for Human Settlement (KRIHS) 1985. *Daedosikwon Koanrileul Wihan Jungchaek Yungoo (Study of Management Issues facing Metropolitan City)*. Seoul: KRIHS.

Korea Research Institute for Human Settlement (KRIHS) 1986. *Joogeo Kijoon*

Seoljungae Kwanhan Yungoo (Analysis of Factors Affecting Housing Functions). Seoul: KRIHS.

Korea Research Institute for Human Settlements (KRIHS) 1988. *Soodogwon Gineung Baechiae Koanhan Yungoo (Analysis of Functional Distribution of the Seoul Metropolitan Region).* Seoul: KRIHS.

Korea Transport Research Institute 1987. *Basic Study of Transportation Plan.* Seoul: City of Seoul.

Korea Transport Research Institute 1990. *Basic Study of Transportation Plan.* Seoul: City of Seoul.

Korea Urban Administration Institute 1994. *National Statistical Yearbook.* Seoul: City of Seoul.

Korean Statistical Association 1991. *Korea Statistical Yearbook.* Seoul.

Kwon, Sang Jun 1983. Nokjy Kongganeuy Kaebalkwa Bojeonae Kwanhan Yungoo (Study of open space development and preservation). *Hangook Chokyung Hakhoyjy (Journal of Korean Landscape Architecture).*

Kyonggi-do Province 1985. *Kyonggi-do Province Daehakchon Jungbigichim Pypunggajaryo Jaksungae goanhan youngoo (Critical Analysis of University Campus Development for Kyonggi-do Province).* Kyonggi-do Province.

Lee, Jong Cheon 1983. Kong Won Jeong Chaek Yuksajeok Kochalkwa Jeongchaek Bang Hyang (History of urban park policy and future directions). In: *Si Jeong Yungoo (City Administration).* Seoul: City of Seoul.

Lee, Kue Yul 1982. Dosi Kaehiok Buebjae Baljachwy (Historical perspectives on city planning). In: *Dosi Moonjae (Urban Affairs).* Seoul: City of Seoul.

Lee, Sang Hee 1985. *Gibang Jaejeong Ron (Theory of Local Finance).* Seoul: Kaemyungsa.

Lee, Tae Il 1987. Tojikoohoikeuy Baljuenjuek Jaepyungga (Reevaluation of city development and planning). In: *Dr. Rho Hoykap Kinyum Nonmoonjip.* Seoul: City of Seoul.

Lim, Sung Bin 1984. Jihachul gwa Dosigyotong (Subway and urban transportation). In: *Seoul Si Jung.* Seoul: City of Seoul.

Ministry of Construction 1982. *2nd Gookto Jonghap Gaebal Gaehoyk (Second National Development Plan).* Seoul: Ministry of Construction.

Ministry of Construction 1987. *Dosi Jaekaebal Saueb Jichim (Policies for Urban Renewal).* Seoul: Ministry of Construction.

Ministry of Home Affairs 1971–1981. *Bureau of Local Finance.* Seoul: Ministry of Home Affairs.

Ministry of Labour 1993. *Survey Report on Establishment Labour Conditions.* Seoul: Ministry of Labour.

National Statistical Office 1992. *Report on Mining and Manufacturing Survey (Region and Country).* Seoul: City of Seoul.

Park, Hyung Suek 1983. Daedosi Jaejung Juenriakkwa Seoulsieuy Jaejung Woonyong (Metropolitan government finance and public finance for Seoul). In: *Seoul Sijueng (Seoul Administration).* Seoul: City of Seoul.

Park, Moon Bae 1989. Jootaek Keumyung Hyunhwanggwa Baljeon Banghyang (Directions for housing finance). In: *Jootaek Keumyung (Housing Finance).* Seoul: City of Seoul.

Park, Sam Ok 1989a. *Giyouk Youngoo (Regional Studies).* Seoul: City of Seoul.

Park, Sam Ok 1989b. Soodogwon saneop Ipgi Donghiangkoa Daechawk (Industrial location for the Seoul Metropolitan Region). In: *Dosi Moonjae (Urban Affairs).* Seoul: City of Seoul.

Seoul Development Institute 1993a. *Transportation Volume and Trip Generation Study*. Seoul: City of Seoul.

Seoul Development Institute 1993b. *Land-use Improvement Study for Seoul*. Seoul: City of Seoul.

Seoul Development Institute 1994a. *Seoul Development Institute Forum (2)*, No. 5. Seoul: Seoul Development Institute.

Seoul Development Institute 1994b. *Seoul Si Jung Yeon Ku (2)*, No. 1. Seoul: Seoul Development Institute.

Seoul Metropolis 1960. *Budget Summary*. Seoul: City of Seoul.

Seoul Metropolis 1962a. *Dosi Kaehoik Baekseo (City Planning Handbook)*. Seoul: City of Seoul.

Seoul Metropolis 1962b. *Seoul Dosi Kaehoik Kwakuewa Jangrae (Past and Future of Seoul City Plan)*. Seoul: City of Seoul.

Seoul Metropolis 1971. *Youido Master Plan, 1971*. Seoul: City of Seoul.

Seoul Metropolis 1972. *Sijueng Jonghap Kaehoik (Overall Plan for City Administration)*. Seoul: City of Seoul.

Seoul Metropolis 1977. *Seoul 600nyunsa (600 Years of History for Seoul)*. Seoul: City of Seoul.

Seoul Metropolis 1983a. *Housing Construction of Seoul*. Seoul: City of Seoul.

Seoul Metropolis 1983b. Danji Sahoieuy euyeuy, Yogunkwa Woorynara Danji Sahoi Hyungsungeuy Yunhyukjeok Kochal (Survey of apartment complex development history and their meaning). In: *Dosi Moonjae (Urban Affairs)*. Seoul: City of Seoul.

Seoul Metropolis 1984a. *Togigoohoikjungrisaoeb Yunhyukgi (Survey of Land Readjustment Projects)*. Seoul: City of Seoul.

Seoul Metropolis 1984b. *Seoul Civil Income*. Seoul: City of Seoul.

Seoul Metropolis 1986–1994. *Comparative Statistics for Major Cities*. Seoul: City of Seoul.

Seoul Metropolis 1987. *Joseonsidae Dosi Sahoi Yungoo (Study of Society During Yi Dynasty)*. Seoul: Ilgisa.

Seoul Metropolis 1987–1993. *Seoul Administration*. Seoul: City of Seoul.

Seoul Metropolis 1989a. *Seoul Jusodeukcheung Siltae Paakkoa Daechak Sooripae Koanhan Yungoo (Survey of and Development of Policies for Low Income Families)*. Seoul: City of Seoul.

Seoul Metropolis 1989b. *Seoulsi Nojumsang Siltae Boonseokkoa Hioyouljeo Koanri Banganae Koanhan Yunkgoo (Survey of Informal Sectors and Policies for Effective Solutions)*. Seoul: City of Seoul.

Seoul Metropolis 1990a. *2000nyundaereul Hyanghan Seoulsi Dosi Kibon Kaehoik (Basic Plan for Year 2000, Seoul)*. Seoul: City of Seoul.

Seoul Metropolis 1990b. *Kyotonggook (Transportation)*. Seoul: City of Seoul.

Seoul Metropolis 1991. *Urban Planning of Seoul*. Seoul: City of Seoul.

Seoul Metropolis 1992–1993. *Municipal Yearbook of Korea*. Seoul: City of Seoul.

Sohn, Jung Mok 1983. Danji Sahoieuy euyeuy, Yogunkwa Woorynara Danji Sahoi Hyungsungeuy Yunhyukjeok Kochal (Survey of apartment complex development history and their meaning). In: *Dosi Moonjae (Urban Affairs)*. Seoul: City of Seoul.

Sohn, Jung Mok 1987. *Joseonsidae Dosi Sahoi Yungoo (Study of Society during Yi Dynasty)*. Seoul: Ilgisa.

Yang, Byung Yee 1985. Dosi Kongwonhwa Wndongeuy euymiwa Baekyung (Movement for urban parks). In: *Dosi Moonjae (Urban Affairs)*. Seoul: City of Seoul.

Yeo, Hong Goo 1982. Sigaji Jaegaebal Sauebeuy Kibon Kaehoykmit Banghyang (Basic concept and direction for urban redevelopment). In: *Dosi Jaekaebal (Urban Renewal)*. Seoul: City of Seoul.

Yoo, Hoon 1985. *Kongkieopron (Theory of Public Corporation)*. Seoul: Buebmoonsa.

Further reading: English language publications

Amsden, A.H. 1989. *Asia's Next Giant: South Korea and Late Industrialization*. New York: Oxford University Press.

Arnold, K. 1971. *Office Dispersal and Regional Policy*. Cambridge: Cambridge University Press.

Bahl, R., Kim, C.K. and Park, C.K. 1986. *Public Finance During the Korean Modernization Process*. Cambridge: Harvard University Press.

Berry, B.J.L. 1973. *The Human Consequences of Urbanization*. London: Macmillan.

Black, J.K. 1991. *Development in Theory & Practice*. Boulder: Westview Press.

Castells, M. 1989. High technology and urban dynamics in the United States. In: *The Metropolis Era: a World of Giant Cities*. Vol. 1. Dogan, M. and Kasarda, J.D. (eds), pp. 85–110. Newbury Park: Sage.

Choe, Sang Chuel 1987. *Urbanization and Urban Policies in North East Asia*. Sheffield University Monograph. Sheffield: Sheffield University Press.

Choe, Sang Chuel 1990. *Growth and Management of Mega-Cities: the Case of Seoul*. Paper presented at the conference Mega-City and the Future: Population Growth and Policy Responses. October 22–25 1990, Tokyo, Japan.

Chung, Sae Wook 1994. *Local and Regional Council Elections in 1991: Features and Political Implications*. SDI Monograph Series No. 94-M-1. Seoul: Seoul Development Institute.

Clark, D.N. (ed.), 1991. *Korea Briefing, 1991*. Boulder: Westview Press.

Clifford, M.L. 1994. *Troubled Tiger: Businessmen, Bureaucrats, and Generals in South Korea*. New York: M.E. Sharpe.

Crowther, D. and Echenique, M. Development of a model of urban spatial structure. In: *Urban Space and Structure*. Cambridge: Cambridge University Press.

Deyo, F.C. (ed.), 1987. *The Political Economy of the New Asian Industrialism*. Ithaca: Cornell University Press.

Friedmann, J. 1973. *Retracking America*. New York: Anchor/Doubleday.

Gereffi, G. and Wyman, D.L. (eds) 1990. *Manufacturing Miracles: Paths of*

Industrialization in Latin America and East Asia. Princeton: Princeton University Press.

Gravier, J.F. 1947. *Paris and the French Desert*. Paris: Flammarion.

Haggett, P. 1972. *Geography: a Modern Synthesis*. New York: Harper and Row.

Hall, P.G. 1989. Urban growth and decline in Western Europe. In: *The Metropolis Era: a World of Giant Cities*. Vol. 1. Dogan, M. and Kasarda, J.D. (eds), pp. 111–127. Newbury Park: Sage.

Hardt, J.P. and Kim, Y.D. (eds) 1990. *Economic Cooperation in the Asia–Pacific Region*. Boulder: Westview Press.

Harvey, D. 1989. *The Urban Experience*. Baltimore: Johns Hopkins University Press.

Henderson, G. 1968. *Korea – the Politics of Vortex*. Cambridge: Harvard University Press.

Huntington, S.P. 1968. *Political Order in Changing Society*. New Haven: Yale University Press.

Jacobs, J. 1961. *The Death and Life of Great American Cities*. New York: Vintage-Random House.

Kim, Choong Soon 1993. *The Korean Culture of Korean Industry: an Ethnography of Poongsan Corporation*. Tucson: University of Arizona Press.

Le Corbusier 1951. *The Heart of the City*. London: Lund Humphries.

Lee, Chong Sik (ed.) 1990. *Korea Briefing, 1990*. Boulder: Westview Press.

Marris, P. 1963. A report on urban renewal in the US. In: *The Urban Condition*. Duhl, L. (ed.). New York: Basic Books.

Misra, B.J. 1982. *Japanese Experience in Physical Development and Land Management*. Paper presented at the International Conference on Local and Regional Development in the 1980s sponsored by the UN Centre for Regional Development, Osaka.

Ogle, G.E. 1990. *South Korea: Dissent within the Economic Miracle*. London: Zed Books.

Owen, W. 1972. *The Accessible City*. Washington, DC: The Brookings Institution.

Phillips, E.B. and LeGates, R.T. 1981. *City Lights: an Introduction to Urban Studies*. New York: Oxford University Press.

Richardson, H.W. and Hwang, M.C. (eds) 1988. *Urban and Regional Policy in Korea and International Experiences*. Seoul: Korea Research Institute for Human Settlement.

Schon, D.A. 1971. *Beyond the Stable State*. New York: Norton.

Soleri, P. 1969. *Arcology; the City in the Image of Man*. Cambridge: MIT Press.

Sullivan, J. and Foss, R. (eds) 1987. *Two Koreas – One Future?* Lanham: University Press of America.

UN Centre for Human Settlements 1987. *Global Report on Human Settlements: Habitat*.

William, C.M. 1965. *The City in the World Economy*. New York: Penguin Books.

Woo, Jung En 1991. *Race to the Swift: State and Finance in Korean Industrialization*. New York: Columbia University Press.

Woronoff, J. 1992. *Asia's 'Miracle' Economies*. New York: M.E. Sharpe.

Further reading:
Korean language publications

Cho, Jung Jae 1990. *Dosi Kyung Young* (*City Administration*). Seoul: Beobmoonsa.
Choe, Jae Seok 1983. APT Giyuk Joomin Goosung koa Geunrin Gawngae (The rights of apartment residents). In: *Dosi Moonjae* (*Urban Affairs*). Seoul: City of Seoul.
Choe, Sang Chuel 1976. *Han Gook Ingoomoonjae oa Daechak* (*Problems and Solutions for Population Problems for Korea*). Seoul: City of Seoul.
Choe, Sang Chuel 1984. Worinara Daedosikwon Hyoungsungkoa Koajae (Korea's metropolitanization). In: *Dosi Moonjae* (*Urban Affairs*). Seoul: City of Seoul.
Choe, Sang Chuel 1986a. Do Si Gi Nung Mit Gong Gan Gu Jo Yeon Gu Seo Sul (Introduction to urban spatial analysis and city functions). *Journal of Environmental Studies*, **18**, 1–18.
Choe, Sang Chuel 1986b. Hankook Dosi Kaehoik Bansaeky (A half-century of Korean city planning). In: *Dosi Moonjae* (*Urban Affairs*). Seoul: City of Seoul.
Choo, Won 1978. *Jaekae Hoigo* (*Review of Finance*). Seoul: City of Seoul.
Chuldochung (Bureau of Rail Service) 1988. *Chuldo Tonngkae Yunbo* (*Annual Statistical Review of Rail Service*). Seoul: City of Seoul.
Daehan Gookto Gaehoyk Hakhoy (Korea Planners Association) 1989. *Dosi Jeongbo* (*City Information*). Seoul: City of Seoul.
Economic Planning Board 1981. *Chong Saeopchae Tonggae Josa Bogoseo* (*Statistical Report on Small Businesses*). Seoul: National Government Printing.
Economic Planning Board 1988. *Jangrae Ingoo Chooy* (*Special Population Reports*). Seoul: National Government Printing.
Economic Planning Board 1989. *Teukgip Ingoo Chorok* (*Population Projection for Korea*). Seoul: National Government Printing.
Han, Kunbae 1990. *Dosiyongdojiyukkwehwek* (*Land Use Planning*). Seoul: Taelim-moonhwasa.
Hong, Kee Yong 1986. *Dosi Bingon Sangtaewa Jungchaek* (*Policies and Conditions of Urban Poor*). Seoul: Dangook University.
Hwang, Myung Chan 1979. Dosi Kyungjae Goojoa Saneop Ipji (Urban economic structure and industry). In: *Dosi Moonjae* (*Urban Problems*). Seoul: City of Seoul.

Hwankyungcheong 1988. *Hwankyung Bojeon* (*Environmental Preservation*). Seoul: City of Seoul.

Kang, Byungki *et al.* 1984. *Dosiron* (*Theory of City Planning*). Seoul: Bupmoonsa.

Kang, Man Kil 1987. *Yljaesidae Binmin Saenghwalsa Yungoo.* (*Research on the Urban Poor During the Japanese Domination*). Seoul: Changjaksa.

Kim, An Jae 1988. *Dosi Jaejueng* (*City Finance*). Seoul: City of Seoul.

Kim, Hyoung Joon 1986. *Soodokwon Ingoo Boonbae Jungchakae Koanhan Yungo* (*Depopulation of the Seoul Metropolitan Region*). Seoul: City of Seoul.

Kim, Hyung Gook 1976. *Gookto Kaeblakoa Ingooidong* (*National Development and Population Movement*). Seoul: Korea Development Institute.

Kim, Hyung Gook 1983. *Gookto Gaebal Iron Yungoo* (*Study of National Development Theory*). Seoul: Pakyoungsa.

Kim, In 1987. *Soodogwon Giyuk Yungoo* (*Analysis of the Seoul Metropolitan Region*). Seoul: City of Seoul.

Kim, Jeong Ho 1989a. Jootaek Konggeub Mit Gagyuk Cheukmyunaeseo Bon Soodogwon Sindosi Geonseol (New Town Development in the Seoul Metropolitan Region: Housing Supply and Price). In: *Dosi Moonjae* (*Urban Affairs*). Seoul: City of Seoul.

Kim, Jeong Ho 1989b. Sindosi Geonseolkwa Jootaek Jeongchaek (New town development and housing policy). In: *Togi Kaebal.* Seoul: City of Seoul.

Kim, Yong Suk 1985. *Dosibinminron* (*Theory of Urban Poor*). Seoul: Aachim.

Kim, You Hyuk 1985. *Yoonrimyunaesu bon Dosi Byungri Sogo* (*Urban Pathology and Morality*). Seoul: Gosigae.

Konghae Choobang Woondong Yunhap 1990a. *1990 Jigoo Nal Jaryojip* (*Information on the 1990 Earth Day*). Seoul: City of Seoul.

Konghae Choobang Woondong Yunhap 1990b. *Saengjonkwa Pyunghwa* (*Life and Peace*). Seoul: City of Seoul.

Korea Environment Institute 1980. *Seoulsinae Daeki Oyum Boonsan Hyunhwangkwa Cheukjeong Oyumdowa Bykyo Boonseokae Kwanhan Yungoo* (*Comparative Analysis of Air Pollution and Measurements in Seoul*). Seoul: City of Seoul.

Korean Urban Administration Institute 1986. *2000nyuneul Hyanghan Jibang Haengjeong Yungoo* (*Analysis of Local Public Administration for 2000*). Seoul: City of Seoul.

Korean Urban Administration Institute 1990. *Soodokwuen Gwangyuk Haengjung Chaegaeae Kwanhan Yungoo* (*Analysis of the Administrative System for the Seoul Metropolitan Region*). Seoul: City of Seoul.

Kwon, Sang Jun 1994. *Green Round: Ji Gu Hwan Kyung U Gyung Je Sa Hwoe Jung Chek* (*Green Round: Socioeconomic Policies for Environment*). Seoul: Moon Woon Dang.

Kwon, Won Yong 1983. Dosi Cha Saneopkoa Dosi Gaehiok (City planning and urban transportation). In: *Dosi Moonjae* (*Urban Affairs*). Seoul: City of Seoul.

Kyotong Kaebal Yungoowon 1987. *Seoul Metropolise Kyotong jungbi Kibon Kaehoikae Koanhan Yungoo* (*Study of the Seoul Metropolitan Region Transportation System*). Seoul: City of Seoul.

Lee, Chongik 1985. *Jaemoohangjongron* (*Theory of Public Finance*). Seoul: Pakyongsa.

Lee, Jong Cheon 1930. *Kyung Seong Dosi Kaehoykseo* (*City Planning for Seoul*). Seoul: Choseon chongdokboo Naemookook.

Lee, Keon Young oae kongjeo 1989. *Dosi Kyotong Jeongchakron* (*Theory of Urban Transportation*). Seoul: City of Seoul.

Park, Chan Seok 1983. Dosi samcha saneob Gaenyumkoa Boonriu (Concept of urban tertiary industry). In: *Dosi Moonjae* (*Urban Affairs*). Seoul: City of Seoul.

Park, Eung Kuouk 1984. *Daedosi Ingoo Sungjangkoa jung chaek (Population Problems and Policies for Metropolitan City)*. Seoul: City of Seoul.

Park, Soo Young 1990. *Do Si Haeng Jung Ron (Urban Public Administration)*. Seoul: Bak Young Sa.

Park, Yang Ho 1989. *Dosi Moonjae (Urban Problems)*. Seoul: City of Seoul.

Park, Woo Seo 1989. Koogka Baljeonkwa Kongkong Haengjung (National development and public administration). In: *Hoykap Nonmoonjip*. Seoul: City of Seoul.

Pyunchan Wewonhoy of Seoul Metropolis History 1985. *History of Hanriver*. Seoul: City of Seoul.

Seoul Metropolis 1980. *Seoul 2000nyun Dosi Gaebal Jangki Goosang Joongki kaehoik (Future Planning Concept of Seoul for Year 2000)*. Seoul: City of Seoul.

Seoul Metropolis 1982a. *Hankang Chonghap Kaebal saeop Hwankyung Yunghiang Pyunggaseo (Evaluation of Han River Development)*. Seoul: City of Seoul.

Seoul Metropolis 1982b. *Dosi Jaekaebal (Urban Renewal)*. Seoul: City of Seoul.

Seoul Metropolis 1984a. *Seoul Simin Sodeuk Chukae (Total Expenditures for Residents, Seoul)*. Seoul: City of Seoul.

Seoul Metropolis 1984b. *Seoul Dosimboo Jaekaebal Kibon Kaehiok (Basic Plan for Urban Redevelopment)*. Seoul: City of Seoul.

Seoul Metropolis 1984c. *Toji Koohiok Juengli Sauep yunhyukjy (Annual Survey of Land Readjustment Projects)*. Seoul: City of Seoul.

Seoul Metropolis 1984d. *Gooklip Kyunggijang Kibon Kaehoikmit Seolkae (Design for National Sports Complex)*. Seoul: Environment Planning Institute.

Seoul Metropolis 1985a. *Hanok Jigoo Dosi Kaehoik (Development Plan for Traditional Korean Housing District)*. Seoul: City of Seoul.

Seoul Metropolis 1985b. *Seoulsi Kongwon Nokji jeongchak Banghyang Yungoo (Analysis of Open Space and Urban Parks for Seoul)*. Seoul: City of Seoul.

Seoul Metropolis 1987a. *Chojik Byunchoensa (Changes in City Organizations)*. Seoul: City of Seoul.

Seoul Metropolis 1987b. *Sijung Kaeyo (City Administration Review)*. Seoul: City of Seoul.

Seoul Metropolis 1987c. *Seoulsi chojik Byunchuensa (Changes in City Organizations)*. Seoul: City of Seoul.

Seoul Metropolis 1987d. *Kunchook Haengjueng (Architecture Administration)*. Seoul: City of Seoul.

Seoul Metropolis 1988a. *Olympic Sunsoo, Kijachon Kongsajy (Olympic Village Plan)*. Seoul: City of Seoul.

Seoul Metropolis 1988b. *Seoulsi Paegimool Cheori Kibon Kaehyok (Basic Plan for Sewage)*. Seoul: City of Seoul.

Seoul Metropolis 1988c. *Dosi Kosokhwa Doro Tadangsung Chosa (Feasibility for Urban Expressways)*. Seoul: City of Seoul.

Seoul Metropolis 1989a. *Seoul Metropolis Kyotong Jonghap Daechaek (Analysis of Transportation Problems for Seoul)*. Seoul: City of Seoul.

Seoul Metropolis 1989b. *Seoul Sijung (Seoul Administration)*. Seoul: City of Seoul.

Seoul Metropolis 1989c. *Seoulsi Dosi Gibon Kaehoik (Basic Plan for Seoul)*. Seoul: City of Seoul.

Seoul Metropolis 1989d. *Olympic Baekseo (Olympic Handbook)*. Seoul: City of Seoul.

Seoul Metropolis 1989e. *Transportation Comprehensive Countermeasures*. Seoul: City of Seoul.

Seoul Metropolis 1990a. *Seoul Metropolis Jikjae (Study of Seoul Metropolis)*. Seoul: City of Seoul.

Seoul Metropolis 1990b. *Seoul Metropolis Tooja Gigwan Hyunhang* (*Industrial Locations for Seoul Metropolitan Region*). Seoul: City of Seoul.

Seoul Metropolis 1991. *Reports on Establishment Census, Volume 2, Region*. Seoul: City of Seoul.

Seoul Metropolis Sijung Yungoodan 1988. *Seoulsijungae Daehan Gicho Josa Yungoo Jaryo* (*Basic Information for City Administration*). Seoul: City of Seoul.

Seoul Metropolis Sijung Kaehyuk Yungoo Wewonhoy 1989. *Seoul Metropoliseuy Sijung Baljueneul Wehan Juengchaek Yungoo* (*Seoul Metropolitan Regional Development Plan*). Seoul: City of Seoul.

Seoul National University 1991. *Junhwangi Hangook Sahoi* (*Korea's Turbulent Society*). Seoul: Sociology Institute, Seoul National University Press.

Seoul National University 1994. *Go Ji Do Ro Wa Go Seo Ro Bon Seoul* (*Seoul from Old Maps and Books*). Seoul: Gew Jang Kak, Seoul National University Press.

Sohn, Jung Mok 1989. *Iljae Kangjumgy Dosikyaehoik Yungoo* (*Analysis of City Planning During the Japanese Domination*). Seoul: Ilgisa.

Yang, Kyung Yuk 1986. *Dosi Joogue Danji Kaehoik* (*Site Development for Apartment Complex*). Seoul: Jipmoondang.

Ym, Jung Duk 1986. Dosi Kyung Jae 20nyun Byunchun (Twenty years of changing patterns for urban economy). In: *Dosi Moonjae* (*Urban Affairs*). Seoul: City of Seoul.

Ym, Seong Bin 1984. Jihacheolkwa DosiKyotong (Subways and urban transportation). In: *Seoul Sijung* (*Seoul Administration*). Seoul: City of Seoul.

Yoo, Jae Hyun 1989. Jootaek Jungchaek Jipyo Seoljungeul wihan Kaenyumboonseok (Analysis for housing policies and concepts). In: *Jootaek Keumyoong* (*Housing Finance*). Seoul: City of Seoul.

Yoon, Jong Joo 1966. *Seoulsi Yipingooae koanhan Yungoo* (*Analysis for in-migrants to Seoul*). Seoul: City of Seoul.

Index

Page references in **bold** refer to figures and plates, page references in *italic* refer to tables. The abbreviation "SMR" refers to Seoul Metropolitan Region.

Index compiled by Liz Granger